LEARNING POLICY

Learning Policy

WHEN STATE EDUCATION REFORM WORKS

DAVID K. COHEN AND HEATHER C. HILL

 Yale University Press | New Haven and London

Designed by April Leidig-Higgins.

Set in Minion type by Copperline Book Services, Inc., Hillsborough, North Carolina.

Printed in the United States of America by Vail-Ballou Press, Binghamton, New York.

Library of Congress Cataloging-in-Publication Data

Cohen, David K., 1934–

Learning policy : when state education reform works / David K. Cohen and Heather C. Hill.

p. cm. Includes bibliographical references (p.) and index.

ISBN 0-300-08947-3 (alk. paper)

1. Education and state—California. 2. School improvement programs—California. 3. Mathematics—Study and teaching—California. I. Hill, Heather C. II. Title.

LC90.C2 C64 2001   379.794—dc21   2001026537

A catalogue record for this book is available from the British Library.

The paper in this book meets the guidelines for permanence and durability of the Committee on Production Guidelines for Book Longevity of the Council on Library Resources.

10 9 8 7 6 5 4 3 2 1

CONTENTS

PREFACE

This book reports on one of the more significant school-improvement policies in late-twentieth-century America: California's decadelong effort to change and improve mathematics teaching in the state's public schools. We studied the policy and its effects for three chief reasons. We are interested in the relations between policy and practice—between deliberate public or private efforts to improve public institutions and the ground-floor practices that such improvements require. We are especially interested in what it might take for intellectually ambitious efforts to succeed in a school system that has generally eschewed ambitious work. And we believe that the evidence we present can improve both policy and our understanding of educational improvement.

We write neither as partisans nor as opponents of the policy in question. We see it as one more wave in a long succession of efforts to push math teaching toward deeper understanding of central disciplinary ideas and greater respect for students' thinking. Though we think these are sensible goals, we do not write out of the conviction that this policy was either a desirable or a deficient path toward them. When we write of the policy's success or failure, we write as analysts, not partisans. We see many ways in which the California effort to improve math teaching and learning could have been improved, and we deal extensively with some of them in the chapters that follow. We also can see some ways in which the policy was better, or different, than its critics charged. For instance, many critics argued that it was eroding the teaching of basic skills—in effect, that the math reform was a quantitative version of "whole language." But we found little or no evidence of that.

That is not to say there is no reason to worry about such erosion. The worry reasonably arises from a long history of misguided efforts to "improve" schools. Self-styled liberals, including many self-appointed but hopelessly misguided acolytes of John Dewey, improvised a flock of disastrous reforms in the 1920s, '30s, and '40s that corroded and debased teaching and learning. Some of the supposedly progressive efforts in the 1960s were cut from similar cloth, as, more recently, were some of the reading reforms of the 1980s. California math reform contained elements of this foolishness—the passion for cooperative learning is a case in point—but liberals have no monopoly on educational foolishness. Some conservatives opposed the mere idea of public education in the mid-nineteenth century. Later, at the turn of the twentieth century, others argued vigorously for offering only the most rudimentary education to working-class and immigrant children. Conservatives were in the vanguard of attempts, through the first six or seven decades of the twentieth century, to deny even a semblance of decent education to African-Americans. Many efforts to influence schools have been caricatures at best, often deeply mean-spirited; reformers have "dumbed down" the curriculum and have detracted from ambitious work under the banner of improving it.

If the California math reforms had some elements of liberal foolishness, though, they also had large and serious academic ambitions for all students in the state's public schools. One reason that we spent a great deal of time studying the state's effort to improve math teaching was our sense that efforts to realize these high ambitions deserve serious attention.

We also wrote this book because we wanted to bring evidence on policy implementation to bear on analysis of educational policy and innovation. Educational reforms can, as Don Campbell wrote, be viewed as experiments. If they were so viewed, evidence would be carefully collected and analyzed to clarify what the experiment was, how it was enacted, and what happened as a consequence. Unfortunately, most educational policymakers and reformers proceed as if the nature and effects of these experiments were already established. Reformers typically make no serious effort to bring evidence and analysis to bear on the operation and effects of their innovation. That tends to deprive policymakers and innovators of knowledge that could improve their work, and teachers and students of opportunities to improve *their* work. If education were medicine, this kind of mindless "experimentation" would get the enterprise a bad name at best and perhaps would get some licenses revoked. We have worked hard on this study because we think that it shows that a fairly small research team, working on a modest budget, can collect and analyze information from which many practitioners, policymakers, and researchers could learn a good deal. We don't write this to toot our own research horn; this study has room for improvement, as we try to make plain. Rather, we want to show that even such a modest effort as this could improve understanding of and debate about policy and practice in U.S. education. We hope that it will help convince policymakers and practitioners that more and better work of this sort would be a good investment.

As is nearly always the case, we could not have completed this work, or avoided many mistakes, without extensive help from colleagues. At Michigan State University, where our work began, we want to thank Deborah L. Ball, Ruth Heaton, Penelope Peterson, Richard Prawat, Ralph Putnam, Janine Remillard, James Spillane, Suzanne Wilson, and others who began observational studies of the California math reform in the late 1980s. Ball, Peterson, and Wilson were leaders on that research team and were crucial in developing the intellectual framework for the original research. They also, in concert with Joan Talbert of Stanford University, played a central role in conceiving and developing the teacher survey on which we report here. Joan Talbert, along with Andrea Lash, Rebecca Perry, Zierlein Aclan, and others, then oversaw the execution of the survey. She also helped us more times than we can even remember as we began to work with the data set; she has been an extraordinary colleague.

Once we had a reasonable draft of the manuscript, both Lorraine McDonnell and Suzanne Wilson read it and commented on it extensively. They represented the best sort of reviewer—sympathetic to the enterprise, but merciless concerning various features of its execution. They encouraged us to make changes that saved us pain later on, and we are grateful for their assistance.

Early, incomplete drafts of this work were read and commented on by Jennifer O'Day, Mike Smith, Susan Fuhrman, Linda Darling-Hammond, Gary Natriello, Gary Orfield, and James Spillane. Though we spared them from reading the entire manuscript, their support for the work and warnings about assorted problems helped us to improve it. Richard Murnane and several anonymous reviewers read and offered very helpful advice on an article that summarized several key features of the study, improving both the intellectual frame and statistical analyses. Steve Raudenbush performed the same service for an early draft of that article, and formulated the statistical approach taken in Appendix F. Statistical and software assistance was provided by Adam Berinsky, Joseph Hesse, Robert Miller, and Kathy Welch. Susan Kaminsky, Jennifer Minton, and Geoff Phelps provided assistance with other aspects of this project.

Finally, we offer thanks to two groups without whom the study could not have been done. The first is the roughly six hundred teachers who responded to the survey. All of them, taking time from their own work or private lives to respond to questions from distant and unknown inquirers, gave generously of their time and knowledge, we imagine, in hopes of improving the enterprise of which they are such a critical part. We think of it as the educational equivalent of anonymous blood donation. The second group is our funders —the National Science Foundation, and especially Larry Suter, the Carnegie Corporation of New York, especially Vivian Stewart and Michael Levine, the Pew Charitable trusts, especially Robert Schwartz, and the Consortium for Policy Research in Education, which supported the original Michigan state research with a grant from the Office of Educational Research and Improvement. Their encouragement and support underwrote the enterprise.

None of these colleagues, commentators, or funders is responsible either for the views we express or for any errors we may have made.

ABBREVIATIONS

AIMS   Activities in Math and Science
CAP   California Assessment Program
CCD   Common Core Data
CDE   California Department of Education
CLAS   California Learning Assessment System
CMC   California Mathematics Council
CMP   California Mathematics Project
CSU   California State University
CTBS   California Test of Basic Skills
EQUALS   A workshop geared to equity issues
FLE   Free Lunch Eligible
ITIP   Instructional Theory into Practice
LEP   Limited English Proficient
NCES   National Center for Educational Statistics
NCTM   National Council of Teachers of Mathematics
OLS   Ordinary least squares
PACE   Policy Analysis for California Education
PQR   Program Quality Review
SES   Socioeconomic status
SIP   School Improvement Plan
TERC   Technical Education Research Centers

Chapter 1

POLICY, TEACHING, AND LEARNING

America is alive with efforts to improve its schools. Governors, state legislatures, business leaders, presidents, members of Congress, and educators have all urged improvement of schools through reform legislation and new academic standards and assessments. This remarkable reform effort began with the publication of *A Nation at Risk* in the early 1980s and has grown ever since. Standards-based reforms have been enacted in most states, and several states took quite aggressive action. By the early 1990s, school improvement was a leading political issue in many states; most had enacted new standards, and many had tried to put schemes into place that would hold schools accountable for students' performance. Only a few states, however, did much to support local school improvement, and by the late 1990s many policymakers and observers were beginning to worry about whether states could improve schools across the board. As we write, anxiety is increasing about whether state reforms will succeed. Reports of problems with state reforms have grown, and test scores, especially those of disadvantaged students, remain low. During a recent education summit, in Washington, D.C., the *New York Times* printed a front-page story reporting that many governors and some university leaders were worried that the reforms were about to plunge over a cliff (Steinberg 1999).

In this book we aim to improve understanding of how state policies that support better teaching and learning can succeed. It is based on a decade's detailed study of a high-profile California effort to improve teaching and learning in mathematics. California's was one of the first major state reforms. It was led by a coalition of state educators, business leaders, and politicians. The goal was to provide much more academically demanding work for students: not just higher standards, but more complex and intellectually demanding work, and improvement for all students, not just an academic elite. The reform offered more detailed guidance for teaching and learning—in assessments, curricular frameworks, student curricula, and professional education—than has been common for most state governments during most of our history.

Like all such reforms, California's mixed pedagogy with politics. The political elements included vigorous leadership from state education officials, pressure on local schools for better performance, education of the public about public education, and confrontation with powerful interest groups, like textbook publishers. The pedagogical elements included stronger direction to teachers and other educators about how mathematics should be taught and learned, encouragement of professionals outside government to play key roles in writing new curricula and improving professional education, revision of the state's assessments to reflect the aims of reform, and improved professional education. Pedagogical and political elements of the reform merged as state leaders tried to align curricula, assessment, professional development, and other sources of guidance to schools and teachers with each other and the new math frameworks. These features of the California reform were later adopted by other states.

When Reform Works

Our central finding is that California's effort to improve teaching and learning did meet with some success, but only when teachers had significant opportunities to learn how to improve mathematics teaching. When teachers had extended opportunities to study and learn the new mathematics curriculum that their students would use, they were more likely to report practices similar to the aims of the state policy. These learning opportunities, which often lasted for three days or more, were not typical of professional education in U.S. schools. Also, teachers whose learning was focused around study of students' work on the new state assessments were more likely to report practices similar to the aims of the state policy. And teachers who had both of those learning opportunities reported practices that were even closer to reform objectives. The shorter-term professional development of most other teachers was keyed to special topics, like diversity in mathematics classrooms and cooperative grouping. These shorter-term learning opportunities, which were typical of professional education in California and elsewhere, did not allow teachers to learn about either student curricula or their work on assessments, and these teachers did not report practices close to reformers' goals.

Our observations are based on field research on the professional education available to California teachers in the early 1990s and on evidence from a survey of nearly six hundred California elementary-school teachers, undertaken by researchers from Michigan State University and Stanford University and completed in 1994–95. We focused on professional learning, because policymakers' aims were ambitious. Reformers in California sought to introduce a very different sort of math teaching from that typically found in U.S. classrooms. A conventional lesson on comparing fractions like $\frac{3}{8}$ and $\frac{12}{20}$, for instance, might begin with a teacher explanation of the procedure for finding a common denominator—multiply the denominators and convert the numerator, or record sets of equivalent fractions until a common denominator is found. Students would then practice the procedure, often using worksheets or problems in texts or workbooks. They would have little chance to connect the procedure to more concrete representations of size and equivalence, to develop and use alternative methods for fractional comparisons, or to begin their study by making comparisons in the context of realistic situations.

Seeing Fractions, a student curriculum package, was produced for the reforms to replace an upper-grade textbook unit on fractions—earning it and other such units the title "Replacement Units." *Seeing Fractions* offers an approach that is very different from conventional math instruction, first by introducing equivalent fractions in the context of *rates,* an often overlooked use of fractions, and then by allowing students to develop their own ideas about this topic. Teachers would start by posing a concrete problem to their classes:

I was at the amusement park last Saturday. I bought gumballs from one machine—I got three gumballs for eight pennies. My friend JoAnne told me that she'd found a different machine where gumballs were twelve for twenty cents. How could we compare them to find out which was the better buy?

Students would work for some time, using concrete materials, called "manipulatives," to aid their thinking. After developing solution methods, students would present their methods to the class and listen as others presented their own ideas. The curriculum materials asked teachers to ensure that students could talk through their strategies with reference to the concrete model, and defend their methods to peers. Only then were teachers to show a conventional method for comparing fractions. Small groups of students then would practice the method or methods they felt comfortable with; meanwhile, the teacher monitored their work by asking about methods and solutions.

In this case and many others, the student work of reform involved the development of new mathematical ideas and strategies, proof and justification, discussion and some practice. Students would also be working on new classroom tasks, ones which allowed for multiple interpretations or a variety of different solution methods. Teachers using this set of student materials would have to learn the new instructional methods and something about the mathematics students might invent or encounter along the way. Replacement units themselves tried to meet teachers' needs by describing such things in more detail than did typical mathematics textbooks. A teacher note on this lesson on comparing fractions, for instance, explains not only the method of finding equal denominators but also a method of finding equal numerators and a method of finding the unit cost. The lesson also identifies typical student misunderstandings of the mathematical content, and elsewhere the materials discuss the value of concrete materials, student-invented methods, and proof in mathematics. Such curricular material was meant to be instructive for both teachers and students.

To aid teachers further, these student units were accompanied by "replacement unit workshops"—two-and-a-half day sessions in which teachers would do the mathematics themselves, talk with each other about the content, and observe examples of student work on the materials. Similar workshops were developed around the California Learning Assessment System (CLAS), the test designed to assess schools' progress according to state frameworks. Teachers completed the student test items, examined student work and typical mistakes on such items, and learned about the mathematics involved.

Only a small fraction of the state's teachers had substantial opportunities to learn about the replacement units or new student assessments, but they made a big difference. Teachers whose opportunities to learn were grounded in specific curricula and assessments reported more of the sorts of practices that reformers had proposed than teachers whose opportunities to learn were not so grounded. Those practices included more sustained work on problems, fostering mathematical discussions and individual or group investigations of mathematical ideas. Teachers whose opportunities to learn were grounded in new curricula or student work reported fewer of the things reformers found undesirable—primarily worksheet drills and computational testing—than teachers whose work was not so grounded.

These workshops differed substantially from others offered in the state at the time, which were keyed to topics like diversity in mathematics classrooms and cooperative grouping methods. Most of these special-topics workshops did not allow teachers to learn about new student curricula, assessments, or students' work on either. Instead, teachers might try out one or a few "hands-on" activities, activities that in some ways embodied reform yet were not linked to one another, planned around students' response to the activities, or designed to develop a mathematical idea or process in depth. This more superficial sort of opportunity for professional growth is endemic to U.S. education.

Important as teacher learning was, reformers' main aim was to improve students' learning. We found that where teachers had opportunities to learn about student materials or assessments, students posted higher scores on the state's assessment of math achievement in elementary schools. Our conclusion was based on linking schools' average student scores on the reform-oriented 1994 state mathematics assessment with our data on teachers to learn whether state policy influenced student learning. Teachers' opportunities to learn about new student curricula and assessments were a critical link between state reform and student learning. These opportunities did not just describe the broad themes of these new policy instruments but were grounded in the actual mathematics and student work on curricula and assessments that were instruments of practice.

These findings imply a departure from conventional research on policy implementation. When researchers have tried to explain problems of implementation, they have typically pointed to complex causal links between state or federal agencies on the one hand and street-level implementers on the other. Those links often have been weakened by such things as bureaucratic difficulties, weak incentives to comply, and differences in the preferences of policymakers and implementers.

Our account adds a major category to these considerations: implementers' opportunities to learn. When California teachers had significant opportunities to learn how to improve students' learning, their practice changed appreciably and students' learning improved. Some policies depart further from existing practices than others, and the more they do, the more implementers have to learn. California's effort to improve mathematics teaching and learning was quite ambitious. Because it called for classroom practices that dramatically departed from conventional schoolwork, professionals' learning was a key element in connecting policy with practice.

One implication of this idea is that policy should be distinguished from the instruments deployed in its support. The 1985 Mathematics Framework for California Public Schools announced the policy, and if reformers had followed past example, they would have left matters there; the policy would have been little elaborated. We found, however, that teachers' knowledge of the framework was only modestly related to changes in teaching. The things that made a difference to changes in their practice were integral to instruction: curricular materials for teachers and students to use in class; assessments that enabled students to demonstrate their mathematical performance —and teachers to consider it—and instruction for teachers that was grounded in these curriculum materials and assessments. These instruments elaborated the framework ideas in much more detailed form, which was usable in instruction.

When the objectives of policies and the actions that implementers need to undertake are thus elaborated, policies are more likely to work. One reason is that everyone concerned can see more clearly what the policy calls for. The goals of the California reforms, for instance, were given instructionally salient shape in examples of students' work on the new assessment and in workshops on the replacement units. Another reason is that such instruments build a basis for implementers' learning. The replacement unit student curricula were turned into materials from which teachers could learn not only the new mathematics their students would study, but how students might make sense of the subject and how teachers might respond. The most important policy instruments in the California math reform were those which enabled teachers to work with learners in the ways reformers had envisioned.

A second implication of our analysis is that consistency among policy instruments is an important influence on the success of reforms like that in California. Inconsistencies among assessments, curricular materials, and teacher education would create opportunities for different and divergent interpretations of the policy, and that would reduce consistency in implementation and policy effects. Policymakers took steps to create such consistency at the state level. They developed curricular frameworks that set out the aims and direction for the changes in math teaching and learning. They used those frameworks to evaluate commercial math texts, in an effort to guide the creation of math materials that could improve teaching and learning. And they used the frameworks to guide creation of new state assessments that were designed to test students' performance on the sorts of tasks that the curriculum and frameworks specified. Reformers also used the frameworks to guide development of instruments of practice, like new math curriculum units for students and teachers. It took only a few years for professionals in firms and universities to develop roughly a dozen new math curriculum units, but it took several more years to revise the state math assessments so that they were consistent with the new frameworks and curriculum.

Reformers also took steps to create coherence among the instruments of policy at the level of practice. They encouraged curriculum developers and other education professionals to create opportunities for teachers to learn about the new curricula and assessment methods. As a result, some teachers' learning was grounded in serious study of the curriculum they would teach, and that curriculum was the focus for their learning. This enabled teachers to learn many things that are unusual in U.S. professional education, including how students might deal with the material. Since the frameworks, new curriculum units, and new assessments had been designed to be at least roughly consistent, learning about one was at least indirectly informative about the others—but learning in detail about all three sorts of guidance was even more informative. Teachers who did learn from the CLAS and replacement units encountered coherent guidance for instruction that was embedded in practice, not just in remote instruments of policy. That was dramatically different from most state policies and most professional education.

If the state's initiative was innovative, though, it was not the most powerful effort of its sort. It was made entirely by one agency of the state's executive branch—the State Board of Education—not by the governor or the legislature, or both. Hence, its authority was limited. Moreover, because political traditions of local control made state agencies reluctant to mandate local educational action, the policy was only advisory; teachers could not be compelled to comply. The state education agency also was technically and administratively weak. Even if it had mandated compliance, it had very modest resources to monitor or offer help. It had fewer than three staffers in mathematics, in a state that is larger and more populous than most countries. Thus, the state depended on other agencies and individuals to enable implementation. Though the state took the official initiative and made several key contributions to the math reforms, much of the work in curriculum development and professional education was done by private professionals who supported improved math learning and teaching.

Researchers and policymakers often have been skeptical about the likelihood of connecting policy with practice in education. One researcher has likened policy to storms that stir the surface of oceans but fail to change much below that surface. The ideas we advance here, and the evidence presented in the following chapters, reflect a very different view. Policies that aim to improve teaching and learning depend on complex chains of causation. Making the policies work depends both on their elaboration and on connecting the links in those chains. One crucial element in many of those links is their instructional content: policies that offer professionals suitable opportunities to learn and coherent guidance for teaching and learning increase the opportunities to connect policy and practice.

This reasoning led us and colleagues in this research program to an "instructional" view of the relations between policy and practice (Cohen and Barnes 1993). Relations between the surface of policy and events far below in practice can be close or remote, depending on the extent to which instructionally fruitful connections between the two are both built and used.[1]

When Reform Does Not Work

The policy was a success for some California teachers and students, and most of this book is devoted to exploring that success story. It led to the creation of new opportunities for teachers to learn, rooted either in improved student curriculum or in examples of students' work on state assessments, or both. Teachers were able to work together on serious problems of curriculum, teaching, and learning in short-term professional communities. The policy also helped to create coherence among elements of curriculum, assessment, and learning opportunities for certain teachers. Such coherence is quite rare in the blizzard of often divergent guidance for instruction that typically blows over U.S. public schools. Only a modest fraction of California elementary teachers—roughly 10 percent—had the experiences just summarized.

One reason for this was the fragmentation of educational governance. State policymakers had fashioned the reforms coherently in Sacramento, but the coherence usually eroded as the policy made its way through the layers of district, school, and professional organizations that made some claim to guide instruction in the state. Some teachers found themselves with opportunities to learn about new student curriculum, for instance, but no opportunities to learn about the linked student assessment. Because teachers made professional development decisions independent of one another —and sometimes independent of their district or school's priorities— teaching in some schools was not consistent; teachers in adjacent classrooms and consecutive grades were taking very different stands on mathematics teaching and practices. Fragmentation of reforms also meant that many teachers who tried to engage new ideas and practices did not receive substantive support from their principals or districts, and principals and districts often did not receive support from teachers. For most California teachers, reform was substantially less coherent in their school than it was in Sacramento. That limited the effects of the reform.

Another reason for the many missed opportunities was that the reformers' efforts to create coherent relationships were superimposed on the existing market-driven professional development system and were in most cases overwhelmed by it. As fast as reformers could create novel ideas and opportunities for professional growth, the existing system transformed them into less powerful and more conventional experiences, such as one-day workshops on student curriculum units. Some of reformers' ideas were also offered as part of a much larger array of far more typical sorts of professional development, and neither teachers nor administrators could distinguish between the two types. That inability to distinguish effective from ineffective professional development also hampered reform efforts. The sheer numerical dominance of conventional opportunities to learn also meant that most teachers did not have extended opportunities to learn about new mathematics instruction, opportunities to work with other teachers on how students thought about mathematics, or opportunities to examine how students worked new and more complex problems on the revised state assessment. Even if they had known how to choose effective learning opportunities, there were relatively few to choose from. As a result, many important connections remained unmade, and many opportunities to learn were never created.

Policy and Research

The ideas summarized above strongly suggest, contrary to most research on education policy, that state policy can have a constructive influence on teaching and learning. They also strongly suggest that such influence depends on forging connections among often disparate elements of organizations, on teachers' having opportunities to learn that are grounded in practice, and on coherence among the instruments of policy. They also open up a new way of thinking about education policy, one that bears directly on current debates in state and national policy. Most reformers, including many governors, President George W. Bush, and many business officials concerned with schools, have argued that schools need to be shaped up with stronger academic standards, stiffer state tests, and accountability for students' scores. Our research shows that these efforts are unlikely to succeed broadly by themselves. Standards, assessments, and accountability are more likely to succeed if they are accompanied by extended opportunities for professional learning that are grounded in practice. That is not easy, for it requires extensive attention to the practice-related instruments of policy, and coherence among those instruments at the classroom as well as the state level. Few policymakers argue for such things, and fewer still have tried to create them.

Our analysis also opens up a new cognitive, or instructional, approach to policy analysis in education and perhaps in other social sectors. It shows that effective implementation of instructional policies depends not only on making connections among often disparate agencies, but also on creating adequate opportunities for professionals to learn what the policy requires of them. Talk of linking policy and professional development has become quite popular in the years since we began this study, particularly with the contributions of Guthrie (1990), Cohen and Barnes (1993), and Spillane (2000) to our understanding of the relationship between individual cognition and implementation. Our analysis shows, however, that not all opportunities to learn are created equal. In California, only those which were grounded in practice and in which teachers had a chance to study and use student curriculum and assessments and see examples of student work had a constructive effect. This finding accords with other research on effective professional development (Kennedy 1998; Brown, Smith, and Stein 1996).

The findings we summarize here would probably not have been noticed in conventional policy research. We assumed that implementation would be quite variable, and we designed the survey and its analysis to identify factors that accounted for variation in implementation. We did so in part to avoid asking the conventional policy research question: On average, did the policy work? Such questions make sense only if a policy turns out roughly the same in all sites of practice. As we will show, though, the variations in the implementation of the California math policy were quite extensive. Hence, to inquire whether the policy "worked" depended on specifying what the policy implemented was. Policy research that fails to make such distinctions can quite seriously mislead everyone about the nature and effects of policy.

The work on which we report here has taken seven or eight years and cost about $3 million. It has not been easy, and more work should be done to probe our analyses. Yet all the research we and our colleagues did represents a very modest investment of time and money, compared with the potential benefits the research offers. We would not have been able to do the work, and the potential benefits never would have been possible, had it not been for the help of two private foundations and the National Science Foundation. Neither the professional organizations that backed the California reforms nor the state education agency made any effort either to learn systematically from experience or to report findings to professionals, the public, and policymakers. Though professionals in these organizations were happy to help us, their approach to educational improvement did not seem to include systematic learning about the implementation and effects of their efforts. They did not hold themselves to the same standards of reflective work or quality of argument they advocated for teachers and students in California.

That practice seems shortsighted and potentially damaging. We would not tolerate it if our physicians made decisions about our health care that were as inadequately based on research as most critical decisions in public education have been. If, as most Americans believe, education is a leading item on the public agenda, decisions about it should be much better informed. Better research on the attempts at and effects of school improvement should be a central part of those efforts.

Chapter 2

THE NEW NEW MATH IN CALIFORNIA

California's attempt at reform was as inventive as it was ambitious. One reason was that the reformers worked from a weak base. Politically, the state government's influence on local schools was modest, and its technical and professional capacity to encourage and support local change was meager. If reform was to have much effect in classroom practice, something more than the standard approach would be required. That led state officials and professionals outside government to collaborate in devising several unusual approaches to linking policy and practice.

Reformers' ambitions were another reason that the reforms were innovative. They wanted to greatly improve the intellectual challenge and quality of schoolwork, and they saw that most influences on instruction cut in the other direction. That led them both to try to change many instruments that guide instruction and to create coherence among them. Though large elements of California's math reforms were lost in political warfare, many more states now have adopted versions of California's approach.

We sketch the developments that led California reformers to their policy innovations and summarize the instruments they devised and deployed.

Policy, History, and Politics

The 1985 Mathematics Framework for California Public Schools was an early product of a national movement for school reform. The earliest national evidence was the 1983 report of the National Center for Education and the Economy, *A Nation at Risk,* which criticized schools for lax intellectual work and set out an agenda for more rigorous academic content and more demanding teaching. The report artfully straddled the camps in the war over whether schools should push the "basics" or intellectually more demanding work, by arguing for a version of the latter but referring to it as "the new basics," and avoiding many specifics. As its sponsors had hoped, *A Nation at Risk* helped galvanize concern about schools across the nation, for it spawned hundreds of other study groups, commissions, and reports. Within a few years, it was no exaggeration to speak of a "movement" for school reform, for the commissions and reports were quickly followed by actions on the part of both professional and governmental bodies. Several state education departments began efforts to revise curricula in the middle of the decade; the Coalition of Essential Schools, which encourages grassroots school transformation, was formed at about the same time; the National Council of Teachers of Mathematics (NCTM) decided to begin the work that led to its curricular standards; and a few years later President George H. W. Bush met with the governors to announce national education goals. All these endeavors shared a rhetoric that emphasized the need for more intellectually challenging work in schools.

California's 1985 framework was thus part of a swelling stream of thought and action in which the problems of schooling were depicted as the result of too much drill and practice, too much reliance on traditional, didactic, teacher-centered pedagogy, and too little respect for disciplinary knowledge and students' thinking. These ideas were hardly new. California's earliest mathematics frameworks, published in 1963 and 1972, contained many themes of the first "new math" movement of the post-Sputnik era: teachers were urged to pay more attention to mathematics and students' thinking. Robert Davis, an entrepreneurial mathematician, math educator, and professional developer, and a leading figure in the new math, used a National Science Foundation (NSF) grant and monies appropriated by the state legislature to create a program called Miller Math. The project brought hundreds of teachers together for two-week summer workshops based on the Discovery

Math lessons for students that Davis had written earlier, in the 1950s and '60s. Miller Math also supported the training of mathematics specialists to work in districts.

The later reforms benefited from these initiatives, which helped recruit bright teachers to learn a novel approach to mathematics instruction and created a tradition of child-centered, hands-on instruction in mathematics. Marilyn Burns, who become a major force both in mathematics education and in the California reforms after 1985, recalls Davis and Miller Math as inspirations, the beginning of her career as a math educator and of the current movement for reform. She also reports that she and, she thinks, other reformers of that time had little idea either about how much teachers would have to learn about mathematics and teaching math to teach in the way reformers then proposed, or about how much work it would take for them even to begin (interview with Marilyn Burns, November 20, 1997).

Since every action in U.S. education seems to provoke at least an equal reaction, the earlier math reforms were partially eclipsed as California swung back to basics in the 1970s and early 1980s, along with most of the United States. Miller Math was canceled, and the next state mathematics framework, published in 1974, called for more emphasis on basic skills like computation and less focus on overarching mathematical themes like set theory and numeration (Webb 1993). Although the 1974 document retained language about the merits of hands-on learning and the application of mathematical concepts, the next framework, published six years later in 1980, moved even further in the same direction: a section on proficiency standards and mathematical remediation was added to old language about problem solving (Webb 1993). The later 1970s and early 1980s were a time of national emphasis on the basics, on "effective schools," and on minimum competency testing. Programs like Madeline Hunter's Instructional Theory into Practice (ITIP) were immensely popular in California and elsewhere and were understood to support basic skills. Reformers from the Miller Math era and their ideas slipped from view for most practitioners and policymakers.

Max Rafferty, who had presided over the state's school system in the preceding decade, might be regarded as one of the creators of modern school politics, for he used the superintendency and the media to project partisan ideas about teaching and curriculum forcefully and to attack his opponents, including education professionals. Wilson Riles, Rafferty's successor, was of a decidedly liberal persuasion, but he was an equally adept political practitioner. Both men used their office to define issues, woo voters, and educate citizens and professionals. Both greatly strengthened the state's rhetorical presence in California schooling. Both vigorously politicized public education, and both broke new ground in using state policy instruments in efforts to shape local instruction. The state had a large role in textbook adoption, and Rafferty tried to shake liberal (or "red") ideas from texts, especially in social studies and literature. A state assessment system began in 1972 and represented another major expansion of the state role: the state began to collect and publish school-by-school evidence on student performance.

If these innovations added weight to the state presence in public schools, though, there were no concerted efforts to use the instruments of policy to re-educate professionals. Whatever their politics, policymakers in Sacramento did not break new ground in using curricula, teacher education, professional development, or student assessment either to change what educators knew or to stimulate classroom change. This situation left reformers in the late 1980s with a stronger state education establishment but no well-developed traditions of using state policy instruments to support implementation of state initiatives.

The 1985 mathematics framework drew on many themes of the earlier, pre-Rafferty frameworks, painting a dramatically different picture of mathematics teaching and learning than was conventional in public schools. It argued that mathematics taught solely through isolated rules, formulas, and procedures produces too many students who cannot apply these techniques to problems and who quickly forget mathematical operations. It contrasted traditional mathematics instruction with something it called teaching for understanding, the latter being cast as a solution to students' difficulties in learning math. Teachers were advised to pay more attention to students' construction of knowledge, to notice how students make meaning of mathematical ideas, and to aim instruction at improving conceptual understanding. The recommended instructional processes included providing students with concrete materials for learning (commonly referred to as manipulatives) and using real-life situations to engage students in complex problem-solving experiences. The 1985 framework further argued that building mathematical understanding is a social process: if students had opportunities to participate in classroom discussion and cooperative learning groups, they would compare ideas, challenge one another's thinking, and learn how to inquire. The frameworks also urged a renewed attention to the discipline of mathematics itself and widened the scope of what is usually taught in elementary classrooms to include numeration, measurement, geometry, estimation, statistics and probability, logic, and algebra.

As a broadside for reform, the 1985 document was a useful piece, but as guidance for action by educators, it offered very little help. It was thin, just under fifty pages, and presented only the most general sort of advice about practice. It fell far short of recommending specific curricular or instructional methods, not even telling readers where they might go for more ideas about how to do what the document urged. A few years later, the California Department of Education (CDE) published a thicker and somewhat more practice-oriented *Model Curriculum Guide,* intended to fill in a few of the missing pieces for those who wished to follow the state's advice. The guide did offer some helpful ideas about materials and academic tasks, but it still was sketchy and far from a teachers' guide to a year's work in mathematics. If teachers had begun searching on their own, their efforts would soon have been swamped by more new frameworks in other school subjects: the 1985 math framework was followed in 1988 by a no less novel English and language arts framework, and in 1989 and 1990 by frameworks for foreign language and science respectively.

The avalanche of new guidance for instruction was inspired in part by an energetic and reform-oriented new state superintendent, Bill Honig. Honig, who had been a teacher, was the scion of a wealthy northern California family. He was articulate and tireless. He had been elected in 1982 on what seemed a cautious platform of attention to the basics, but he shortly made clear that he would press for sweeping change in the state education system. His ambitions soon became a topic for black humor among California educators, as they archly wondered which subject would have to be entirely overhauled this year, and which next. If Honig's ambitions seemed impressive in Sacramento, in the schools they looked like a tidal wave. Many teachers reported that they did what they could in the subject of the year and then moved on.

The torrent of advice about teaching and learning was aided by the 1983 passage of the Hughes-Hart Educational Reform Act, Senate Bill (SB) 813. Among the eighty provisions of this legislation were increased graduation requirements, incentives to lengthen the school day and year, tightened discipline, improved teacher selection, and an $800-million boost for the state's schools. Reforms of this sort became standard for state education initiatives during the 1980s, and though relatively easily put into practice, they did not require fundamental change in schools or curricula (Fuhrman, Clune, and Elmore 1988; Murphy 1989). The real power of SB 813 lay instead in small passages. One called for making the state tests—the California Assessment Program (CAP)—more comprehensive and focused on higher-order thinking, and the other authorized curricular alignment and the development of a "model curriculum" to guide districts, schools, and teachers. Their effects were not immediately felt, but they enabled Honig and other reformers to begin efforts to change classroom instruction substantially.

In 1992, the state published a new math framework. It was much more detailed and was an even more radical departure from conventional classroom practice than the 1985 version had been. For example, the 1992 framework advised teachers to delay instruction on "number facts"—such as memorizing answers to multiplication problems—until students understood the processes that underlie those operations. This document was a more significant resource than its predecessor for teachers seeking to change their practices, for it offered descriptions of desired student mathematical thinking, suggested roles for teachers and students in the classroom, and proposed ideas for mathematical units. It also illustrated contrasts between conventional mathematics practices and those the framework's authors favored. The document introduced the idea of student "investigations," which were inquiries into mathematical ideas in novel problem-solving situations that could take a week or more to complete, and contrasted them both with traditional problem solving, which might take the student a minute or two, and with mathematical exercises—traditional addition or multiplication problems—which may take less than thirty seconds. The first type of task was designed to encourage student encounters with major mathematical ideas and was displayed as exemplary by the framework. The last, practiced alone, was discouraged.

The 1992 framework also used strongly egalitarian language, often adding the phrase "for all students" to recommendations made for instruction, materials, and mathematical content. The framework warned against tracking students by ability and advised teachers about teaching mathematics to diverse groups of students. That included students whose English proficiency was limited, who by 1991 made up one third of elementary students statewide.

Although the 1992 document provided more guidance for teachers who were trying to adopt new views of mathematics instruction and student learning, it still was far from what teachers would need to support extensive instructional change. Though the document provided many more examples of desirable and undesirable practices than its 1985 counterpart, for example, it offered no help at all to teachers who might want to learn how to undertake new approaches to math teaching. The 1992 framework was a proposal, not a guide to new practices or a curriculum for learning them. California politics prohibited the state from mandating curricular or instructional practices in classrooms, and that may have constrained the framework authors from giving much explanation of what teachers should do in specific grades for specific topics. Because state education governance mixed very active state guidance with a long-standing commitment to local control, reformers in the CDE had to work carefully.

In addition, as state influence grew, so did attacks on liberal policies and state power. The political frame of school politics had changed through the 1970s and 1980s, as the devastating effects of Proposition 13 and a long recession in the early 1990s drained resources from the system and shifted influence to Sacramento. Tax revenues fell, and the Republican governors Deukmejian and Wilson argued that revenues aside, state government was bloated and needed to shrink. One result was less money for the CDE to use in pressing any initiative, and another was more trouble for that agency. The number of state policy initiatives grew in public education, though, as the legislature increased its efforts to manage the schools and compete with executive branch agencies. This development was encouraged by the decline in the strength and discipline of political parties and resulting proliferation of individual policy entrepreneurs who hawked their pet solutions to social problems. Growing ideological divisions, fueled in part by a strong conservative movement in California, crosscut this activism and increased legislative conflict. Partisanship increased in the administrations of Governors Deukmejian and Wilson, as did contention over education policy. These developments also brought more political conflict over state reform efforts.

As state school reform initiatives increased, state support for professional development in education diminished. One of the many programs severely cut in the late 1980s was state professional development aid, which left the CDE with much less money to help teachers to learn the reforms in mathematics. That was a problem, because most teachers had a great deal to learn: few were mathematically literate, and they had few opportunities to learn or practice any improvements in math teaching, let alone adopt the reformers' ambitious proposals. Mathematics was not the most important subject in the elementary curriculum; in California classrooms that the Michigan State University (MSU) research group observed, math lessons rarely consumed more than fifty minutes of the school day, and they often took less. Reading, writing, and language arts consumed half or more of the school day, and there was more enthusiasm for change in reading. It was relatively easy for teachers to invest in such work, for they were already literate and did not need to learn to read to use literature in the classroom.

Paradoxically, then, although policy and political activity had increased at the state level, and the CDE had more power on paper, state guidance for instruction was less consistent, conflict over state policies more common, and funding to support state initiatives scarcer. The typical teacher could not revise her practice simply by reading the 1992 framework: she probably would not understand a great deal of it, and she would require opportunities to learn about students' mathematical thinking, new instructional methods, elementary school mathematics, and the instructional techniques that could turn the new ideas into usable instruction. Teachers seeking to transform their math classrooms would also need instructional materials to support their daily activities, but even if the CDE had had a lot of experience doing such work, it had neither the money, the staff, nor the political support for such detailed intervention.

The Instruments of Policy

Despite diminishing resources and increasingly partisan politics, reformers in California would have to find ways to help teachers overcome these obstacles if reformers were to have much influence on classrooms. Though they did have appreciable authority, and some impressive instruments with which to shape instruction, they did not have much experience. Their efforts in the late 1980s and early 1990s combined false starts with ingenious improvisation.

Reformers had a reasonable beginning in the 1985 mathematics framework, the K–8 model curriculum guide in 1987, and SB 813 and accompanying reform documents. All of these provided important platforms from which educational reformers might spread their ideas, but none offered teachers and schools much help in figuring out how to take up the new

ideas. One problem was that the frameworks and other state reform documents merely advised districts, which meant that local educators could ignore them. Before 1985, this practice seems to have been customary—
frameworks were published and quickly forgotten. Another problem was
that no one in California had much experience with making the sort of
wholesale, fundamental changes in instruction for which the frameworks
called. Reformers did have a mental list of things not to do—like leaving
teachers out of the planning or ignoring the interests of other players—but
they did not have a repertoire of tried and true measures that could support
changes in classroom practice.

They did have some significant new ideas, however. The most important
was that Honig and some of his advisers and colleagues on the State Board
of Education believed that if state policy could use the various policy instruments they controlled—curriculum guidance, text adoption, assessment, and the like—to send a consistent message about teaching and learning to schools, the messages would have a much better chance of being
heard, accepted, and put into practice. This idea about consistency within
instructional policy later came to be called systemic, or standards-based, reform, and it has been quite widely used by states in the last fifteen years in
attempts to improve public education. The idea seems to have been the
nearest thing to a broad strategy that reformers had. It led them to try to influence a range of policy instruments—curriculum, assessment, and teachers' learning—that might shape practice. Nonetheless, their approach was
not well developed, for they had no detailed plans. Reformers, as they altered elements of the state's educational apparatus to encourage local educators to pay attention and change, repeatedly improvised, as they discovered how much there was to do and tried to cope with increasing conflict
over the reforms.

Curriculum materials. The 1985 framework itself stirred little controversy,
but shortly after it was issued, the Curriculum Commission of the State
Board of Education used it to guide textbook adoption, and that produced
something of a political firestorm. In California, as in several other states,
the state board reviews and approves textbooks, and state approval carries
weight, because localities get state aid if they use approved texts. The state
board claimed that the commercially published textbooks available in 1985
were not suitably aligned with the framework and rejected all but one text.
After much debate, some negotiation, appreciable political pressure from

publishers, and a good deal of acrimony, some of the books were somewhat revised, and the board declared most of them fit for children's use. Yet by some reports, the texts came back to the Curriculum Committee with only 10 percent of their pages changed, and many people argued that the books only weakly supported the new framework (interview with Walter Denham, December 19, 1997).

The controversy, and the publishers' lobbying, helped mobilize opposition to the state's new approach. It also highlighted a dilemma for reformers. The 1985 framework recommended a truly novel approach to mathematics, one not widely practiced among the state's or nation's teachers, and there was no early evidence that educators were flocking to the new ideas. Why should textbook publishers radically revise texts at enormous expense if there was no sign that the new ideas would find a "market" among local districts? Yet, if the publishers did not make the change, reformers would lack a crucial element in revising instruction, for without suitable materials to use with students, teachers would have little to work with in trying to implement the framework.

To remedy that problem, state officials encouraged the development of small, topic-centered modules, which they termed replacement units. In 1989, the CDE contracted with Susan Jo Russell, a curriculum developer at the Technical Education Research Center (TERC) in Cambridge, Massachusetts, to produce a fifth grade fractions replacement unit. Joan Akers and Walter Denham, two state officials who worked on the math reforms, reported that the replacement unit strategy had several purposes. One was to begin to fill the gaping hole in support for reform created by the absence of suitable curriculum. Another was to devise materials that would make converts for reform. Choice of topics was critical, for the CDE officials needed units that would have a good chance of being widely used, which might sell teachers on the reforms by helping them and their students, and which might show publishers and others that there was a large market for less conventional instructional materials.

State officials settled on fractions. This topic involves mathematically important material that was typically treated very conventionally and often unintelligibly, as a matter of pure computation. Nearly all teachers taught fractions, but many had trouble with them themselves and knew that fifth graders often had difficulty understanding mathematical representations and manipulations of fractions. Students frequently misapplied algorithms, for instance, confusing the addition and multiplication procedures. By providing teachers with new materials that made fractions more intelligible and offered a method for teaching the topic in a way that would improve student understanding, state officials hoped they could make many converts. They reasoned that by building a grass-roots market for such materials, they could help to convince textbook publishers that there was, or could be, a market for a "thinking curriculum." Akers and Denham had their eyes on the state textbook adoptions that were set for 1994; they wanted to lay the groundwork for commercial production and state adoption of high-quality, reform-oriented materials.

Replacement units thus would be a temporary and transitional measure, intended to offer missing curricular assistance for reform while building support for much better commercial materials. To help ensure success, Akers and Denham took the unusual step of arranging special training in the curricula for twenty-five of the state's strongest fifth grade teachers. Once these teachers had taught the units in their own classrooms and reconvened to discuss the experience, they would work in pairs, offering two-and-a-half-day workshops on the new curriculum to other teachers around the state.

The *Seeing Fractions* unit was ready within five months of being commissioned. State-sponsored professional development workshops were announced to districts and educational organizations in the spring of 1990. To everyone's surprise, the eighteen workshops were wildly popular—one thousand teachers subscribed within three weeks of the announcement. The master teachers scheduled an additional eight workshops, which quickly filled, as well. Overall, about 1,500 teachers had access to these opportunities to learn about this replacement unit, and more learned about it in subsequent waves of county- and district-hosted workshops offered by some of the teachers who had attended the original series. Denham told us that "we paid a lot for that, but it was worth every penny."

Since the replacement unit was a big hit among teachers, the message spread quickly. In the years before the 1994 textbook adoptions, seven more elementary-level replacement units, on subjects from decimals to geometry to measurement, were produced and disseminated by private curriculum developers. The second unit, titled "My Travels with Gulliver," covering

measurement and proportion, was produced at the Educational Development Center in Massachusetts, and the state again paid for the initial training of twenty-five California teacher-disseminators. A third unit, on multiplication, was written by Marilyn Burns for the third grade. Workshops
for teachers were held through both Burns's own company and the state-
sponsored train-the-trainer approach in the summer and fall of 1991. More
than four hundred teachers were trained by Marilyn Burns Associates alone.

After publication of the initial replacement units, including one for the
middle grades, the state took itself out of direct provision of professional development and curriculum. By the mid-1990s, replacement units had become a small industry in California. Curriculum developers printed and disseminated their own work, often turning themselves into small publishing
companies in the process. Sharon Ross's Chico State project, for instance, was
responsible for the *Beyond Activities* elementary-grade units. Her project
was funded by federal Eisenhower professional development grants, and it
produced three replacement units through an intensive process in which
roughly two dozen teachers co-wrote, piloted, revised, piloted, revised, and
then disseminated the curricula between 1991 and 1993. Ross told us that her
office had sold 20,000 units in one year alone, mostly to California teachers.
Marilyn Burns Associates, already a major publisher of innovative books and
materials, sold 49,500 of their unit nationwide by the end of 1994.

State officials were satisfied that they had established a market for novel
curriculum materials and had in turn spurred mathematics specialists and
teachers to develop more units. Walter Denham reported that "we nearly had
to beat them [developers] off with a stick." Yet the state education agency retained no authority over the term "replacement unit." This meant that it gave
up the opportunity to control quality and that state officials later complained about the content of some of the units.

Professional development supporting the workshops mushroomed too,
as organizations like the California Mathematics Project, the California
Mathematics Council, and county and district professional development
offices offered teachers opportunities to learn about and obtain replacement
unit materials. Although some of these workshops were shorter than state
officials and curriculum writers would have liked—some teachers who
used the unit taught half-day workshops to others in their school—there
was remarkably wide dissemination of the curriculum materials. Many
replacement-unit authors later sold their rights to small commercial pub-

lishing companies like Creative Publications, and the material is now available to teachers across the country.

Walter Denham and Joan Akers judged the replacement-unit strategy to be a success. They had advanced the reform with useful curriculum modules. They had stimulated demand for novel curricula. And they had sent a message to publishers about the existence of a major market for innovative, reform-oriented materials as they looked toward the 1994 textbook adoption. They later reported that publishers responded, producing markedly improved—but still not ideal—texts, which were approved by the state and adopted by many districts. Since then, Denham and Akers told us, professional development has focused less on replacement units and more on helping teachers use the new commercial texts. Starting from a base of little experience and modest resources, state officials and reformers had built impressive curricular support for reform in the short run and changed supply and demand for materials in the longer run.

Professional development. New materials were a significant step for the reforms, but to make a difference, they would have to be usable. That would require helping teachers learn to use them, when most teachers knew only a conventional version of arithmetic, few had any deeper knowledge of mathematics, and most taught in a very conventional, facts-and-skills manner. If they were to respond constructively to the reforms, teachers would have a great deal to learn. Learning the new mathematical ideas in the replacement units was one major concern; learning how students would make sense of the more challenging materials was another; and learning how to help students learn a new version of mathematics was yet another.

Meeting those challenges was at least as formidable a task as creating new materials, and the reformers had less of a grip on it. Professional development soaks up a lot of money in states like California, but little of it is focused on serious matters of curriculum or student learning—there simply is no tradition of extended or thoughtful work on such matters. Most workshops were short and superficial. In addition, this was not a domain in which the state had a great deal of influence. Most of its funds for such activities had been cut in the late 1980s Sacramento budget wars, and local districts were taking an even larger role in professional development. Many districts contracted with external "experts," some cultivated in-house teacher-experts, and larger districts did both. The resulting opportunities for professional education consisted chiefly of short workshops for large

numbers of local teachers, dealing with matters that were easily appre-
hended and directly useful.

As the math reforms began, professional developers focused on the elements they could most easily adapt to the culture and organization of the
very decentralized nonsystem sketched out above. The Michigan State research group's interviews revealed that the most popular new offerings concerned "math manipulatives" and "concrete materials." Local districts and
county offices offered countless workshops for teachers, helping them learn
how to use blocks, beads, beans, and other objects to represent the four basic
arithmetical operations. A former teacher, Mary Baratta-Lorton, had published a book titled *Math Their Way* in 1976, and its popularity soared with
the reforms. The book was organized around the use of manipulatives, and
it became one of the chief texts for professional development and a key supplement for many primary-grade teachers.

As the reforms developed, the replacement units got more attention. The
state-sponsored workshops described earlier seemed to initiate a waterfall
effect, stimulating districts, county offices, and private providers to offer
their own versions of workshops for teachers. Still other workshops focused
on CLAS, the assessment that had been designed to be consistent with the
frameworks. These introduced teachers to new views of math, novel problems, and examples of student work. If some workshops focused on replacement units and CLAS, though, many others focused on elements of the
reforms that seemed less directly related to curriculum and instruction. The
chief contender in this department was "cooperative learning," a practice
recommended by the framework as a way to encourage mathematical conversation among students but which became widely popular as a generic approach to classroom organization, with little reference to curriculum or to
the disciplined student inquiry that reformers also meant to foster. Cooperative learning seemed to be everywhere in California in the late 1980s and
early 1990s.

A different approach to professional development was funded by the California State University (CSU) system. The system supported the California
Mathematics Project, which used its own and federal grants to fund university mathematicians and math educators to host teachers in several small,
weeklong (or longer) summer workshops and ongoing professional support. There were seventeen of these projects, and their content varied according to the tastes and capacities of their university hosts. Some focused

on the National Council of Teachers of Mathematics (NCTM) standards and California reforms, but others did not. The state's share of federal Eisenhower monies, available through state applications, also supported some professional development, as in the case of the Chico State project. Finally, a number of freestanding professional organizations and entrepreneurs offered teachers opportunities to learn about the frameworks and curricula. The California Mathematics Council (CMC), the state's NCTM affiliate, held annual conferences at which major reform ideas were discussed, and the CMC encouraged its regional and county affiliates to offer sessions to educate teachers. The Lawrence Hall of Science at Berkeley offered training in EQUALS, *Family Math* activities, and CLAS. And Marilyn Burns, in addition to writing the replacement unit, offered a series of five-day Math Solutions workshops geared toward helping teachers and schools implement the NCTM standards. All this professional development was intended to advance the reform, and some of it was undertaken by state or state-funded agencies. None, however, were initiatives over which Honig and his staff had any influence. The multiplication of state agencies, the interest of federal agencies, and the efforts of reformers meant that teachers heard different versions of the reform message, from many different sources.

Considered historically, there had been appreciable progress in creating opportunities for teachers to learn new approaches to math teaching. Workshops focused on the new curriculum materials, the new state assessments, and other features of the reforms, and thousands of teachers took them. Though this situation represented an advance over the relative lack of such opportunities in 1985, reformers had only scratched the surface, considering the need. Additionally, although professional development paid much more attention to reform, it had done so chiefly by absorbing bits and pieces of the reform agenda into the pre-existing scattered and superficial framework of professional development. The reform agenda that was available to teachers became more diffuse as its elements were disseminated. The state had great difficulty exerting much leadership, partly because of political and budget wars in Sacramento and partly because the political organization of public education in the state was designed to inhibit the sustained exercise of state influence. State reformers' efforts helped advance reform, but the results revealed how much more would be needed to reach more than a fraction of elementary school teachers.

Assessment and accountability. As ideas about standards-based reform developed in the 1980s, reformers began to portray assessment as a key element for "driving" instruction. Bill Honig, Lauren Resnick of the University of Pittsburgh, Mike Smith and Jennifer O'Day of Stanford University, and others argued that aligning the state assessments with the frameworks would ensure that the state was sending the same messages about teaching and learning with all policy instruments at its disposal. That would be a significant innovation in a school system in which varied guidance for instruction flowed from scores of different sources, with little or no effort at coordination. But if giving coherent advice about instruction to teachers, students, parents, and others was one reason to "align" the state's policy instruments and thus to change the tests, another was changing the incentives. Reformers who wanted to make instruction more "accountable" argued that teachers would not move far from algorithms and rote memorization if the old tests, which called for exactly such work, remained in place. New tests, tied to the new framework, would remove the incentive for teachers and students to focus solely on "the basics" and might provide an incentive for teachers to modify instruction to match the framework more closely. Those who cared about performance on the test might be motivated to investigate new forms of instruction or curriculum. Teachers who saw students struggling or succeeding with new mathematical problems might be motivated to learn more about those problems. Assessment might influence performance by offering teachers opportunities to learn, incentives to perform, or both. Commentators and reformers often take sides on assessments as a means of accountability, but the assessments are potentially more complex than the arguments about them.[1]

California's annual California Assessment Program had reported on students' and schools' performance since 1973. Those assessments gauged performance on standardized, multiple-choice tests on the "basic skills" of writing, reading, and mathematics and in the content areas of science, history, and literature.[2] State officials worked through the late 1980s and into the 1990s to reconcile conflicting messages by revising the tests to accord with the new frameworks. They wrote items and developed assessment formats that would gauge students' mathematical thinking, as well as their more conventional skills and knowledge.

The new tests were first given in the spring of 1993, after years of political tussles, field tests, technical difficulties, and a hastily contrived teacher-education campaign. The new CLAS was administered to fourth, eighth, and twelfth grade students. In English language arts, students were asked to read texts and respond to open-ended questions about that text. In mathematics, the assessment asked elementary school students to solve novel problems and justify their answers. Students' work was scored, and the scores were averaged to the school level and then published in 1993. State officials then organized unusually extensive opportunities for teachers to use CLAS as a way to learn about the new mathematics by learning about how students made sense of it. Teachers were invited to help grade students' work on the open-ended items on the test in the summer of 1993, and they used the grading to learn the math underlying these items, as well as to learn how students thought about the math.

Judged from the perspective of those who saw external incentives as the chief policy instrument, CLAS offered only weak school accountability, for the state attached no sanctions for poor performance or failure to improve. But there could be some incentive in publication of schools' scores, which could be a wake-up call for parents or officials and could give teachers an opportunity to see how students did on the new kinds of mathematics. Furthermore, CLAS was not the only string in the state's bow: California also required a school-level Program Quality Review (PQR). All schools receiving School Improvement Program (SIP) funds—that is, most schools—had to undergo review every three years. Teams were appointed to make site visits, and review criteria were promulgated by state officials. Criteria for school and district performance were drawn from the state's frameworks, and local educators reported on their performance. Site visitors assessed local progress on the criteria. Although PQR sought accountability, and state officials used it to encourage alignment, it entailed appreciable learning, as teachers gathered to read the frameworks and review curricula and instruction within schools (Barnes 1997; Perry 1996).

The picture on assessment and accountability was as mixed as it was for other elements of the reform. Important progress was made toward more coherence among the instruments that state policymakers used to encourage change, and a serious effort had been made to create opportunities for teachers to learn in and around the new assessments. The reforms only scratched the surface in these areas, however. No more than a tiny fraction of the state's teachers had any serious opportunity to learn about the assessment. A slightly larger but still very small fraction of teachers had had such chances to learn about the replacement units. Additionally, several of the most important policy instruments, like pre-service teacher education, were entirely outside the CDE's jurisdiction. There was little chance to deal with these matters, for political troubles engulfed the CLAS soon after it began, and it was canceled. This innovative assessment was soon replaced by a more conventional testing system.

The California math reform was unusual. State officials and supporters in the private sector deployed a broad array of instruments to promote change in math teaching and learning. They began to devise a new curriculum and paid a good deal of attention to its usefulness and strategic value for further reform. They began to change professional development in ways that were grounded in the student curriculum and assessments tied to the reforms. Officials created a new assessment system, linked to the new frameworks, and began to offer teachers opportunities to learn from it. In these ways and others the reformers offered many teachers hitherto unimagined opportunities to learn new approaches to math teaching.

These initiatives were especially impressive given the absence of much experience with basic instructional change in a mass education system. They required substantial innovation, extraordinary collaboration among many individuals and agencies in and outside government, and sustained hard work. The progress that was made was due in large part to remarkable innovation, not only in policy but also further down the line toward practice. The reformers were remarkably inventive in devising the instruments —assessments, curricula, and teacher development—that might support improved instruction.

The effort also was remarkable, though, for the absence of much evidence to guide reform, and the lack of any effort to learn systematically from experience. None of the individuals or agencies used research and evaluation to learn how the reforms were playing out, what approaches to change seemed most and least useful, and what helped students most. The sort of thoughtful practice, including learning from students' work, that reformers urged on teachers and students was not prominently on display in the reformers' work with educators. A few researchers interested themselves in the California math reforms, and professionals in California report that they found the work useful. It is curious, however, that this is the first effort to consider the statewide progress of reforms that were intended, among other things, to prod students and teachers to view their work much more self-consciously and learn from it.

Chapter 3

LEARNING ABOUT REFORM

California reformers argued that teachers' conventional practice and superficial treatment of mathematics were central reasons that students' mathematics learning was so routine and mechanical. Teachers would have to perform quite differently if students' learning was to improve. If teachers were to teach as the framework proposed, however, and if most teaching was as conventional as reformers argued, implementation of the state reform would depend on many teachers learning a great deal (Cohen and Barnes 1993; Guthrie 1990). According to this view, teachers were both a source of the policy problem and a key to its solution. Their learning could turn that paradox into a success story.

These ideas suggest that the questions researchers ask about policymaking and implementation should not be limited to issues of compliance, incentives, and bureaucracy but ought also to include the sort of questions one might address to any case of teaching and learning: What was taught—that is, what content were the learners (in this case, the teachers) exposed to? What opportunities did they have to engage and assimilate it? How deeply did these opportunities to learn penetrate the subject matter, how extensive were they, and how broadly were they distributed across the population of teachers? For if few learners had substantial opportunities to explore new ideas about mathematics, or if their opportunities to learn were superficial, we would expect weak enactment, on average, and unimpressive policy outcomes.

These ideas were not as clear to policymakers and reformers early in the reform as they later became. The 1985 framework said little about how teachers might learn or where the relevant resources for learning might be found. Perhaps that silence meant that reformers expected teachers to learn easily, or perhaps reformers simply did not focus on the matter. Several of them later reported that they had been shocked when research showed how modest many teachers' responses to the reforms were, and how much they had to learn. As we wrote in Chapter 2, though, early experience with efforts to implement the new policy encouraged policymakers to invent several innovative approaches to improving math teaching and learning and to helping teachers learn.

If learning potentially has an important influence on policy, then it is necessary to understand the influences on learning. In this chapter we take a step toward exploring the nature and extent of those influences, by reporting on the instruments that policymakers and others used to encourage teachers to learn. Our survey sorted those instruments into four categories. One was reform documents that teachers could read; a second was professional development activities in which they could learn about the reforms and about teaching and learning mathematics; a third was professional networks in which they could participate and thereby learn about the reforms; and a fourth was the state mathematics assessments, which could be used as an occasion to learn either about how students would be tested or about how students responded, or both.

These four activities, which might appear to analysts as the instruments of policy, can also be regarded as the curricula of reform for those who learned from them. If learning has an important influence on the implementation of policy, those curricula could form a key connection between policymakers' ideas, on the one hand, and teachers' practice on the other. The content of these curricula might encourage teachers to adopt reformers' new ideas and practices, or it might impede the process, or it might have no effect at all. Because learning plays such a key role in our story of the California reforms, it is worth examining in some depth the instruments that were deployed to encourage learning. We first discuss the survey on which the analysis is based and what it tells us about teachers, their schools, and students. Then we turn to a discussion of the instruments that policymakers and others deployed to support teachers' learning and to some analysis of the distribution of opportunities to learn across the teacher population. In Chapter 4, we turn to what teachers reported about learning from those instruments.

The Survey

The Sample. One goal of the survey was to situate the original Michigan State University case studies in a wider picture of mathematics practice in California elementary schools. The MSU research group wanted to know how general their case study findings about the response to reform were, and they wanted to get a better sense of what the average teacher knew and believed about math teaching. They might have simply polled a thousand randomly sampled teachers from the state about their views on mathematics reform, but this would have yielded more responses than necessary from teachers in high-population areas like Los Angeles, and not enough from those in rural areas to represent those areas accurately. Instead, the survey employed a multistage cluster sampling design: first, school districts were selected from a sampling frame in which they were stratified by size; then schools were selected from those districts. That allowed the researchers to draw enough schools from each size category to ensure an accurate representation of the views of teachers in them, while maintaining efficiency— and the "cluster design" of four teachers per school might allow the estimation of between- and within-school variances for some measures.

The resulting stratified sample is shown in Table 3.1. One teacher per grade for grades 2 through 5 was selected at random from each of the 250 schools; to each, a long-form survey was mailed. Because some schools did not support four teachers for these grades, the final number of teachers in the sample is 975, rather than 1,000.[1] Sampling weights were constructed to account for the unequal probability of each school's and teacher's entry into the sample. Using these weights in combination with a correction for non-response—that is, overweighting those in strata where response rates were low—allowed us to obtain estimates of the population parameters for the measures discussed in this chapter. The sampling and nonresponse weights were also used for later analyses.

Table 3.1. Sampling Frame

Stratum	District enrollment	Districts sampled/ total districts in stratum	Number of schools sampled/district
1	600,000+	1/1	10
2	35,000–125,000	10/10	5
3	10,000–34,999	50/98	2
4	1,000–9,999	70/368	1
5	Less than 1,000	20/421	1

The survey instrument was developed during the spring and summer of 1994 by the MSU researchers and Joan Talbert. (Talbert is a principal at Stanford's Center for Research on the Context of Teaching.) Survey development focused on the issues discussed in Chapters 1 and 2, but questions were culled from previous surveys,[2] both because other studies had revealed something about the validity and reliability of such items and because using the items allowed comparisons among projects (Ball 1990; Mayer 1999). Twelve experts on mathematics, instruction, and survey research reviewed a draft of the survey, and eight California teachers piloted the instrument before it was mailed to respondents in late fall 1994. Teachers were offered twenty-five dollars in instructional materials for completing and returning the hour-long survey. The survey design and administration were overseen by Talbert, to whom we owe a great debt.

Careful sampling and follow-up on nonresponses means that the sample of teachers, when properly weighted, probably comes very close to representing the population of teachers in the state. Those who did not immediately respond were sent reminders by mail. Of the 975 teachers who were surveyed, 559 (57 percent) responded in these early efforts. As a check for possible nonresponse bias, the survey staff made an intensive effort to convince a small sample of 70 nonresponding teachers to complete the survey. Thirty-six teachers from this group eventually completed the survey, bringing the total response to 595 (61 percent) and allowing some estimation of differences between this group and the main sample. That stage was completed by the spring of 1995. In addition, 13 teachers in the nonresponding group answered some questions by phone, and another 149 nonresponding teachers completed a second, shorter questionnaire. No analysis will be conducted here of the information collected from this short-form group, although it provides an important perspective on possible nonresponse bias, which we discuss in Appendix A.[3]

Demographics. One reason for our confidence in the sample's representativeness is that the demographic profile it presents is similar to other data on teachers in the state. The average teacher in our elementary school sample, for instance, was forty-three years old and had been teaching for thirteen and a half years; a respected data source for the state reports that the average K–12 teacher in the state at roughly the same time was forty-four years old and had taught for fifteen years (Kirst, Hayward, and Koppich 1995).[4] Whereas our average teacher was squarely in midcareer, though, nearly a quarter (23 percent) were in the first five years of their tenure, and another quarter reported teaching for twenty years or more. A bit more than 86 percent of the teachers in our sample were female, and 76 percent were white. Persons of Latino descent accounted for 10.4 percent of the sample, Asian-Americans another 6.5 percent, and African-Americans 3.2 percent. The remaining 4 percent were divided between American Indians and nonrespondents to the question. This racial breakdown mirrored the breakdown found in the statewide teacher population (Kirst, Hayward, and Koppich 1995), although teachers in our sample were slightly less likely to be white.

Teachers in California in 1994 were thus mostly veterans at the job, mostly female, and mostly white. Almost by definition, they also were relatively advantaged. This profile contrasts with what we know about their students. In pursuit of solid evidence on student characteristics, we merged demographic data from the 1994 National Center for Education Statistics (NCES) Common Core Data (CCD) file for the state into our school records (Table 3.2).[5] Three schools did not have matching records, but in the others, an average of 54 percent of students qualified for a free lunch. This is a measure commonly used to designate students as low-income, and it indicates a family income of equal to or less than 1.3 times the poverty level (which itself was $18,660 for a family of four in 1993–94). The school records, when averaged, also show that fewer than five in ten of the students were white, more than three in ten were of Hispanic origin, and fewer than one in ten were of either Asian-American or African-American ancestry during that year. These data square roughly with statistics on statewide student populations available in a 1995 report on education in California, assuming growth in minority student population over the years.[6] Thus, the teacher population included more whites and fewer members of minority groups

Table 3.2. School Characteristics

	Mean	Standard deviation	Minimum	Maximum
Number of students per school	618	218	26	1572
Average Asian student population	10%	.51	0	79%
Average black student population	9%	.54	0	93%
Average Hispanic student population	36%	1.16	0	98%
Average white student population	46%	1.31	0	100%
Average free lunch eligible (FLE) student population	55%	1.20	0	95%

Note: Figures taken from the 1994 NCES CCD database and weighted to represent California school population. N = 245.

than the population of students they instructed. Yearly PACE sourcebooks also record tremendous growth in the number of students attending public school in California. In 1984–85, at roughly the time the math reforms began, the state enrolled 1.9 million children in K–5 education (Guthrie and Kirst 1985); by 1994, that number had climbed to 2.6 million (Kirst, Hayward, and Koppich 1995). These changes, alone, were an important context for the teachers in our survey: schools and classes had become more crowded, and little financial aid was forthcoming from Sacramento to help ease the situation. Teachers who returned our survey reported that their average class size was thirty students in 1993–94, and class size in the sample ranged from eight to forty-one students.

California teachers also had to cope with more linguistic diversity and more poor students than they had a decade earlier, conditions that were complicated by the deep recession of the early 1990s. Table 3.3 shows that teachers reported that nearly a third of their students were classified as Limited English Proficient (LEP), and nearly half received Chapter 1 services. These two estimates, however, may be compromised by the amount of data missing for each question—about a quarter of the sample for the LEP question and somewhat more for Chapter 1.[7] This might artificially raise the estimates of both, given that teachers with more of either type of student might have been more aware of these categories and their students' classification. A Policy Analysis for California Education (PACE) sourcebook on California education for 1995, for instance, reports that 22 percent of the

Table 3.3. Teachers' Reports of Classroom Characteristics

	Number of teachers responding	Mean	Standard deviation	Minimum	Maximum
Number of students per class	582	30	3.4	8	41
Number of LEP students per class	425	10	9.6	1	35
Number of Chapter 1 students per class	359	15	9.2	1	35

state's students were classified as having limited English proficiency (Kirst, Hayward, and Koppich 1995).

Such averages mask great differences. The schools on which we report range from tiny to huge, with student populations from 11 to 1,715; the average school served roughly 600 students. Some of these schools had nearly entirely affluent students, whereas the populations of others had almost entirely poor. Standard deviations for the rest of the variables discussed here (Tables 3.2 and 3.3) give a sense of the range into which most schools in our sample fall.

The survey also queried teachers about their professional education (Table 3.4). Not surprisingly, nearly all (99.2 percent) had completed their bachelor's degree, and another 33 percent had a master's degree;[8] but their preparation in mathematics was much less extensive. Nearly all had taken high school algebra and geometry, which are typically ninth and tenth grade courses, but slightly less than a third reported taking trigonometry, and less than a fifth had taken advanced math or calculus in high school. About half had taken an algebra course in college, and four in ten reported having taken a statistics course. Only a very small proportion, though, had taken any other math courses in college, and the average teacher had taken her last course for college credit in mathematics in 1980, nearly fifteen years before the survey. Almost nine in ten had taken a math methods course as part of their professional education.

Teachers' Opportunities to Learn

We argued that implementation of reforms would depend on the creation of opportunities for teachers to learn about mathematics, teaching, and

Table 3.4. Teachers' Coursework

	Percentage of teachers completing course
High school mathematics	
Algebra	94.1
Geometry	90.2
Trigonometry	28.9
Advanced math or calculus	17.9
Teacher education courses	
Supervised student teaching (including mathematics)	71.4
Mathematics teaching methods	71.8
Instructional use of computers	46.0
College mathematics	
College algebra	49.0
Trigonometry	10.5
Probability and statistics	39.6
Discrete mathematics	4.5
Calculus	11.5
Mathematics for elementary school teachers	86.5
Geometry for elementary or middle school teachers	20.9

learning. The survey was designed to reflect those opportunities, as well as to learn what teachers thought they had learned. Teachers reported a broad array of opportunities to learn: they read documents, attended workshops, listened to educational leaders discuss the reforms, discussed the reforms, read a variety of new curriculum materials, adopted some of them, and familiarized themselves with the new fourth grade math assessment. The breadth and variety was impressive, as was teachers' engagement with the process; but if breadth and variety are important, so is depth. We attend to both in efforts to map how teachers in California learned about the reforms.

Documents. Official documents are often regarded as a poor way to convey knowledge of policy to teachers, on the grounds that few would bother with such things. Yet reformers took care to communicate their ideas and

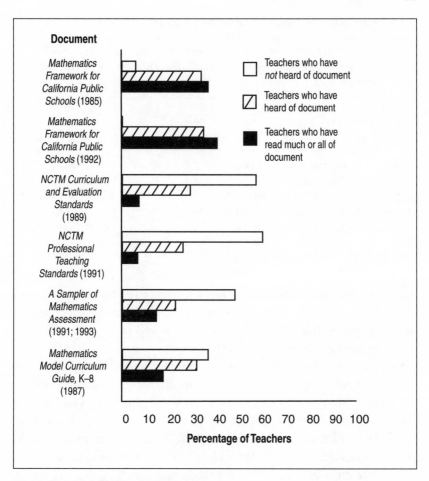

3.1. Teachers' Familiarity with Reform Documents

proposals in nontechnical language, and results from the survey suggest that the 1985 and 1992 California state mathematics frameworks would have done well on a statewide policy best-seller list. Figure 3.1 shows that only a few teachers who responded to the survey reported that they had not heard of the frameworks, and just under half (49 percent) reported that they had read either the 1985 or 1992 framework.[9] Additional calculations revealed that three in ten (31 percent) reported reading both.[10]

This was fairly broad coverage. Most teachers knew of California's two math frameworks, and about half had read much or all of both. This would

Table 3.5. Resources for Teachers' Instructional Planning

Q: Suppose you were getting ready to begin a unit on fractions with your class. How much would you draw on each of the following in preparing the overall unit and particular lessons?

	Not at all			To a great extent
Lessons or problems you have used before	.9	4.6	19.8	37.5	37.1
A textbook teacher's guide	8.8	16.3	31.8	28.3	14.8
Pages or ideas from the student textbook	5.7	12.9	36.2	30.8	14.4
An official district curriculum document	42.5	26.2	19.8	7.5	4.0
An official state curriculum document	39.3	27.0	18.8	10.7	4.3

Note: Numbers represent percentage of those selecting category.

have been welcome news to reformers, for these represented the Magna Carta of math reform, in defining terms and goals for student learning, describing appropriate instructional techniques and tasks, and delineating eight key mathematical content strands.

Nevertheless, these documents were limited by their generality. Even though teachers might have read, for example, that they should encourage students to "think and talk about their work" (1992, p. 50), they could have had little sense of what to talk about regarding two-digit addition, or fractions. The 1992 document was more specific than most state mathematics policies, but it fell far short of providing teachers with the kind of detailed guidance many would need to change their practice.

Teachers agreed. We inquired about the uses teachers made of the reform documents, including a specific question about what resources teachers would use to develop a lesson regarding fractions. The data in Table 3.5 show that fewer than five out of every hundred teachers reported that they might rely "to a great extent" on a policy document. By contrast, just under four in every ten reported that they would rely "to a great extent" on lessons they had used before, and most also reported relying on a teacher's guide or on the student text. This is not surprising, for the state documents were not meant to serve as day-to-day guides for instruction. It does, however, illustrate the limitations of documents like frameworks in educating teachers: although many reported reading them and may have learned broadly about directions in teaching or curriculum, teachers did not regard them as directly useful for teaching.

Teachers who answered the survey were much less familiar with documents that offered more specific assistance in revising instruction. Fewer than fifteen in every hundred teachers reported reading California's *Sampler of Mathematics Assessment*, an introduction to the state's revised tests. A little fewer than eighteen in every hundred reported that they had read much or all of the *Mathematics Model Curriculum Guide* (K–8), a more detailed discussion of possible classroom work and materials that the State Education Department published following the 1985 framework. So even when more detailed guidance was available, only a few teachers knew of it.

Teachers were not broadly familiar with several other important documents. Only seven in every hundred teachers reported having read the *NCTM Curriculum and Evaluation Standards* or the *NCTM Professional Teaching Standards*. Many said they had never heard of them. For many teachers, then, the reform stopped with the frameworks. Only a few mentioned having any exposure to the state's attempts to make the math reforms more concrete and specific. This would have been less of a problem if the frameworks had been a complete guide to new math teaching, but they were not.

Professional development. Documents were hardly the only way to link policy goals to classroom practice. Reformers also relied on further education for teachers. That made sense, both because documents are a limited way to learn about a practice that centers on face-to-face interactions and because staff development sessions were a ready-made forum, ubiquitous and widely attended. Most districts allocate a specific number of days that teachers must spend on professional development, and most states support it financially. Only seven teachers in our sample reported no professional development activities in 1993–94.

A year's worth of professional development for the typical American teacher consists of a few one-day or half-day workshops offered by the school district, local university, or colleagues from the district. The workshops may be very generally oriented toward instruction, but they tend to focus on topics tangential to knowledge of the subject matter and teaching it. When workshops do focus on instruction, it usually is via easily learned activities that teachers can bring directly back to their classrooms — in professional parlance, "make and takes." It is quite uncommon for professional development to focus on anything for more than a few hours or to go in any depth into matters of curriculum, instruction, or student learning (Little 1993; Lord 1994).

As mathematics reform gathered steam in California, state officials and reformers outside the government tried to revise professional development to make it support the frameworks. The encouragement of state and national agencies and the work of independent operators like Marilyn Burns produced a sizable number of professional development projects that supported improved math teaching. The California Mathematics Project, which offered teachers fairly extensive summer learning and leadership training, was one. The Mathematics Renaissance, a middle school initiative, was another; EQUALS, a series of workshops oriented toward equity issues in the new approach to math teaching, was still another. Many other workshops were offered by local districts, county education offices, and private providers. By the time our survey was in the field, a sizable fraction of California's professional developers were offering learning opportunities that were related to the reforms.

To assess teachers' responses to such opportunities, one section of the survey invited respondents to list the time spent improving their own skills and knowledge during the year before the survey. We wanted to know about both the time and the content of these learning opportunities. In one question, reproduced in Table 3.6, teachers were asked to report very generally on what kinds of opportunities to learn they had had—and how long they had engaged in the activities.

The data support several observations. Most teachers reported attending two or fewer days of staff development in mathematics in the previous year, an outcome that fits with other studies of professional development. Only one fifth reported more than two days of workshops, and this total included a broad array of professional meetings, workshops, and conferences. Teachers spent more time in professional development for mathematics than in "other subjects." Despite the folk wisdom that teachers did "math this year, reading the next," we found a modest positive correlation between the mathematics and other measures ($r = .25$, $p < .001$). Teachers who participated more in professional development in one subject were likely to participate more in others.[11]

The information reported in Table 3.6 does not reflect the content of teachers' learning opportunities in mathematics, or their duration, or whether they were aligned with the state frameworks. To investigate these matters, we

Table 3.6. Teachers' In-Service Education—Time

Q: How much total time have you spent on in-service education about mathematics (or the teaching of mathematics) and about other subjects during the past year? Include attendance at professional meetings, workshops, and conferences, but do not include formal courses for which you have received college credit.

Approximate hours of in-service education during the past year	In mathematics, California	In mathematics, national*	In other subjects, California**
None	16.9	34	2.1
Less than 6 hours	34.3	32	14.2
6–15 hours	29.2	20	32.8
16–35 hours	10.6	8	28.7
More than 35 hours	8.9	6	22.2

Source for national data: 1993 National Survey of Science and Mathematics Education: Compendium of Tables, Horizon Research, 1995, p. 3.42. This project surveyed teachers in Grades 1–4. The item that generated this response read: "What is the total amount of time you have spent on in-service education in mathematics or the teaching of mathematics in the last twelve months? Include attendance at professional meetings, workshops, and conferences, but do not include formal courses for which you have received college credit."
**Thirty missing cases.

asked teachers a third question, reproduced in Table 3.7, about how much time they had invested in each of five mathematics-related activities within the past year. The activities were selected to reflect the range of professional development options in math available in California at the time, in offerings whose content we could identify with confidence.[12] The five kinds of workshops listed in Table 3.7 differed not only in organizational arrangements, such as sponsor or location, but also in the curriculum each offered teachers and how that curriculum related to the frameworks.

The table shows that "cooperative learning" was a popular theme in professional development; almost half the teachers in our sample said they had attended a workshop associated with such learning in mathematics during 1993–94. The frameworks had urged teachers to organize their classes so that students could work together as they worked on problems, on the assumption that competence and problem solving are social and that students would benefit from discussing ideas. The MSU research group's earlier ob-

Table 3.7. Teachers' In-Service Education—Content

Q: Which of the following mathematics-related activities have you participated in during the past year and approximately *how much total time* did you spend in each?

	None	1 day or less	2–6 days	1–2 weeks	More than 2 weeks
EQUALS	96.5	2.4	.9	.2	0
Family Math	81.7	12.9	4.2	.8	.3
Cooperative learning	54.5	28.9	13.7	1.8	1.1
Marilyn Burns	83.2	9.8	5.3	1.3	.3
Mathematics replacement units	58.9	22.7	14.2	1.7	2.5

Note: Missing data treated as "none."

servations suggested, however, that cooperative learning was often treated as a generic approach, and none of their classroom observations in California turned up deep or sustained student discussion of mathematics. None of the approaches to this innovation appeared to be closely associated with any school subject; rather, cooperative learning was often presented as a new approach to classroom organization, requiring little more than new managerial skills, and it seemed to have been quite widely promoted in California that way. Cooperative learning also was widely offered by school districts employing local staff, a trend that helps explain why a larger fraction of teachers participated in cooperative-learning workshops than in any other.

In contrast, EQUALS, a project at the University of California, Berkeley, focused on issues of gender, race, and language skills in mathematics instruction, as well as on promoting new ideas about teaching and learning math. Teachers spent time learning activities they could use with students and receiving materials they could take to their classrooms. These seemed consistent with themes in the frameworks, but EQUALS did not offer a coherent curriculum around specific mathematical topics. Its central theme was equality. Admission to EQUALS was limited, so participation was intentionally modest. Only about 4 percent of the teachers answering our survey reported participating in EQUALS during the year preceding the study.

Family Math was developed beginning in 1981 by EQUALS staff who obtained a grant to write a text to help teachers involve parents in their children's math learning. The text was published in 1986 and was intended to be the curriculum for a series of six- to eight-week workshops for parents and children. The goals included familiarizing parents with changes in their children's curriculum, improving parents' facility with mathematics, and improving their ability to help students with homework. Potential workshop leaders (both parents and teachers) could attend a *Family Math* workshop to learn about the curriculum and leading local workshops, and nearly 20 percent of the teachers who responded to our survey reported that they had done so.

The other projects listed in Table 3.7 were more closely tied to the academic content of the reforms. The California Department of Education initially commissioned the creation of a replacement unit on fractions and indirectly encouraged others on central topics in the elementary curriculum. If curriculum developers created discrete units covering key topics in ways that were closely aligned with the frameworks, teachers could use the units in place of text chapters, and reformers could get new materials developed and put into use without facing difficult issues of text adoption.

Professional development for the units was offered by unit authors themselves, by the California Mathematics Project, and by local district staff. Eight elementary-level replacement units had been finished when our survey went into the field, and they were generally thought to be of high quality. That 41 percent of teachers in the survey had participated in a replacement unit workshop suggests the units were widely available by the winter of 1994.

Marilyn Burns is a respected curriculum developer and author who has also been a leading figure in mathematics education in California. Her firm is a major provider of professional development workshops and mathematics curriculum materials around the country, but unlike some others, Burns's firm did not franchise its workshops to other providers. It kept fairly close control over selection and training of its own staff and over the workshop curricula, factors that may help explain why participation rates in the Burns workshops, while substantial, were more modest than other replacement units.

Time and content coverage varied within and among the projects. Many professional developers, including the creators of several replacement units, tried to reach more teachers by way of the "trainer-of-trainers" model. Teachers who attended the prime sponsor's extended workshops were encouraged to return to their districts or schools and offer workshops locally.

Some were taught a bit about such work, but others were not. The local workshops were reported to be much shorter than the originals, perhaps consisting of a day or an afternoon, and even apart from the time spent, most local offerings probably were weaker on content than the sponsors' workshops.

The five curricula listed in Table 3.7 did not exhaust the available math-related professional development opportunities in California. There were many more offerings on the local or county levels, or provided privately, that were unrelated to those shown in the table. Yet two thirds of the teachers who responded to our survey participated in professional development activities of at least one of these five types. That is significant, for by reshaping the content and agenda of some professional development, reformers were able, in less than a decade, to teach a sizable fraction of the teaching force something about curriculum, teaching, and classroom work that was associated with an aspect of the frameworks. This was a remarkable accomplishment.

The breadth of these opportunities to learn was not matched by their depth, however. Our chief indicator of depth was the amount of time that teachers spent. Time is no guarantee of more substantial content, but having more time creates opportunities for substantial work that would be less likely to occur if there were less time. Most teachers spent only a little time in mathematics-related professional development. More than eight in ten teachers spent fewer than fifteen hours (Table 3.6), and between seven and nine in ten teachers spent either no time or a day or less in each of the five sorts of professional development (Table 3.7). A much smaller number spent between two days and a week in such activities. A very small fraction managed to spend more than a week in one of the professional development efforts.

We could place these results in context by comparing them with results for teachers elsewhere in the nation, but few studies contain similarly detailed reports on teachers' professional development. Iris Weiss's 1993 National Survey of Science and Mathematics Education, however, suggests that California teachers may have received only slightly more time in staff development in mathematics than their peers elsewhere in the nation (Matti, Soar, Hudson, and Weiss 1995; Weiss 1993). Of first through fourth grade teachers, 14 percent nationwide had attended more than sixteen hours of staff development during the preceding year, whereas nearly 20 percent of second through fifth grade California teachers reported attending sixteen hours or more total staff development in the last year alone (Table 3.6). Most California teachers who took any of the five curriculum workshops spent only a day or less (Table 3.7). That accords with what other observers report: the average teacher's professional development typically consists of a few days of learning each year about a discrete topic (Little 1993; Lord 1994; O'Day and Smith 1993). A few teachers connected up with relatively rich learning opportunities, but most did not.

One reason the replacement units were an important innovation was that some developers grounded teachers' professional education in the improved student curriculum that teachers would teach. By linking the two, the developers realized part of the logic of systemic reform. Previous efforts to improve instruction had typically focused on one element, like the curriculum (the NSF had long supported such work) or on specific instructional methods (Madeline Hunter's ITIP is an example). Such efforts had had mixed results at best. The NSF-sponsored reforms of the 1950s and 1960s had no discernible broad effects on instruction (Welch 1979; Dow 1991), in part because they focused on only one element of instruction. Similarly, Jane Stallings's research raised doubts about the staying power of Hunter's methods (Stallings and Krasavage 1986). Embedding professional development in improved curriculum might avoid such problems by focusing on more than one element in instruction—that is, by linking teachers' learning to the student curriculum.

Only a few teachers had such opportunities. The combination of state budget problems and reformers' inexperience with ambitious instruction meant that longer and more substantive opportunities to learn better ways of teaching math were limited. More access would have required reformers to overhaul the entire professional development system so that it focused on central issues of teaching and learning, for the changes reformers sought would require basic alteration of core elements in teaching, along with relearning of professional practice. Recent research suggests that this would require extended opportunities to learn, support from peers and mentors, and the chance to practice, reflect, and practice again (Heaton and Lampert 1993; McCarthy and Peterson 1993; Ball and Rundquist 1993; Wilson, Miller, and Yerkes 1993; Schifter and Fosnot 1993). These were not on offer in the existing system of professional development.

Professional networks. California teachers also had access to professional networks or leadership opportunities in which they would have been likely to encounter reform ideas. The California Mathematics Project (CMP), for instance, which began in 1983 as a spinoff of the Bay Area Writing Project, invited teachers in for intensive four-to-six-week summer training institutes at universities statewide to learn about new ideas in mathematics, grow a support network of innovating peers, and develop the ability to become instructional mentors in their respective schools. The CMP staff included college- and university-based mathematics educators, as well as former CMP students, many of whom had been involved in the broader California math reforms effort in some way. Though the workshops were diverse in focus and content, they all aimed to improve math teaching. Teachers could return in subsequent summers for more learning, and they often taught workshops in their home districts. Some teachers took these workshops in their home district, while others went to a CMP summer site.

The California Mathematics Council is the state affiliate of the National Council of Teachers of Mathematics and was very active statewide and through its regional affiliates. At the time of our survey, the CMC and affiliates' main activity was hosting regional conferences; by one estimate, nearly ten thousand teachers might have attended those conferences at three sites every year.[13] These meetings supported teachers by offering opportunities to meet others interested in mathematics, share ideas, attend workshops, and assume leadership roles in improving mathematics teaching. The CMC actively promoted the math framework, and CMC meetings enabled teachers to hear about innovations in curriculum and assessment, including replacement units, and to attend panels on mathematics policy and practice.

Teachers also had opportunities to be active in districts and schools. Many schools and districts encouraged them to teach workshops or to participate in professional networks like the CMP. Teachers also might have served on district or school mathematics committees that revised math curricula, reviewed textbooks, or worked on the Program Quality Review teams. Such professional activities differed from the workshops, for they enabled teachers to work together over more extended periods of time and perhaps even to sustain conversation with colleagues about mathematics, curriculum, and instruction. In addition, the expectation in many of the math projects was that teachers would return to their schools with new ideas and mentoring skills. That may have offered more opportunities for teachers to participate extensively and to learn actively than the teacher-as-recipient/expert-as-teller mode, which seems to prevail in most other professional development (Firestone and Pennell 1997; Lieberman and McLaughlin 1996).

There was no assurance, however, that teachers would learn about the frameworks or mathematics reforms in district committee work, especially when schools did not perform program reviews. Even in activities specifically designed to advance the math frameworks, like the Program Quality Reviews, no specific effort was made to enhance teachers' learning; and in carefully designed activities designed to support learning—including some esteemed programs—workshop leaders had difficulty sustaining attention to teachers' understanding of mathematics (Wilson, Lubienski, and Mattson 1996). There is a difference between leadership activities that afford teachers greater engagement in decision making or empty "empowerment" and those which expand teachers' professional community, knowledge of subjects, and instructional skill (Lichtenstein, McLaughlin, and Knudsen 1992). Many "networks" seemed quite loosely organized, and there has been little systematic study of how and what teachers learned from work in them.[14]

Teachers' modest participation was an even more fundamental problem with network and leadership opportunities, for only a small fraction of the state's teachers took part in such activities in the year directly preceding the survey. The percentages in the first column of Table 3.8 show that the overwhelming majority of teachers who responded to our survey participated in no network or leadership activity. The total participation in the California Math Project, which is often cited as a model program for teacher change (Firestone and Pennell 1997), was less than 6 percent of our sample. Even if we assumed that all of the opportunities in Table 3.8 were both powerful and closely tied to the math framework, few teachers would have profited from them.

CLAS. State officials also used the revised statewide assessment to offer teachers opportunities to learn that would be consistent with the reforms. This professional development took several forms. In 1993, as the first administration of CLAS neared, CDE testing experts asked districts for volunteers to pilot items from the test in their classrooms. Eventually, a small number of teachers did, and educators reported that teachers learned about the sorts of performance that reformers expected. Little other professional development touched on the new assessment before its first administration, though, in part because of the limited time legislators had given the CDE for test development.

Table 3.8. Teachers' Participation in Reform Leadership and Networks

Q: Which of the following mathematics-related activities have you participated in during the past year and approximately *how much total time* did you spend in each?

	None	1 day or less	2–6 days	One week or more
Participated in a California Mathematics Project	94.3	2.4	1.9	1.5
Attended a national mathematics teacher association meeting	94.2	5.0	.8	0
Attended a state or regional mathematics teacher association meeting, including California Mathematics Council affiliates	87.5	7.2	5.0	.2
Taught an in-service workshop or course in mathematics or mathematics teaching	86.2	10.4	2.7	.8
Served on a district mathematics curriculum committee	86.3	6.6	2.7	4.4

Note: Missing data treated as "none."

Once the test had been administered, more teachers were invited to help score student responses to open-ended items. State officials saw their inclusion as a way to reduce the expense of scoring those items—a necessary savings, because the Sacramento budget wars had left them with little money for such work—while educating some teachers about the assessment and the sorts of mathematics it contained. Between 150 and 200 teachers, many affiliated with the state's mathematics projects, spent a week in the summer of 1993 scoring the open-ended items. Observers reported that as teachers learned to score the tests, they also learned how fourth graders thought about the math and learned more math. The sessions built in a good deal of time for this learning, and the workshops were said to be powerful learning opportunities.

The participating teachers were encouraged to return to their districts and hold workshops for their local colleagues, and many did. Others offered workshops in association with the California Mathematics Council or its regional affiliates, and the California Mathematics Project sponsored workshops on performance assessments as well. In the year between the two administrations of CLAS, the work of these teachers and organizations was complemented by others, like the California Assessment Collaboratives and the Lawrence Hall of Science, which offered teachers opportunities to learn about performance-based assessment and perhaps the CLAS itself.

One survey question asked teachers to describe the content of CLAS-related learning. Roughly one third of those responding to the survey reported that they had learned about the CLAS through practice scoring, taking practice tests, and developing scoring rubrics, and the like.[15] Those activities exposed teachers directly to concrete examples of the kind of learning the frameworks were meant to encourage. One third of the teachers also reported administering the assessment in their own classrooms in either 1993 or 1994. Though there was a good deal of overlap, the two groups were not identical.

Learning in Context

To learn is always to learn some particular thing in some situation, and the situations can influence what is learned. The opportunities to learn that we have thus far considered were situated outside schools and classrooms, and many were far from teachers' home districts. Still, teachers' schools, classrooms, and districts could have influenced their learning about instruction or their use of information or techniques learned elsewhere. Teachers who worked with colleagues to improve their teaching probably would be more likely to try to do so than those who worked in schools whose staff did not support it. Similarly, teachers who worked in schools whose principal or teachers supported the math reforms probably would be more likely to engage with the reforms, and perhaps learn about them, than colleagues who worked in schools whose staff did not support them (Talbert and McLaughlin 1993). School and district professionals could have provided information about learning opportunities available through district or state networks, or incentives for teachers to attend to the innovations in mathematics or encouragement to experiment with new ideas.

Many teachers reported that they worked in schools or districts that promoted the math framework. The responses to the first statement in Table 3.9 show that roughly half of the teachers thought that their principal was "well informed" about reform documents. The responses to the second statement in the same table show that roughly half of the teachers believed that their

Table 3.9. Teachers' Estimates of Local Support for Reform

Q: Now indicate your opinion about how well each statement applies to your school and district.

	Strongly disagree				Strongly agree	Don't know
The principal of this school is well-informed about one or more of these [reform] documents.	5.3	7.5	15.1	15.3	29.3	27.5
There is a schoolwide effort to achieve the kind of mathematics education promoted by one or more [reform] documents.	5.6	13.9	20.7	16.8	33.2	9.7
Our district is providing extensive staff development based on one or more of these documents.	19.6	20.7	23.4	11.7	14.7	10.0

school promoted the reforms. One quarter reported, in response to the third statement, that their district was providing "extensive" staff development associated with reform ideas. These reports offer evidence that a sizable fraction of teachers found significant support at their school and in the district for novel and controversial ideas about math instruction. Nevertheless, plenty did not. Roughly half the teachers either disagreed or were neutral in response to the statement about their principal's knowledge of the math reforms or didn't know enough to respond; these probably included teachers who suffered from lack of knowledge or poor communication and who in addition may have held the view that the principal was poorly informed. Half saw no schoolwide effort to support the reforms or didn't know if one existed, and three quarters saw no evidence of "extensive" staff development based on reform documents.

These data concern general perceptions about support. Given their mixed nature, we consider school-level support for improved teaching. Table 3.10 reports evidence on five conditions of math teaching in the schools sampled for this project. Roughly 60 percent of teachers agreed or strongly agreed that they perceived support from peers to try new ideas and that they felt support from the school administration for undertaking innovations in math education. Yet appreciably fewer teachers—about a third—said that

Table 3.10. Teachers' Reports of Mathematics Conditions in Their School

Q: Now consider conditions of *mathematics teaching*. How well does each of the following statements describe conditions in your school?

	Strongly disagree				Strongly agree
I feel supported by other teachers to try out new ideas in teaching mathematics.	3.8	8.6	26.8	26.8	34.0
The school administration promotes innovations in mathematics education.	6.2	11.6	24.0	29.7	28.5
Teachers in this school regularly share ideas about mathematics instruction.	8.2	28.4	29.2	22.6	11.7
I regularly work with other teachers on mathematics curriculum and instruction.	20.8	34.0	23.7	13.9	7.6

teachers regularly shared ideas, and even fewer—about a fifth—reported that they regularly worked with others on mathematics curriculum and instruction. These reports fit with other research: even if peers and administrators encourage innovation, most teachers work alone. Support for reform or other innovation thus is largely rhetorical: solo labor means that few teachers could have concrete evidence of collective effort for change.

The analysis can be pushed a bit further with a set of items that tapped teachers' perceptions of the extent of collective work in their schools (Table 3.11). We divide these items into two sets. One concerns general activities like offering advice or sharing ideas (the third and fourth items) or nondescript activities like promoting innovative practices (the fifth item). Numerous teachers who responded to the survey reported that many of their colleagues engaged in activities of this sort. The second set, however, concerns behavior that would push the boundaries of privacy: working together to develop curriculum and instructional materials and observing each other teach (the first and second items). These activities could reveal serious work together on the reforms, but only a small fraction of teachers reported that most or all teachers in their school engaged in either one.

This evidence supports a few conclusions about school and district influences on teachers' work and on their learning new teaching practices. One is that many teachers believed they heard strong support from administrators

Table 3.11. Teachers' Reports of Norms of Collaboration

Q: This question concerns how teachers interact in your school. Please indicate about how many teachers in your school do each of the following.

	No teachers	Some teachers	Most teachers	All teachers	Don't know
Work together to develop curriculum and instructional materials	4.4	63.8	22.1	6.8	2.8
Observe each other teaching	29.3	59	7.7	1.0	3.0
Offer advice or help to each other	1.2	36.4	43.0	17.9	1.5
Share ideas on teaching	0	31.9	45.8	21.5	.7
Promote innovative teaching practices	1.7	48.6	35.5	12.5	1.7

and colleagues for the reforms, but a second is that few teachers saw many concrete manifestations of extensive school or district support for such innovation. A third is that few teachers saw much evidence of collective work together on improved instruction. A fourth conclusion, therefore, is that most teachers believed they had plenty of room to learn new approaches to math teaching on their own, but few saw much evidence either of specific support from the school or district or of work together with colleagues. This corresponds with extant research on teaching and schools, which portrays teaching as a primarily isolated endeavor, with little collective work or instructional coordination. We find scant evidence here that California districts and elementary schools offered much concrete support for serious change in mathematics teaching.

We have reported three impressive features of the effort to enable teachers to learn about the California math reform. There was a broad array of opportunities to learn: teachers could read documents, attend workshops, become familiar with the new assessments, and participate in professional networks. Many teachers took advantage of these opportunities. About half reported reading the state's chief documents describing the reforms, and nearly two thirds attended at least one workshop associated with the reforms. Only a tiny number reported no such opportunity. The breadth of this coverage is impressive. California is larger than most nations in the world, and the CDE and other reformers succeeded in reaching more than half the elementary school teachers in a short time.

State officials and reformers devised some remarkable opportunities for teachers to learn. The leading case in point was tying teacher education to new curricula that reflected the state's ambitions for improved instruction. Producing and disseminating the replacement units and linking professional education to them meant that teachers could ground their learning about teaching and learning math in materials that embodied the reform ideas and which they could use with their students. These workshops had appreciable depth and allowed teachers to investigate more seriously individual mathematical topics, like fractions, in the context of student curriculum. Moreover, these relatively more extensive opportunities to learn were aligned with what students were doing, and with the CLAS—a major innovation that resembled standards-based reform. Such integration may seem obvious, but it is rare; very little professional learning in the United States is so closely tied to curriculum and instruction.

State officials and reformers were less successful in other respects, though. Most teachers did not have substantial opportunities to learn. Although about half the surveyed teachers reported reading at least one of the two frameworks, the documents offered little help in reorienting classroom work. A much smaller number of teachers reported reading documents that tried to offer more specific help with instruction. The widest audience received only superficial guidance, whereas more detailed guidance reached a much narrower audience.

Similarly, only a small percentage of teachers had access to professional development that enabled them to learn much of substance about improving instruction. Only a few hundred of the state's teachers spent as much as a week learning about the new assessments and students' work on them. And only about a fifth of the teachers in the survey reported spending two days or more learning about one of the new replacement units. Teachers often strung together one or two different brief workshops related to mathematics in a single year. Some of the limitations were the result of what teachers wanted, and others were the result of what was available through districts, schools, or the state.

Finally, neither the successes nor the problems were attributable simply to state agencies. Most of the opportunities to learn were provided not by the state but by nonstate parties: curriculum developers, individuals associated with the CMP, the CMC, and universities. Though the state encouraged and in some cases subsidized these activities, it was not directly responsible for supplying most opportunities to learn about policy. The impressive accomplishments were due to collaboration between the state and strong professional and other private agencies, but so were the less impressive accomplishments.

Chapter 4

TEACHERS' IDEAS AND PRACTICES

California teachers had an unusual range of opportunities to learn. Public and private agencies deployed several innovative instruments to encourage professionals' learning, meanwhile using several others that were more conventional. These opportunities varied considerably in depth and extent. Though many elementary teachers had a range of relatively modest opportunities to learn about what reform might entail for classrooms, a much smaller number had relatively more substantial opportunities to learn.

The fact that teachers had some opportunities to learn about the new state math policy, however, tells us nothing about what they learned, nor does it tell us whether teachers used what they learned in their classrooms. Studies of past reforms have shown that many instructional innovations did not reach a wide audience and that, even when they were widely disseminated, it often was difficult to persuade teachers of their virtues. Even if they were persuaded, teachers often found it difficult to alter their practice substantially. If we think that learning may influence policy implementation, it is critical to relate evidence on the policy to evidence on what teachers learned, and to relate both to evidence on how policy was implemented.

We begin to probe those relationships in this chapter, by exploring the knowledge, ideas, and practices that teachers reported. These are the domains in which teachers may have learned in response to the policy, and we want to discern any patterns in teachers' beliefs and practice. We will compose a picture of what attitudes teachers held, what they knew about the policy, and what classroom practices they reported when the policy had been operating for nearly a decade. We also will compare those patterns of practice and ideas to the ideas that reformers and policymakers had advanced, for that will enable us to begin to make some judgment about the success of the policy. Once we have elucidated these patterns of belief and practice, in Chapter 5 we will probe their relation to teachers' opportunities to learn.

The MSU researchers had these matters in mind in designing the survey. In addition to the measures of teachers' opportunities to learn, which we discussed in Chapter 3, the survey contained several sets of items that measured the possible results of those learning opportunities. One group of items tried to gauge teachers' familiarity with reform itself—their knowledge of the policy. Another group solicited teachers' ideas, or attitudes, about student learning, mathematics teaching, and assessment. These items investigated teachers' ideas or attitudes about both the mathematics reform and more conventional instruction. The survey also contained a set of items that inquired into classroom practice, including such things as how frequently students worked from mathematics textbooks or wrote about how to solve a math problem.

Teachers' attitudes, knowledge, and practices all differed widely. Much of the variation existed among groups of teachers who reported different ideas and practices, but teachers also varied internally, as they adopted attitudes and practices that many reformers, and critics of reform, regard as contradictory. Perhaps the most important point in this department is that a substantial group of teachers, although apparently knowledgeable about and receptive to ideas about reform, also seemed reluctant to part ways with conventional practice. This turns out to be a central theme in our book, and the evidence we present in this chapter supports the theme by showing that nearly all teachers still made extensive use of conventional practices in mathematics and most reported quite selective implementation of reform practices. The claim about insufficient attention to basic skills and computation, which many Californians argued was a consequence of state policy, finds no support in our survey results. The evidence we report here begins to lay the foundation for judgments about the success of the policy but also makes plain that there is no easy, one-dimensional way to make such judgments. Teaching looks much more complex than much of the discussion about it.

Because we want to present a comprehensible picture of teachers' ideas and practices, we stick mostly to reporting raw frequency counts of sets of items from the survey. Because the accuracy and validity of teachers' reports of practice is an important issue, in Appendix B we also present evidence concerning these matters. We begin with a discussion of teachers' ideas and then turn to their practices.

Teachers' Ideas

One broad gauge of the success of mathematics improvement efforts is whether teachers actually knew about the reformers' aims; if these ideas stayed in Sacramento, they would have little chance of affecting what happened in classrooms. Another gauge is what teachers made of the ideas, for if they were not persuaded of their merit, few classrooms could change. We explore both issues.

Teachers' familiarity with policy. Our purpose here was not to "test" the teachers responding to our survey or to discover how many had learned an authoritative catechism of reform. Rather, we wanted to know how familiar teachers were with some leading ideas about reform and how accurately they could distinguish them from more conventional views of instruction. Thus we designed a set of seventeen items that were consistent either with the ideas contained in the frameworks or with more conventional ideas about teaching mathematics. There is no Ultimately Authoritative Guide to Reform Principles, so we framed statements that, on the basis of documentary evidence and many interviews with reformers, seemed to represent both leading reform ideas and features of conventional practice fairly. Mark items, teachers were instructed, that "you see as *core ideas* of the new mathematics standards, whether or not you agree with them." Items corresponding to more conventional views of math instruction were to be left unmarked.

Teachers knew a great deal about the new policy. The average teacher properly identified fourteen of the seventeen items as either reform or conventional instruction. One third of teachers incorrectly identified only one or no items, and only 5 percent incorrectly identified half or more of the items, as could have been expected if respondents had guessed randomly. Most teachers easily negotiated the broad generalities of the reform.

When we divide the seventeen items into groups of statements oriented toward either reform on the one hand or the traditional approach on the other, the view changes a bit. Seven of the nine reform statements were identified correctly by more than 90 percent of responding teachers, and even the most commonly misidentified item was answered correctly by almost three quarters of respondents (Table 4.1). This result suggests that teachers gleaned the framework's new views quite completely. But the story is different for items associated with conventional views of mathematics, which were not endorsed by reformers (Table 4.2). This set of items shows that teachers commonly identified a number of these concepts as part of the reforms; in fact, many associated with the reforms the very things that reformers wanted to reduce or eliminate in mathematics classrooms. It is particularly striking that slightly more than half of the teachers in the sample reported that "Students need to practice basic skills in order to be prepared to solve mathematical problems" was a core idea of the mathematics reforms. Another third said that the statement "The elementary mathematics curriculum should emphasize computational skills" should be likewise classified. Few reformers would have agreed with either view, and several reform documents specifically cautioned teachers against the view that mathematics learning consisted chiefly of drill on facts and skills.

It is noteworthy, though a bit less striking, that many teachers associated statements 3, 4, and 6 in Table 4.2—which commonly would be identified with conventional practice—with the reform.[1] The 1992 frameworks and other documents emphasized that students learn best through exploration of difficult ideas, and that confusion and disagreement are to be expected. Reformers held that students should be offered opportunities to figure out how to attack unfamiliar problems, on the grounds that learning how to do that is essential to mathematical sense-making. Teachers in conventional classrooms might explain why zero is an even number, but reformers wanted teachers to turn "Is zero an even number?" into a problem for students to explore and reason about. If teachers did this, students might work on the problem for several days, be confused about the correct answer, and learn to reason mathematically. That a sizable minority of teachers identified statements about the need for teachers to clear up confusions, which re-

Table 4.1. Percentage of Teachers Identifying Reform Ideas with Reform

	Percentage identifying statement as relating to reform
1. It is important that teachers observe and listen to how students think about mathematics.	97
2. Students learn from one another when they work together on mathematics problems.	96
3. The curriculum should emphasize the application of mathematics to the real world whenever possible.	96
4. All students should have a challenging, problem-solving and conceptually oriented mathematics curriculum.	95
5. Alternative assessments—including portfolios, performance assessment, and group projects—are an important means of documenting students' learning.	93
6. Students should be encouraged to justify their ideas in mathematics.	90
7. Writing about mathematics should be a regular part of mathematics instruction.	90
8. Neglected topics such as probability and geometry need to be included in the elementary curriculum.	88
9. A mathematical idea is best learned if a student is first exposed to a concrete example.	72

formers would have linked to conventional practice, as part of the reform suggests the difficulties of conveying a complex policy to practitioners.

Tables 4.1 and 4.2 contain appreciable evidence that teachers were more familiar with leading ideas in California's mathematics reforms than with reformers' views of conventional practice. One explanation for the difference is miscommunication: perhaps the policy message had not been clearly articulated. The policy itself was not well elaborated, and the 1992 framework contained few particulars about the kinds of mathematics instruction teachers should avoid in their classrooms. Nowhere did it state whether it was desirable that "students not have mathematical misconceptions at the end of class," even though several reformers took the view that students

Table 4.2. Percentage of Teachers Identifying Conventional Ideas with Reform

	Percentage identifying statement as relating to reform
1. Students need to practice basic skills in order to be prepared to solve mathematical problems.	55
2. The elementary mathematics curriculum should emphasize computational skills.	31
3. It is important that students not have mathematical misconceptions at the end of class.	30
4. Students should demonstrate that they can perform computations "by hand" before being allowed to use calculators.	22
5. Teachers should clearly explain to students how to solve a particular kind of problem they have never seen before.	21
6. Whenever students ask how to solve a mathematical problem, teachers should provide a thorough explanation.	18
7. Students should demonstrate mastery of a particular mathematics concept before proceeding to the next concept.	18
8. Students should work individually in mathematics to ensure that they master the skills and are able to work on their own.	17

might well have a muddled understanding over some period of time. The 1992 document itself recommends only "postpon[ing] emphasis on facility with basic facts" (p. 74), rather than cautioning teachers more succinctly against "drill and skill."

Another source of miscommunication might have been reformers' uncertainty about the role of critical thinking and basic skills, uncertainty that might have been increased by the political storms in California. As this survey was sent to teachers, reformers were on the defensive against advocates of conventional math teaching who argued that state policy would leave students without computational skills. In response, some reformers incorporated a revised version of the basic skills argument into their own: fostering deeper understanding was not inconsistent with fostering computational ability, and it was a major goal of reform for students to master both. Even before the political storms blew into the state, though, there was no clear consensus among reformers on this and other matters. Some self-identified reformers might have agreed with the statements about computational skills, while others would have disagreed. Teachers' responses might have reflected both kinds of ambiguity.

Selective perception is yet another explanation for teachers' inability to identify conventional practices as clearly as reform practices. Enmeshed as they were in the demands of practice, teachers might more easily have heard the elements of reformers' message that they could put into practice with the least effort and ignored elements that would have demanded more challenging work and deeper alterations in practice. A concept like "teachers should observe and listen" was relatively easy to embrace, for it is something good teachers would do no matter how they teach mathematics.[2] Statements like "It is important that students not have mathematical misconceptions at the end of class" are much more difficult. Reformers may make a case for the value of disagreement, extended puzzling, and confusion, but such an agenda may make many teachers quite ambivalent, because they see their job in part as helping students to get things clear.

Whatever one thinks about this issue, the evidence should give pause to nearly anyone concerned with the math reforms. It raises doubts about critics' claims that the state's "experiments" had replaced old-fashioned drill and practice, for, even at the height of the reform movement, more than half the elementary teachers in the state saw teaching of basic skills as a component of the reforms. That result would also have given reformers who wanted to get rid of basic skills food for thought. Whatever else one may say about these reports, they show that elementary school teachers in California had a much more complex view of reform, one that included many elements of conventional teaching, than did many reformers and critics.

Teachers' ideas about mathematics teaching and learning. One reason we attend to teachers' ideas is that they may shape their teaching. Teachers who see mathematics as a set of rules to be memorized, for instance, will differ in their presentation of material from teachers who view math as a set of principles and concepts to be comprehended and used. Teachers who view students as passive recipients of knowledge will teach differently from those who see students as active problem solvers who can use new approaches. More generally, Jere Brophy (1991) wrote: "Similar students learning about ostensibly similar content from different teachers may have very different experiences if their teachers have very different beliefs about the nature of the subject matter, about the reasons why it is included in the curriculum, and the purposes to be accomplished by teaching it, or about what learning experiences will be most effective for moving students toward the extended outcomes" (xii). Recent research in education has provided examples of how teachers' understanding of student learning affects their work (Peterson, Fennema, and Carpenter 1991; Carpenter, Fennema, Peterson, Chiang, and Loef 1989). It also shows how teachers' notions of subject matter and instruction influence the way they implement novel reforms (Borko 1995; Cohen 1990; Thompson 1992; Wilson 1990).

The role of ideas is especially salient in schemes for changing instruction. Reformers of a "constructivist" bent argue that math instruction should change dramatically; but if that is to happen, teachers will have to unlearn their existing notions of mathematics, student learning, and instruction and absorb new knowledge and beliefs concerning each point. Brophy observed that "many teachers may need to be re-socialized to new beliefs about and orientations toward [mathematics] before they can fully understand and appreciate the recommended changes in instructional methods" (1991, 353). Such change in teachers' views cannot be accomplished overnight or by working through bureaucratic channels. Teaching practice remains private in nearly all schools, and privacy is protected by powerful norms: closed classroom doors and teacher autonomy. Most teachers in the United States believe that their approach to instruction is a matter of personal style rather than evidence on effectiveness (Buchmann 1993). Most seem to feel free to ignore or adopt selectively whatever instructional guidance comes their way, whether it is a new text or a state policy. An important part of any serious reform effort must thus be finding ways to reshape norms and change beliefs, for changing practice seems to require changing the norms of privacy and autonomy that govern teaching.

Reformers tried to change teachers' minds about the rationale for certain instructional activities. One method of doing so was to offer general workshops that introduced teachers to the reforms. Another was to embed opportunities for teachers to observe student performance in novel replacement units or in their scoring of student work on the CLAS. Another was to create a rhetoric that promoted reformers' view of student learning and mathematics instruction. If teachers' learning was such a crucial element of California's reforms, a large part of reformers' work was persuasion—that is, changing teachers' ideas. That is a facet of many recent social policies (Stone 1988; McDonnell 1994).

Ideas are also important because they influence how teachers understand what they are doing, and thus how they discuss it with others and report on it. Even teachers who say that they are doing the very same things, such as leading a discussion, or inviting students to frame conjectures about a problem, understand and carry out these practices quite differently when their ideas about mathematics differ. That effect influences what a survey can discern about instruction and suggests the importance of exploring teachers' ideas about student learning and mathematics instruction.

The survey results reveal—among other things—how sensitive reports of teachers' ideas are to the ways in which the questions are put. The survey took two approaches to asking teachers for their opinions of reform: one was a single-item measure of their attitude toward reform as a whole; the other was a set of several items addressing their attitudes toward specific ideas on reform. Results from the global question show that many teachers seemed enamored of reform. When asked how they felt "about the kind of mathematics education promoted by the new mathematics standards and assessments," teachers could respond on a Likert scale of 1 to 5, extremely negative to extremely positive. A very small fraction—3 percent—circled one of the "negative" possibilities, and another 34.5 percent reported that their feelings were "mixed." More than half said they felt positively about the reform, while fewer than 10 percent said they held no opinion. If we had only this measure of teachers' attitudes about the reform, we would be likely to conclude that most were positive, that a bit more than a third were ambivalent, and that outright resistance to reformers' vision of mathematics was quite muted.

When we turned to teachers' ideas about more specific elements of student learning and mathematics, however, we found considerable variation in their views of reform. Table 4.3 shows that teachers strongly agreed with several statements associated with the policy. Reformers had proposed that students attach more meaning to mathematical operations when those operations arise from real-life situations, like the length of three third graders laid end to end, or how much change a student would get if she paid for a fifty-seven-cent candy bar with a dollar bill. More than nine in ten strongly agreed, or agreed with the first statement, "Students learn best when they study mathematics in the context of everyday situations," and only a small

Table 4.3. Teachers' Ideas about Reform and Conventional Teaching

	Disagree	Neutral	Agree
Reform ideas			
1. Students learn best when they study mathematics in the context of everyday situations.	2.0	8.4	89.6
2. Students learn mathematics by discussing different approaches to a task, even when some of them are wrong.	3.7	12.7	83.7
3. Students should write about how they solve mathematical problems.	4.8	14.7	80.6
4. Teaching a mathematical concept should begin with a concrete example or model.	9.0	24.7	66.3
5. Teachers should make students figure things out for themselves, rather than tell them how to solve a mathematics problem.	11.6	31.8	56.7
6. Students learn mathematics best in classes with heterogeneous groups of students.	18.5	29.3	52.2
Conventional ideas			
7. Teachers should make sure that students are not confused at the end of a mathematics period.	17.9	30.0	52.1
8. Students talented in mathematics need a special curriculum.	27.6	26.9	45.4
9. Students need to master basic computational facts and skills before they can effectively engage in mathematical problem solving.	38.7	25.0	36.3
10. In teaching mathematics, my primary goal is to help students to master basic computational skills.	52.5	34.0	13.4
11. If elementary students use calculators, they won't learn the mathematics they need to know.	72.5	19.2	8.3
12. It is not a good idea to have students work together in solving mathematical problems.	89.7	2.4	9.0

fraction were on the fence.[3] Reformers also suggested that allowing students to develop their own approaches to problems and to discuss them would help increase mathematical understanding. Many teachers agreed with the item written to reflect this idea, "Students learn mathematics by discussing different approaches to a task, even when some of them are wrong." Only a small minority disagreed, and only 12 percent were neutral.

Similarly, that 90 percent of the teachers disapproved of statement 12, "It is not a good idea to have students work together in solving mathematical problems," is not surprising when we consider that group work was one of the most popular ideas in many recent instructional reforms. Reformers also urged teachers to have children in elementary classrooms use calculators, on the assumption that they could help with lengthy computation and provide a means of looking for patterns or structure in numbers. More than seven in ten teachers agreed, rejecting statement 11, "If elementary students use calculators, they won't learn the mathematics they need to know." The growing enthusiasm during the last ten or fifteen years for student writing, including "writing across the curriculum," also helps explain the high approval ratings for statement 3, "Students should write about how they solve mathematical problems." A quick glance at these five items would suggest that the great majority of elementary teachers in California favor the math reforms; yet all these statements might be approved by teachers who employed very conventional approaches to instruction. Such instruction often is loaded with "everyday examples." Researchers regularly observe classes in which teachers report having "discussions" with students, but in which researchers only see teachers fishing for the right answers and ignoring everything else. Many classes in which instruction is quite conventional are nonetheless organized for group work and cooperative learning. Some teachers further encourage students to keep math "journals," yet the writing in those journals consists of copied definitions and procedures instead of students' original thinking about problems or ideas.

Thus far, we have presented mostly positive results on the impact of the new policy. By contrast, teachers' support for reformed approaches to instruction diminished as the statements cut closer to the core of conventional classroom work. It is assumed in most conventional approaches to instruction, for instance, that the teachers' responsibility is to clarify matters for students, rather than to set strategic problems and encourage students to figure things out for themselves.[4] Conventional approaches to teaching and learning assumed that the mind was both plastic and relatively passive, more a product of environmental stimuli than an active manipulator of such stimuli. If teachers made things clear, students would absorb them. Reformers typically rejected this conception of mind and learning in favor of cognitive or constructivist views of mind, which depict it as an active creator of experience, shaping knowledge by complex judgment in both perception and interpretation. According to these views, to learn is to make sense of things actively, not to absorb someone else's finished sense-making.

Two statements in the survey directly engaged these contrasting views of mind and learning. First, teachers' approval of statement 5, "Teachers should make students figure things out for themselves, rather than tell them how to solve a mathematics problem," dropped to 57 percent. A majority favored this central reform idea, but it was a much narrower majority than we found for the statements discussed earlier. Only 12 percent flatly rejected the idea, but nearly one third of teachers were on the fence. A roughly equal percentage of teachers agreed with statement 7, "Teachers should make sure that students are not confused at the end of a mathematics period." Many reformers believed that confusion and struggles to figure things out were beneficial to learning, and that things need not be tidied up every day, but a narrow majority of responding teachers thought that such confusion was a bad thing; only one fifth flatly rejected the idea; another third were on the fence.

These two questions reveal divisions among teachers. Because they deal with issues that touch more closely on the core of conventional practice, they discriminate a bit more precisely among teachers' views of reform. Statements that focus on basic skills highlighted similar divisions. Most reformers would have seen statement 9, "Students need to master basic computational facts and skills before they can engage effectively in mathematical problem solving," as diametrically opposed to the mathematical thought they aimed to encourage. They wanted students to acquire computational and other skills in the course of learning to reason. Yet teachers were almost evenly divided between agreeing and disagreeing with the sentence, and one quarter were on the fence. Slightly more than half (53 percent) agreed with reformers in rejecting statement 10, "In teaching mathematics, my primary goal is to help students master basic computational skills," but even though only 13 percent of teachers agreed with this conventional view, 34 percent were ambivalent. At the same time teachers expressed substantial support for more ambitious math teaching, ambivalence, uncertainty, and opposition were reflected in the substantial divisions among teachers.

Another key reform position was that grouping by ability should cease, and that position too garnered relatively low support from teachers. The 1992 framework devoted five full pages to such matters, starting with the blunt statement "This *Framework* calls for heterogeneous grouping and detracking as a goal and recommends against attempting to group students by ability," (*Mathematics Framework for California Public Schools* 1992, 60). Yet 45 percent of responding teachers supported a special curriculum for students talented in mathematics (statement 8), and another 27 percent were on the fence. Only 28 percent agreed with the framework's view. In a related item (6), barely half the teachers agreed with reformers that students learn math best in heterogeneous groups. These items touched on one of the most controversial aspects of the frameworks; observers reported that reformers' opposition to grouping according to ability was one reason for some parents' mobilization against the math reforms. That conflict was echoed in teachers' opinions.

The survey thus provides evidence of multiple divisions over ideas among teachers. It also provides evidence that teachers were divided within themselves. Reformers might regard the items in Tables 4.3 as exemplars of a general theory of mathematics teaching and learning, but teachers took a more complex view. A factor analysis showed that the statements in Table 4.3 split into two dimensions, reform and conventional ideas. Rather than being two parts of one systematic view of instruction, these items in the aggregate were understood to represent two different big ideas. Even more convincing, when we turned these two sets of statements into scales of conventional and reform ideas, and correlated them, we found them only mildly opposed, at −.25. A teacher's score on the conventional belief scale only modestly predicts her score on a scale of math framework ideas. On the whole, teachers who had *more* reform ideas did not necessarily have *fewer* conventional ideas; the two scales seem to lie in different dimensions. The two modes of instruction, which reformers considered to be almost antithetical, were not opposed in many teachers' minds. Rather than dividing teachers into two opposing camps, each with its own internally consistent view of instruction, many teachers held elements of both views at the same time.

Teachers agreed among themselves, in the main, about things like making mathematics tangible and relevant to everyday life and having students work in groups. The more central to conventional practice the statements became, though, the more diverse teachers' ideas about the statements became. Compare, for example, the first three statements in Table 4.3, which are all easily adopted reform ideas, with statements 5, 7, and 9, which come much closer to the core of practice. The first three reveal very strong agreement about reform, and very modest disagreement among teachers, but the second three reveal much less agreement with reform and much greater disagreement among teachers, of whom many more were either frankly opposed to reform or on the fence. The closer statements about reform got to the core of teaching, the sharper the differences of opinion.

It would be easy to see these as differences between contending groups within the teaching profession; that is how many advocates and opponents of reform saw them, and the last decade of California history certainly shows how deep factional divisions about education can be. At the same time, we found teachers who were internally divided, too, agreeing and disagreeing with themselves—and sitting on their own fences—sometimes with regard to the same ideas (see also Barnes 1997). It was not unusual to find a teacher in strong agreement with one part of reformers' message and in complete disagreement over another. Teachers even seemed to disagree with themselves about very similar items. More than a hundred teachers in the sample, for instance, who agreed with statement 6, "Students learn mathematics best in classes with heterogeneous groups of students," also agreed with a nearby statement, 8: "Students talented in mathematics need a special curriculum." The two differ slightly in their implications for classroom arrangements, but they are closely enough related to strike many observers as requiring some consistency in response. Once again, though, teachers' views on improving math teaching were much more complex than the sectarian wars Californians waged about their classrooms.

Our results do show that by 1994 some reform ideas had gained currency, either because teachers already believed in them or because reformers had successfully persuaded teachers of their merit. The results also show that teachers were serious fans of some reform ideas, opposed to some others, and ambivalent about still others. These findings confirm several studies portraying teachers as engaged mediators between policy and practice (Porter, Floden and others 1986; McDonnell 1994; McLaughlin 1991a). The California elementary teachers we surveyed were active in their consumption of policy and complicated the sharp lines that reformers and policymakers often tried to draw in the political sand around math teaching and learning. What reformers and opponents packaged tidily, teachers disaggregated and reassembled. Their logic was different from and more complex than both the logic put forward by reformers in the frameworks, who saw what we call "conventional" and "reform" ideas about teaching and student learning as opposed to each other, and to the critics of reform, whose view of these matters was at least as black and white as that of the reformers. Though many teachers expressed strong allegiance to the principal reform ideas, most did not discard the corresponding conventional ideas. Moreover, not all reform ideas were popular: reform views of tracking and heterogeneous grouping got mixed reviews. For many teachers, the reforms consisted of disparate parts that they could choose to accept or not.

There is little evidence in the survey that allows us to explain these results, but because they are such an important thread in the study, we offer a few tentative explanations, drawn from other work. One is that teachers are sent many inconsistent and even directly conflicting messages by policymakers about such matters as whether to retain or discard basic skills and tracking (Cohen and Spillane 1993; Cohen, Spillane, Jennings, and Grant 1997; Spillane and Thompson 1997). Some of the inconsistency is temporary, as policy fads change with near-lightning speed, and some arises from intense political disagreement among policymakers and others who seek to influence policy. Other inconsistencies arise from fragmentation in an educational nonsystem, where the state can send one message, districts another, and school leadership yet another. California had at least its fair share of all three, and teachers may have absorbed the divergent messages that politics and policy had been teaching anyone who cared to listen. Or perhaps teachers had learned only that to make sense and survive in such a conflicted polity, they had better cobble together assorted planks to form a consensus platform.

A second explanation is that teachers learn things from experience that reformers, critics, and policymakers can never know because they lack the experience and rarely inquire of teachers. Some reformers might charge teachers with refusing to commit fully to the framework if they persisted in mixing basic skills with innovative materials and practices, and many critics of reform exhorted teachers to cling fast to basic skills and to cast aside any innovative ideas and practices. In other studies, some teachers who embraced the reforms told us that professional experience led them to conclude that many students needed work on basic skills. Others who initially resisted reform said that some methods and materials pressed on them by reformers had in those teachers' experience turned out to be quite useful and improved both their teaching and students' work.[5] Teachers who had come to such conclusions might have viewed the opposing statements in the survey as presenting a needless or even foolish dichotomy and could have responded by trying to assemble a more balanced set of ideas than those the survey suggested. Teaching is more complex than many reformers and critics seemed to realize.

A third explanation arises from the practice of teaching itself. Teachers' views of reform might be a function of how close it comes to the core of conventional practice. The closer it comes, the deeper the divisions. We certainly saw that the reform statements that received the highest approval ratings were those which challenged conventional views of learning and teaching least. It does not require deep rethinking of mathematics teaching to add writing about math and some problem solving to the curriculum; teachers need only invest more time in the activities most already command. Similarly, group work can be instituted simply by seating students in threes and fours instead of in rows; it does not necessarily entail the extended conversations and deep investigations that reformers had in mind. In contrast, reform ideas like having students puzzle out concepts and relationships were more likely to provoke teachers to rethink central tenets of conventional work, and those got much lower approval ratings. This relation should not be surprising, for doing such things would mean altering basic definitions of what it is to teach and to learn, what it would mean to know mathematics, and what students' role as learners would be. Such efforts would make school much more complex and difficult for teachers and students, not to mention more troublesome and controversial for many parents and communities.

All of this suggests one final explanation: learning is often slow and painful, and even when rapid, it attaches to inherited ideas, intellectual structures, and familiar practices. Cognitive psychologists have convincingly argued that students learn by assimilating new knowledge to established ideas and mental structures and do so even when the new and old seem incompatible. Learners add new bits and patches to existing mental edifices, and sometimes, when the inconsistencies seem too acute, modify one part to fit the other. Usually, though, it is easier to add to what exists than to reconfigure the entire structure, rendering it symmetrical and consistent either by discarding previously serviceable ideas and practices or by wholly rejecting new ideas. This supposition seems no less true for teachers learning new approaches to teaching, learning, and mathematics than for their students who are trying to do the same things.

Classroom Practices

It is one thing for teachers to embrace new ideas and beliefs about instruction but quite a different matter to change classroom practice. This issue is at the heart of implementation studies and perhaps of policymaking itself. If California policymakers wanted classrooms to reflect the new standards, teachers' and students' actions were a fundamental criterion of success. In order to explore this issue, the survey invited teachers to report on specific classroom activities and to describe their familiarity with and use of various materials and curricula that were related to the reform. Our analyses of these reports suggests that what teachers said they actually did in classrooms offers a somewhat more conservative picture of teaching and learning than one would expect from their ideas and knowledge of reform. Teachers' reports of classroom work also suggest that some elements of reform were quite widespread, while others were not. We offer our analysis in two categories that correspond to the chief elements of classroom work probed in the survey: the curriculum and materials that teachers and students used, and the work which students were reported to do. In both cases, teachers reported generous amounts of conventional mathematics teaching and learning.

Curricula and materials. One indicator of the extent to which teachers adopted a reform agenda was their use of the actual curriculum of reform: replacement units, curriculum packages, or other programs aligned with reform. Roughly one third of teachers responding to our survey said they relied mainly on a more conventional textbook at the time of the survey; another four in ten said they mixed the textbook and other resources in equal parts; another third still said they mainly used other, newly created curriculum resources (see Figure 4.1).

These results describe a remarkable adoption of reform materials. Most California teachers did not have access to extended NCTM-aligned curricula like Everyday Math (Chicago), Mimosa, or Investigations, around the time of the survey. The textbooks in use at the time were much more conventional, designed around an assumption that teachers would provide explanations of mathematical concepts and students would practice skills or procedures. These texts provided little support for hands-on activities, extended investigations, or contextual problem solving. If such texts seemed to take precedence in about a third of classrooms, two thirds of classrooms seemed to have room for other curriculum or materials—including those

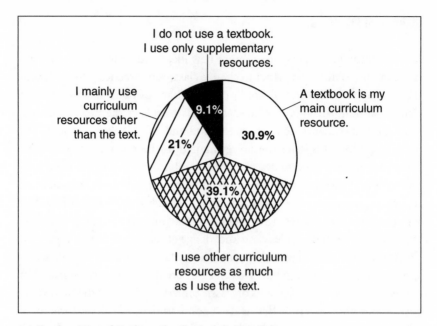

4.1. Teachers' Use of Mathematics Curriculum Materials

which were keyed to the state frameworks or similar reform ideas. Given that the easy option for teachers was to fall back on a conventional text supplied by the district, evidence that they found and used supplemental materials in large numbers suggests that many teachers actively sought out reformers' ideas and used them in their classrooms.

Another indicator of the extent to which teachers adopted elements of the reform was their reported use of just such alternative curricula and materials. We asked about their use of six sets of curriculum materials that were generally identified with the movement for mathematics reform; all were thought to be quite popular and relatively easy to use, but none were closely identified with the state policy. Most were available nationally at the time of the survey, and some, like *Math Their Way*, had been available for ten years or more. Figure 4.2 presents evidence on the percentage of teachers who reported that they had used one of the texts or curricula in their teaching. The figure shows that among the teachers in our sample, these generally reform-oriented texts and curricula had been adopted at impressive rates. More than three quarters of teachers reported using Activities in Math and Science (AIMS), a broad-gauged math and science curriculum reform package that has been very popular in California and elsewhere. True to its name, this Sacramento nonprofit organization offers books, journals, and newsletters filled with hands-on activities for students of various ages. Slightly more than half the teachers reported that they used *Math Their Way*, a primary grade text and "manipulative" materials package, which was developed on the assumption that if students use concrete objects in learning basic mathematical operations and ideas, they will deeply understand the underlying concepts. Roughly 40 percent reported having used *Family Math*, a set of activities intended for parents and children to improve parents' understanding of both mathematics and the math that their children are doing in school. Some teachers who used this curriculum may have attended a *Family Math* workshop, while others may simply have used *Family Math* as a resource for classroom activities. The results show that *Math in Stride*— another set of curriculum materials—and two other packages had been adopted at very much lower rates. Overall, almost 90 percent of teachers reported using at least one of these sets of materials, and almost 65 percent reported using two or more.

While such materials offered teachers a chance to depart from conventional math instruction, their use of these materials did not mean that there had been fundamental classroom change. One reason is that the survey did not invite teachers to explain in any detail what it meant to "have used [one of these] in my teaching." The question was put so generally that teachers could have meant anything, from trying it out for only a few days to using it consistently over an entire year. Another reason was that these materials did not offer a coherent curriculum with which teachers could help children learn concepts associated with specific mathematics topics. Most offered a mixture of hands-on or "real-life" activities that could be used as a single lesson or a bit more but were not part of a systematic inquiry into mathematics. These popular materials and curricula were relatively easy to adopt and to integrate into rather conventional classrooms (Cohen 1990), and teachers often used *Math Their Way* to supplement the conventional account of an arithmetic topic.

The survey also invited teachers to report on their use of manipulative or concrete instructional materials, such as beans, beads, rods, and blocks. The California math frameworks and other reform documents argued that students should work with a variety of mathematical representations, includ-

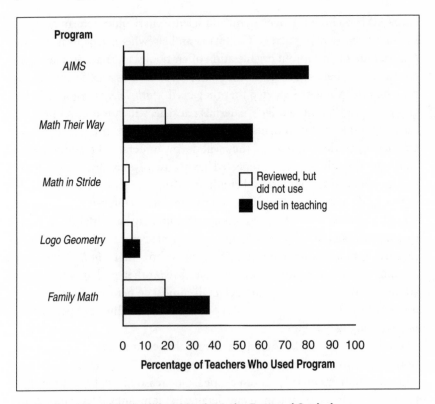

4.2. Teachers' Use of Nontraditional Mathematics Texts and Curricula

ing such materials. One rationale was that if students can work with materials that represent mathematical operations concretely—making three groups of ten beans each as a way of depicting the problem 3 × 10, for instance—they will be more likely to understand what goes on inside the operations that are more abstractly represented in mathematical notation. The idea seems reasonable, and it certainly struck a chord with elementary teachers. Figure 4.3 displays the concrete materials that teachers were asked to report on and reveals that these materials turned out to be even more popular than some of the texts and materials shown in Figure 4.2. Unifix cubes, pattern blocks, and geoboards were the most widely used: about eight in every ten teachers responding to our survey reported employing each of them in class. Two thirds of survey respondents reported using base-ten blocks, and about half used Cuisinaire rods, geoblocks, multilink cubes, and

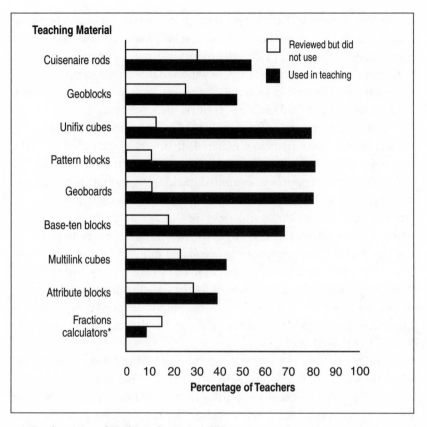

4.3. Teachers' Use of Mathematics Materials
(*Thirty-eight missing cases)

attribute blocks. The least popular of the materials were fraction calculators. More than 95 percent of the teachers who responded had used at least one of the nine, and the average respondent had used between four and five of the nine.

Figure 4.3 shows that this hands-on thread in the reforms was immensely popular. This finding is consistent with teachers' overwhelming approval of the statement, reported in Table 4.3, "Students learn best when they study mathematics in the context of everyday situations" and their strong approval of the idea that "teaching a mathematical concept should begin with a concrete example or model." These ideas suggest that there had been a significant shift in the curriculum and materials used during mathematics education in California. That view gains support from the changes reported in Figures 4.2 and 4.3. Nevertheless, those changes would not have required or even signaled a deep change in mathematics instruction. Our earlier studies of teachers' responses to the state policy showed that although many enthusiastically employed these materials, few used them in ways that diverged much from conventional teaching (Guthrie 1990; Ball 1992).

A more telling measure of change in teachers' practice was whether they reported using new curriculum materials that were specifically tied to the state reforms. After its largely failed effort to change math textbooks, the State Education Department commissioned the creation of two "replacement units," in which curriculum developers created the means to teach and learn an entire topic—fractions was one—that would be closely aligned with the frameworks. Teachers could use the units in place of the relevant text chapters without encountering broad and difficult issues of text adoption. The units were generally thought to be of high quality, and all represented a departure from the kinds of mathematics usually found in classrooms. Because replacement units were specifically designed to help teachers implement the new math standards, and because they required a departure from conventional mathematics instruction, it seems likely that the use of these units represented a commitment to more central features of the reforms than did use of concrete materials or *Math Their Way*.

Given the greater difficulty of putting these units into use and the shorter time they were available, it is not surprising to see in Figure 4.4 that far fewer teachers reported employing them than reported relying on the more accessible texts listed in Figure 4.2. The replacement units were also designed for specific grades, a factor that further reduced the number of teachers in our sample likely to have adopted any given unit. Figure 4.4 shows the percentage of teachers who reviewed the unit but chose not to use it, along with the number that reviewed the unit and used it in their classroom.

Seeing Fractions, the original unit commissioned from TERC by the California Department of Education, and Marilyn Burns's multiplication unit *Math by All Means* were the most widely used; they had also been available for some years prior to the survey. More recent units, and those less well publicized, enjoyed less widespread use.[6] In total, two of five responding teachers reported using at least one of the units listed above. Among third through fifth grade teachers—at whom most of the units were targeted—the proportion approached one in two. That is a remarkable achievement

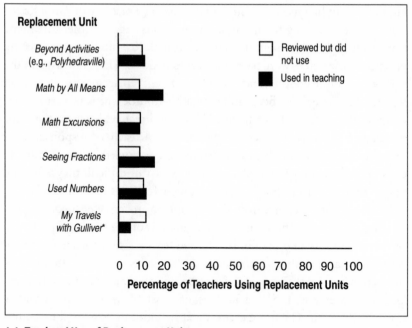

4.4. Teachers' Use of Replacement Units
(*Thirty-four missing cases)

for only a few years' work, but it is still far below the percentages of teachers who reported using the activity-centered texts and manipulatives described earlier.

There is modest indirect evidence that putting these units to use was a meaningful decision for teachers. The survey collected evidence on the relation between considering the units and actually using them, and Figure 4.4 shows that a high proportion of the teachers who reviewed a replacement unit did not adopt it. If we compare these rates to those for manipulatives, for which adoption rates mostly ranged from 60 to 85 percent, we see that replacement-unit adoptions were much lower. The same was true of a comparison of replacement units with other supplementary materials (see Figure 4.2). Nine out of ten teachers who reported reviewing *AIMS* also claimed to have tried some activity from this package; two out of three teachers who reviewed *Family Math* used it, and three out of four teachers who reviewed *Math Their Way* used at least some part of it. Two out of three teachers who reviewed *Math by All Means* or *Used Numbers* did use them, but only about half used *Beyond Activities, Seeing Fractions,* or *Math Excursions 2* after reviewing them. These comparisons suggest either that many teachers found replacement units more difficult to assimilate into existing practice or that there were fewer incentives to do so. That contrast and the wide variations in adoption rates among different replacement units suggest that teachers may have been quite sensitive to differences in various elements of the mathematics reforms. There is indirect evidence for that supposition in our earlier observational studies of teachers' response to reforms: though many teachers searched for innovations that would improve classroom work, they also took note of how easy or difficult they would be to fit into their current practice (Wilson 1990; Jennings 1996; Grant 1998).

We could not generalize from these results to any broader theory of curriculum adoption without an extensive analysis of the texts and packages, replacement units, and manipulatives, and teachers' decisions to use them; yet we can say that the patterns discussed here correspond with observations elsewhere by students of innovation: the closer a text or tool is to the kind of mathematics most teachers feel comfortable with, the more widely it will be adopted. The more easily a text or tool can be altered to fit into teachers' pre-existing frame of reference, the more widely it will be adopted.

Practices. Above all, the California reformers sought to change what teachers and students did in mathematics lessons. Teachers' reports on the adoption of curricula and other materials reveals something about that, but only indirectly. The materials used could not tell us much about what students and teachers actually did as they worked on mathematics. To get some sense of patterns of classroom work in mathematics, and how they squared with reformers' ideas, we devised twelve indicators of classroom activities and asked teachers to report on how often they used each one. These indicators were selected because they were good markers of both the conventional practices that reformers meant to reduce or eliminate and of the innovative practices that they wanted teachers to adopt. Therefore, the indicators range from activities commonly observed in conventional classrooms to those which would be observed if teachers and students were working as the frameworks proposed.

The findings here echo those in the earlier sections: though teachers did embrace many reform practices, they also retained numerous elements of more conventional instruction. Table 4.4 reports the distribution of teachers' accounts of these practices. Two of the practices are considered by most

Table 4.4. Teachers' Reports of Classroom Practices

	Never	A few times a year	Once or twice a month	Once or twice a week	Almost daily
1. Make conjectures and explore possible methods to solve a mathematical problem	1.0	7.4	18.3	42.8	30.4
2. Discuss different ways that they solve particular problems	0.9	5.0	14.6	46.6	32.9
3. Practice or take tests on computational skills	0.6	9.7	33.4	42.6	13.7
4. Work in small groups on mathematics problems	1.2	3.8	20.4	46.4	28.2
5. Work individually on problems from the textbook/workbook	3.0	4.3	9.7	38.1	45.0
6. Work on individual projects that take several days	23.5	36.7	26.5	10.6	2.6
7. Work on group investigations that extend for several days	25.4	36.2	26.1	9.4	2.9
8. Write about how to solve a problem in an assignment or test	11.6	16.9	33.7	28.8	9.0
9. Do problems that have more than one correct solution	8.1	14.1	33.0	32.8	12.0
10. Use manipulative materials or models to solve problems	0.9	5.0	19.7	40.0	34.4
11. Use calculators to solve problems	12.7	20.4	29.1	29.6	8.3
12. Do mathematics in conjunction with other subjects or class projects	1.1	10.1	33.5	36.9	18.3

to be "conventional"—having students work alone on problems from texts (5) and taking or practicing to take computational tests (3). Both were popular: 45 percent of responding teachers reported that their students engaged in individual work on mathematics problems from the textbook or workbook almost daily, and nearly another 40 percent said they did so once or twice a week. Only 3 percent of teachers in our sample eschewed this practice. Practicing or taking tests on computational skills was only slightly less popular; over half our sample said that their classes engaged in such activities at least one or twice a week. Only three teachers in the sample of nearly six hundred reported that their students did not engage in computational testing. These frequencies suggest that for most students of these teachers, some elements of mathematics instruction remained firmly rooted in the practices and activities of past generations.

Responses to items intended to represent reform practice show that even though conventional practices remained popular, some reform practices were extensively implemented. Student discussion and exploration of ways to solve math problems were reported as taking place once or twice a week in the average classroom (2), and manipulatives and models to help solve math problems were employed just as often (10). It appears that the average student also frequently worked on math problems with his peers (4) and did math in conjunction with other subjects at least several times a month (12). These practices were central to the emphasis in the frameworks on constructivist learning. The report that many students were often questioning and building models about mathematics seems to indicate that this aspect of the reforms had taken root.

Popular reform practices, like student group work or use of manipulatives, could be integrated fairly easily into conventional classrooms, a feature that may also explain their high rate of adoption. By contrast, Table 4.4 also shows that some reform practices were much less widely adopted than others. Extended group and individual investigations (items 6 and 7) were the least widely adopted; the average student engaging in both only slightly more than "a few" times a year. Writing about how to solve mathematics problems (8) also seems to have occurred relatively infrequently (on average once or twice a month) in California classrooms, despite state efforts to emphasize the technique as a fundamental part of the reform. Our explanation for these low rates of adoption, based on earlier field studies, is that the practices summarized in items 6 through 8 would be relatively difficult to enact without making significant changes in the organization of teaching and learning; they are elements of reform that could not easily be added on at the periphery of conventional classroom practice.[7] The report that most students "do problems with more than one correct solution" (9) only once or twice a month or less seems consistent with this view.

Without direct classroom observation, we have no way to know how teachers interpreted these statements. Having students "discuss different ways that they solve particular problems," for example, might mean quite different things to different teachers (Mayer 1999). Whereas some teachers might interpret this statement to mean lengthy debates over the principles involved in a particular word problem, others might assume that students "discuss" mathematics while the teacher is presenting the material, simply because those students answer some questions. Yet we would argue that some of the items are more grounded than others and would be less vulnerable to measurement error and the perception of socially desirable responses. Working on individual projects over several days, for instance, is a novel practice that is fairly easily distinguishable. Writing about how to solve problems is an activity, similarly, that is concretely measurable. When we see lower rates of classroom engagement with these practices, 6 through 9 in Table 4.4, we might conjecture that the rates reflect not only the difficulty of adopting such practices, but perhaps also a decrease in measurement error owing to the ease with which the practices can be registered.

Our chief conclusion from these reports of classroom practice stands, despite these difficulties. At the time of the survey, California elementary schools featured a mixture of conventional and reform-based instruction. Conventional math teaching, in the form of seat work and computational tests, remained popular at the same time that some reform practices were widely employed. Though this result is consistent with our earlier analyses of teachers' ideas about instruction and their familiarity with reform, neither reformers nor critics of reform would be delighted with these results. Many of the practices that seemed important to reformers had not been widely adopted by teachers, and many of the practices that conservative critics feared had been driven out of schools were still firmly in place, as critics were attacking their absence and blaming the reforms.

Teachers made their own sense of the reforms, oftentimes constructing classroom practices that might puzzle advocates of conventional or reform mathematics. Some teachers who reported that students work out of textbooks almost daily also reported that students make conjectures almost daily; many who reported that students practice or take tests on computational skills also reported that students discuss different ways to solve a problem at least once or twice a week. A factor analysis of these practice items shows conventional and reform practices on two separate dimensions that correlate only moderately at −.30 when scaled.[8] In the aggregate, the evidence does not suggest that one style of instruction thrived at the expense of another. The conventional instruction that many reformers abhorred coexisted with the reform practices that many traditionalists decried, very often within the same teacher.

These reports are consistent with our earlier analysis of teachers' knowledge of reforms and their ideas about math teaching, in which we saw teachers easily blending elements of new ideas and practices with older instructional traditions. Many of our interpretations are similar. Some observers would regard this as evidence of teachers' confusion, but we think there are other plausible ways to interpret the results. One is that there is a logic of practice, in which both computation and conjectures, test practice and writing about problem solving, make sense. Though that logic defies the tidy lines that reformers and traditionalists often draw, it makes more sense in the complex world of classrooms. A second is that even when teachers felt comfortable with the new forms of mathematics, they were still bound in many districts by traditional skill-based tests or demands for skills practice from parents or both. Their teaching was a compromise between the practices they preferred and those which seemed to be called for by their situation. Third, many teachers were trying out new ideas and practices, learning new approaches to mathematics teaching, and gradually changing their practice, but such learning is slow, and new ideas and practices are typically assimilated into inherited intellectual frameworks and habits of work. Because a one-time survey offers only a snapshot, observers might see a clash where teachers experienced a coherent trajectory of change.

The reforms brought significant change to instruction, but conventional practice had enormous staying power. Teachers were both enthusiastic about the reforms and wary of fundamental alterations in the classroom. Teachers were engaged with new ideas about learning and yet deeply attached to conventional instruction. In most cases, teachers tacked the reforms in bits and pieces onto conventional instruction, rather than replacing it wholesale, or even in large patches. We certainly know that many teachers transformed reformers' ideas to resemble more conventional teaching; whereas some teachers who reported enthusiastic engagement with the reforms had made modifications resembling those the reformers had in mind, most teachers had simply added innovative bits around a conventional core.

The research we report has no baseline for comparison. It is hard to say how much more conjecture or less drill and practice occurred in California in 1995 than in 1990, because the survey was cross-sectional. Yet even the relatively crude measures of change contained in the survey were useful, because we know from interviews and other studies that many of the classroom practices that reformers advocated were nearly nonexistent in schools in the years before reform.

Our analysis also throws light on the relations between policy and practice. Policymakers often act as though they believe that teachers' assignment is to do as they are told: to enforce graduation requirements, teach new curricula, enforce disciplinary standards, and the like. The analyses we report show that although teachers attended to the guidance that California policymakers offered, they exercised judgment about what to attend to, and how. It makes sense to view teachers, in the phrase Andrew Porter and his colleagues coined, as "policy brokers." They actively evaluate the new ideas and practices they are urged to adopt, modify many, adopt some, and reject others. It makes less sense to think of teachers as educational clerks who either follow or disobey orders than as active players who judge and use policy, and make policy as they respond to others' initiatives.

Chapter 5

TEACHERS' OPPORTUNITIES TO LEARN
AND CLASSROOM PRACTICE

Teachers responded differently to the new mathematics policy. The evidence that we have presented so far suggests that some teachers used new curricula and instructional practices in their classroom, but others did not. Some seemed to invest heavily in the reforms, but others invested much less. Many teachers adopted some reform ideas but rejected others. In traditional approaches to studying implementation this policy might be judged part success and part failure, as many teachers moved a short way, and others further, toward implementation.

In this chapter we propose another way to gauge the success of this policy. We ask whether those who had the unusual learning opportunities we described in Chapter 3 report more beliefs or practices aligned with the reforms than those who did not have such opportunities. If so, it would support our proposal that complex policies must rely on learning as a critical element in the causal chain that can connect policy and practice. A related explanation is that changes in teachers' beliefs and practices would depend on their attitudes toward policy; if so, learning would be subsidiary to pre-existing attitudes, not an independent influence on implementation.

We also wanted to know whether some opportunities to learn mattered more than others. Professional developers in California offered teachers a tremendous variety of opportunities that were related to the reform, and the state provided others. All of them varied in several critical dimensions: whether the opportunities concerned instruction, curricula, or student assessments; whether they were grounded in student work or not; whether they were brief or lengthier; and whether they were created by the state and localities or by professional organizations and scholars. Comparing teachers' professional development to teachers' reports of their ideas and practices might shed some light on what makes learning opportunities effective.

We found that teachers' learning is an independent influence on policy implementation. Teachers' reports of implementation depend not only on their general attitude toward reforms but also on their opportunities to learn about the new classroom and assessment practices that reformers promoted. Opportunities to learn proved a crucial link in the chain between policy, on the one hand, and teachers' classroom practice on the other. Still, all opportunities to learn were not created equal. Teachers who took workshops that were extended in time and focused on students' tasks—either the replacement units created for the reforms or new assessment tasks and students' work on them—reported more practices that were similar to those which reformers proposed. In contrast, teachers who took workshops more loosely focused on hands-on activities, gender, cooperative learning, and other tangential topics were less likely to report such practices.

We present evidence to support those findings. We outline our measures of teachers' ideas about mathematics instruction, their classroom practices, and their familiarity with and attitude toward reform. Then we examine the association between teachers' opportunities to learn about policy and the instruments used to promote policy, as well as teachers' ideas and practices. We take teachers' familiarity with and attitudes toward policy into account, as well as the relation between teachers' learning and their preexisting knowledge and beliefs. Finally, we consider whether efforts to foster professionalism among teachers influenced the implementation of reform.[1]

Measures of Ideas and Practice

We developed two types of measures for this analysis. One was straightforward, consisting of teachers' reports of attendance at workshops, use of reform materials, and experiences with the CLAS. We adjusted these reports to reflect the intensity of teachers' investment in those learning opportunities—the time they spent in professional development, or how much attention they paid reform documents, for instance.

The second type of measure concerns ideas and practices that reform might influence. These are the survey items concerning teaching practices and beliefs that we described in Chapter 4. One set of measures focuses on teachers' ideas. A factor analysis revealed that survey items on teachers' ideas fell into two groups: one that represented more conventional ideas about mathematics instruction and one that represented ideas that were closer to the reform. Because teachers might have drawn on different experiences and ideas in responding to the two types of statement, and because of the generally low correlation between items that made up the conventional and reform-related factors (−.26),[2] we created two scales. One was designed to represent more conventional ideas about mathematics learning and was built by averaging the five items displayed in part 1 of Table 5.1, for each teacher. The mean of the five is 2.85, the standard deviation for the scale on "conventional ideas" is .76, and its reliability is .68. The second scale represents more reform-oriented ideas about mathematics learning and was built by averaging the four items that are displayed in part 2 of Table 5.1. The mean of this "framework ideas scale" is 4.18, the standard deviation .63, and the reliability .67. The remainder of the items regarding belief scaled onto smaller factors that we will not use in the analysis.

The second kind of dependent measure concerns teachers' self-reported instructional practices in mathematics. The survey measured those practices with thirteen items—the twelve we listed in Table 4.6, and another that inquired about teachers' use of textbooks. As was the case with teachers' ideas, a factor analysis of these items revealed that responses lined up along two dimensions. The first, which we call "conventional practice," incorporated responses to items that represented more conventional instructional activities (see Table 5.2, part 1) as well as to the item about textbooks. Because of inconsistencies in response categories from item to item, we standardized teachers' responses to each item and averaged by teacher to form

Table 5.1. Items That Make Up Scales of Ideas

	Factor loading— conventional	Factor loading— reform
Conventional ideas		
1. Teachers should make sure that students are not confused at the end of a mathematics period.	.71	−.00
2. Students need to master basic computational facts and skills before they can engage effectively in mathematical problem solving.	.72	−.11
3. In teaching mathematics, my primary goal is to help students master basic computational skills.	.58	−.29
4. Students talented in mathematics need a special curriculum.	.66	−.02
5. If elementary students use calculators, they won't learn the mathematics they need to know.	.57	−.28
Reform ideas		
1. Students learn best when they study mathematics in the context of everyday situations.	−.05	.72
2. Students should write about how they solve mathematical problems.	−.19	.64
3. Teachers should make students figure things out for themselves rather than tell them how to solve a mathematics problem.	−.08	.56
4. Students learn mathematics by discussing different approaches to a task, even when some of them are wrong.	−.11	.75

Note: Varimax rotation. Several items from Table 4.3 did not factor onto either dimension:
- Teaching a mathematical concept should begin with a concrete example or model.
- It is not a good idea to have students work together in solving mathematics problems.
- Students learn mathematics best in classes with heterogeneous groups of students.

Variance explained by each factor:
  Conventional factor: 2.23
  Reform factor: 2.32
  Final communality estimate: 5.65

the scale. The mean for the scale is zero, its standard deviation .75, and its reliability .63.

The second dimension, which is captured in our "framework-practice" scale, consisted of responses to seven items that represented more reform-oriented practices (see Table 5.2, part 2). To devise the scale, we averaged teachers' responses, which gave a mean of 3.26, a standard deviation of .72, and a reliability of .85. The conventional practice and reform practice scales correlate at −.40.[3]

These four scales are the dependent measures in our effort to probe the effects of teachers' opportunities to learn. Within the limits of a cross-sectional data set, we ask how policy-related opportunities to learn were linked to the ideas and practices summarized in those four scales. We shall employ ordinary least squares (OLS) regression to compare the effects of different opportunities to learn, for that will enable us to estimate the effect of each learning opportunity efficiently, while controlling for others.[4] This analytic technique also will allow us to control for factors other than learning opportunities that might influence teachers' relative position on the conventional and framework dimensions, including teachers' familiarity with and view of reform. Familiarity with reform was measured by asking teachers to identify from a list of statements about instruction and student learning the themes that were central and not central to the reforms (see Chapter 4, Tables 1 and 2). We include the percentage identified correctly—"familiarity with reform"—in both our models on ideas and our models on practice, because teachers more familiar with reform themes might have reported ideas and practices more consistent with the reforms simply because they knew the official policy line. Other teachers with similar ideas and classrooms but who had less acquaintance with the reforms might have been less likely to give a socially desirable response. The mean of this measure, .83 on a scale of 0 to 1, indicates considerable familiarity with the leading reform ideas.

The second control is for "attitude toward reform," and derives from teachers' response to the question "How do you feel about the kind of mathematics education promoted by the new mathematics standards and assessments?" Teachers answered this query on a scale of 1 to 5, with 1 labeled extremely negative and 5 extremely positive.[5] The mean of the scale is 3.77 and its standard deviation .93. We included it in our analyses because teachers' general view of reform might have colored their reports of the classroom ac-

Table 5.2. Items that Make Up Scales of Practice

Q: About how often do students in your class take part in the following activities during mathematics instruction?

	Factor loading— conventional	Factor loading— reform
Conventional practices		
1. Practice or take tests on computational skills	.60	−.01
2. Work individually on mathematics problems from the textbook/workbook	.81	−.16
3. Textbook use*	.77	−.19
Reform practices		
1. Make conjectures and explore possible methods to solve a mathematical problem	.04	.82
2. Discuss different ways that they solve particular problems	−.07	.76
3. Work in small groups on mathematics problems	−.34	.53
4. Work on individual projects that take several days	−.25	.57
5. Work on group investigations that extend for several days	−.35	.57
6. Write about how to solve a problem in an assignment or test	−.19	.68
7. Do problems that have more than one correct solution	−.13	.74

Note: Items we did not use are in note 3. Variance explained by each factor: conventional: 3.5; reform: 2.20; final communality estimate: 7.49.

*This item had the following format:
Which statement best describes your use of the mathematics textbook?
1. I do not use a textbook. I use only supplementary resources (9.1%)
2. I mainly use curriculum resources other than the text (21.0%)
3. I use other curriculum resources as much as I use the text (39.1%)
4. A textbook is my main curriculum resource (30.9%)

tivities they engaged in. Past research leads us to think that teachers' opinions about a policy may affect the way they respond to that policy. Perceptions of social desirability may have also played a role in responses: teachers who approved of reform might have reported engaging in more practices that corresponded to it than teachers who did not approve, even though their classrooms would appear quite similar to an observer. We did not include this measure in our analysis of ideas because it is so close to the dependent variable.[6]

The controls, when entered into regressions predicting teachers' ideas and practices, may act as conservative checks on the effects of teachers' opportunities to learn. Some teachers may have known and been enthusiastic about the reforms at the outset; if so, they may have reported teaching practice more in line with the framework as a result of their predisposition rather than in response to the policy. Controlling for teachers' opinions of reform should reduce or eliminate the effects of such a predisposition and effectively parcel predisposition into its own variable, rather than including it in other independent variables. Other teachers, though, were likely to have become enthusiastic or knowledgeable as the result of a policy-related opportunity to learn. Controlling for teachers' attitudes would soak up at least some of this effect of policy learning and partially mask the effect on practice of teachers' opportunity to learn.

Linking Learning and Practice

We explore the conjecture that teacher learning was a key component of policy implementation and try to distinguish why some learning opportunities made a difference in teachers' ideas and practices. We expected that fruitful learning opportunities would be grounded in specific, substantial content related to the reforms, such as improved mathematics curriculum for students, or assessments that inform teachers about what students should know and how they perform. We also expected that there would be consistency, or overlap, among the elements from which teachers might learn—assessments, curricula, and so on. We further anticipated that the more overlap there was, the more likely teachers' learning would be to build coherently, rather than accumulating in small unrelated or contradictory bits. Finally, we thought that teachers who had had longer exposure to such opportunities to learn would be likely to learn more. Our view is informed by the scanty research on teachers' learning (Brown, Smith, and Stein 1996; Carpenter and others 1989; Kennedy 1998).

Our analysis was constrained by the cross-sectional survey. We could not observe teacher learning as it took place over time in California, for changes in the political and professional environments meant that the influences on teachers' ideas and practices would not have been parallel for the first and second waves of the study. This meant that the relationships we observed between opportunities to learn and dependent measures might not reflect any learning, but other factors that might have contributed to teachers' attitudes or practices. We shall discuss some of these problems as we present results from each of the policy instruments that reformers used to shape classroom practice.

Professional development workshops. We showed in Chapter 3 that the vast majority of practitioners learned about the reforms in conventional workshops. Some lasted a day or two, others less, and many were offered by a teacher or administrator to those who volunteered to attend. This pattern matches the profile of typical professional development in the United States (Little 1993). A minority of workshops, however, focused on issues linked to the state's reform effort, and others were grounded in the student curriculum that reformers promoted.

We divided the workshops into two categories (Table 5.3), based on existing expectations about the influences on teacher learning (Kennedy 1998; Wilson and Berne 1999).[7] The two workshops in section B of the table focused on the new mathematics curriculum for students. Replacement units, the curriculum modules designed around specific topics and meant to replace entire units of mathematical texts, were the sole focus of these workshops. Like the Marilyn Burns workshops, they offered teachers more than one-lesson activities; each was designed to enhance teachers' knowledge of student mathematical thinking, instructional methods, and mathematical subject matter in a relatively more integrated fashion than most professional development available in the early 1990s. Marilyn Burns Institutes were offered by experienced trainers whom Burns selected and taught, and they focused on teaching specific math topics; some focused on replacement units that Burns had developed. In some cases, teachers who attended these workshops one summer were able to return the next summer and continue. Thus, the workshops in section B of the table actually mixed two different approaches toward professional development — new materials that students would use, and use of those materials as the curriculum of teacher education. Teacher education was thereby grounded in the student curriculum, which itself was framed in light of the reforms. This was a very significant departure from the usual approach to professional development.

Workshops like cooperative learning, EQUALS, and Family Math — in section A of the table — were more loosely related to the frameworks, for

Table 5.3. Teachers' Opportunities to Learn

Q: Which of the following mathematics-related activities have you participated in during the past year, and approximately *how much total time* did you spend in each?

	None	1 day or less	2–6 days	1–2 weeks	More than 2 weeks
Section A: Special Topics					
EQUALS	96.5	2.4	.9	.2	0
Family Math	81.7	12.9	4.3	.8	.3
Cooperative learning	54.5	28.9	13.7	1.8	1.1
Section B: Student Curriculum					
Marilyn Burns	83.2	9.8	5.3	1.3	.3
Mathematics replacement units	58.9	22.7	14.2	1.7	2.5

Note: Missing data treated as "none."

none of the three focused directly on students' mathematical curriculum. EQUALS centered on inequalities in math classrooms arising from gender, linguistic ability, class, and race. Family Math helped teachers bring parents into math learning, and cooperative-learning workshops came in many different flavors, some focusing on "detracking," some on other topics, but all of them encouraged learning together. It was common for teachers in these workshops to engage in short mathematical activities that they could bring back to their classes. For the most part these were brief exercises intended to provide teachers with "something for Monday morning," and differed greatly from the deeper exploration of subject matter, teaching, and learning provided by the typical replacement unit.

Instead of comparing each workshop individually against our dependent measures, we grouped them by content and created composite variables. The variable "time in student curriculum workshops" marks attendance at workshops that took students' new curriculum as a basis for investigating mathematics instruction. The variable "time in special topics workshops" marks attendance at in-service sessions associated with more tangential aspects of mathematics reform.[8] Roughly 45 percent of teachers had had at least some opportunity to learn about student curriculum in either the

Marilyn Burns or mathematical replacement-unit workshops, and around half the teachers in our sample reported spending some time learning about "special topics" in EQUALS, Family Math, or cooperative learning.

We also created a more general variable known as past framework learning. Because the figures in Table 5.3 capture teachers' opportunities to learn in only the one year directly preceding the survey, we tried to control for earlier learning opportunities. Not doing so could have led to a bias, for teachers who had had an earlier opportunity to learn about the content or curriculum of the new framework would have been lumped in with teachers who had not. This measure showed that about 30 percent of teachers had not attended one of the curriculum or special-topics workshops in the past year yet did report having had some previous opportunity to learn about the frameworks. That a number of respondents in this category also reported using replacement units suggests that they might have attended a replacement-unit workshop in the years before the one immediately preceding the survey.

The regressions in Table 5.4 state a central finding quite bluntly: the content of teachers' professional development made a difference in their practice. Workshops that offered teachers an opportunity to learn about the student math curriculum materials were associated with teacher reports of more reform-oriented practice. The teacher who had attended a student curriculum workshop for two days (the typical length of the workshops) reported having had on average nearly a half a standard deviation more framework practice than did the teacher who had not attended these workshops. Teachers who attended two days of such a workshop engaged in more of the classroom activities that reformers proposed—including extended mathematical investigations, holding discussions about problems and their solutions, and having students write about mathematics. Furthermore, time spent had a potent influence on practice. The typical teacher who attended a weeklong student curriculum workshop appeared about a full standard deviation higher on the framework-practice scale than the teacher who did not attend such a workshop at all. In other words, the more time teachers spent in one of these workshops, the more reform practices they reported using with their students. These observations held true as well of the relation between student curriculum workshops and teachers' ideas.

The relationship works in both directions: teachers who reported two days' attendance at either a Marilyn Burns or a replacement-unit workshop

Table 5.4. Associations Between Teachers' Learning Opportunities and Their Ideas and Practice

	Conventional ideas	Framework ideas	Conventional practice	Framework practice
Intercept	4.92***	3.20***	1.51***	1.95***
(standard error—se)	(.17)	(.15)	(.19)	(.17)
Time in student				
curriculum workshops	–0.09***	0.07***	–0.10***	0.15***
(se)	(.02)	(.02)	(.02)	(.02)
Time in special-topics				
workshops	0.04	0.05	0.05	–0.03
(se)	(.03)	(.03)	(.03)	(.03)
Past framework learning	–0.09	–0.03	0.09	0.02
(se)	(.06)	(.06)	(.07)	(.07)
Attitude toward reform			–0.22***	0.23***
(se)			(.03)	(.03)
Familiarity with reform	–2.39***	1.08***	–0.81***	0.40*
(se)	(.20)	(.18)	(.21)	(.20)
R^2 (adjusted)	0.23	0.10	0.18	0.22
N	592	592	583	583

*Indicates $p < .05$.

**Indicates $p < .01$.

***Indicates $p < .001$.

reported relying less on conventional practices than teachers who did not attend. So the Marilyn Burns and replacement-unit workshops were linked with less frequent use of computational testing and individual computational practice. The same pattern appeared for conventional ideas. These opportunities to learn seemed not only to increase innovative teaching practice but also to decrease use of conventional methods; teachers did not simply add new practices to a conventional core but also changed that core teaching approach. This is quite significant, when compared with the "Christmas tree" approach most teachers bring to learning from professional development, in which they festoon an otherwise stable and conventional practice with attractive new—and often inconsistent—additions (Bryk, Sebring, Kerbow, Rollow and Easton 1998).

In contrast, the variable representing special-topics workshops had nearly a zero association with our dependent measures in all four cases. Workshops not closely linked to student curriculum seemed unrelated either to the kinds of practices that reformers wished to see in schools or to the conventional practices—like worksheets and computational tests—that they would rather not have seen. The workshops were also unrelated to ideas associated with conventional and reform-based perspectives on student learning and mathematics instruction. We suspect that this occurred because special-topics workshops were not chiefly about the mathematical content, though they were consonant with the state math frameworks in some respects. Such workshops may have been useful for some purposes but would probably have been peripheral to mathematics teaching. They might have encouraged cooperative learning or new techniques for girls or students of color, rather than any change in core beliefs and practices concerning mathematics and mathematics teaching.

We extended this analysis to check for linearity in the effects associated with student curriculum and special-topics workshops. We broke each workshop into a set of four "dummy" variables, each representing a discrete investment of time (Marilyn Burns for one day; Marilyn Burns for two to five days, and so on) and then entered these dummy variables into the models predicting framework or conventional practice. In general, greater time investments in student curriculum workshops were associated with teacher reports of more frequent framework practices and with fewer reports of conventional practices (see Appendix C). Greater investments of time in special-topics workshops were not related to either sort of practice. This parallels research on students' opportunities to learn, in which observers have found the combination of time spent and focus on content to be a potent influence on learning. Even large investments of time in less content-focused workshops were not associated with more of the practices that reformers proposed or with fewer of the conventional practices that reformers considered inadequate. The effects of these workshops seemed tangential to the central classroom issues on which the mathematics reform focused, as measured by our practice scales.

These findings bear on our concerns about selectivity. A critic might argue that the results of the models in Table 5.4 could be explained by teachers' having selected themselves into workshops that mirrored their teaching styles and interests. It seems extremely unlikely, however, that teachers would have arranged themselves so neatly by level of enthusiasm and progressive practice into different levels of time investment. When the additional hours or days spent in a student curriculum workshop are linked with progressively higher scores on our framework-practice scale and lower scores on conventional practice, especially when we control for teachers' familiarity with and views of reform, we surmise that learning, not fiendishly clever self-selection, was the cause.

Our two control variables—"familiarity with reform" and "attitude toward reform"—helped to explain teachers' scores on the idea-and-practice scales in Table 5.4. Both measures displayed a negative association with conventional practice and thereby show that teachers who were better acquainted with the reforms and who felt more positively about them reported relying less on conventional teaching practice. Both measures also displayed a positive association with framework practice, an indication that teachers who were better acquainted with the reforms and who felt more positively about them reported making more use of reform-oriented methods. Because this was a cross-sectional study, it is difficult to know exactly what this means. In some part, it could be that individuals more inclined to act on policy are more likely to put it into place, with or without the benefit of professional education. This was probably the case for some teachers. Other stories are equally likely, though, and consistent with the findings presented here; for instance, teachers might have become more enthusiastic about the reforms as a result of their opportunity to learn, and as a consequence "attitude toward reform" may have been an effect of professional development, and professional development another indirect cause of teachers' practices.

This line of thought brings us back to selectivity. Because this was a cross-sectional analysis, we cannot make any conclusive statements about the relation between teachers' attitudes about the reform and teachers' learning about policy. Two types of selection bear on this matter. Teachers might have chosen a workshop because it matched their view of good mathematics teaching, and their learning opportunities would have reinforced an already existing practice. Though plausible, this explanation is unlikely, for reform-oriented practices were reportedly not widespread in the state before the early 1990s. Nearly all the observers and teachers we interviewed reported that the reforms created the innovations that we shall discuss. Several were created entirely afresh, and we could find little evidence in fieldwork and interviews that there was an appreciable pre-existing pool of elementary school math teachers who were already doing what the frameworks proposed. In fact, we found just the opposite.

To try to verify this empirically, we used two-stage least squares regression to control for those factors that may have led teachers to select themselves into certain workshops (see Appendix D). This procedure modeled teachers' choices in two stages. The first stage predicted whether teachers would take part in a certain kind of workshop, given their beliefs and familiarity with reform. Then we used that "predicted" workshop attendance for each to forecast the teacher's individual classroom practices in regressions like those above. That helped mitigate the first kind of selection—that is, teachers assigning themselves to workshops on the basis of their beliefs and practice. The results showed that teachers' decisions to enroll appeared only modestly related to their disposition toward certain types of mathematics teaching and in particular to their broad opinions of reform, as captured in the category "attitude toward reform." Further, the results of the second-stage regression showed that the effect associated with student curriculum workshops held even when teachers' attendance was predicted by an earlier model that included their opinion of reform, familiarity with reform, and other factors that might encourage an interest in it. In fact, insofar as we can tell from these data, teacher selection into workshops did not appear to be rational, in the sense that teachers carefully sought out workshops that fit with strongly held convictions about reform. That observation suggests that our findings hold up, at least with regard to the first kind of selectivity.[9]

This impression is strengthened by other research. In Judith Warren-Little's (1989, 1993) accounts of the "system" for teachers' professional development, she described teachers' workshop choices as usually related to very general subject matter interest like "math" or "technology" but only weakly related to the specific content or quality of a workshop or its potential effects on students' learning. Brian Lord (1994) went one step further, arguing that teachers' staff development choices are "random" with regard to the factors reformers might care about. Ruling out the first kind of selection is one step in demonstrating the worth of these workshops centered on student curriculum: a sizable number of teachers did learn as a result of their attendance.[10]

A second kind of posssible selectivity is that some teachers may have been more open to change than others. To the extent that it did operate, it could have slightly affected our results. If the individuals who opted into certain workshops or read reform documents were already inclined to like what they saw and heard, their instruction might have changed as the result of the interaction between that predisposition and their learning. Such selectivity would consist of individual will interacting with the content of the learning opportunity, and, if so, we could not generalize some of the results discussed here to nonvoluntary teacher-learners. Our controls for teacher attitude and familiarity with reform might in some way measure such predispositions and thus might go a small way toward mitigating this second kind of selectivity, but we cannot use statistical controls to remove their effect entirely.

Assessment. Tests are widely believed to have a significant influence on teaching. Beginning in the 1970s, as some educators lobbied for expanded teaching of basic skills, many argued for more "minimum competency" tests to ensure that teachers and students would work on basics. When a new generation of reformers in the 1980s proposed higher standards, many complained that the minimum-competency tests were responsible in part for the low intellectual content of curriculum and instruction (Resnick and Resnick 1985). The reformers argued that teachers have incentives to teach what is tested, especially when mechanisms intended to increase accountability allow the public and politicians to gauge educational outcomes through published test results. Reformers argued that because most commercially available tests in mathematics before 1990 assessed chiefly such things as basic computation, schools could do little other than formulate instruction around the implied low standards. Reformers hoped that by developing and implementing assessments focused on student understanding and communication of broader mathematical concepts, they could at least replace incentives for simplistic work with incentives for more ambitious and thoughtful work.

It was hence no surprise that California reformers urged that assessments should focus on the new conceptions of mathematics and mathematical performance that were contained in the frameworks. The state began to revise its testing program in the mid-1980s. Reformers argued that newer and more "aligned" tests would help reform instruction throughout California by ensuring that the state sent more consistent messages about curriculum, instruction, and assessment. Since the new tests would be more difficult, scores would drop, the news would be published, and public concern over the lower scores would create an incentive for teachers and schools to invest more in learning and teaching the new curriculum. As teachers used and read the new tests, they would become familiar with the ideas for reform.

By the late 1980s, several other states had embarked on the technically difficult and costly exercise of implementing "alternative" assessments. In Vermont, reformers moved toward portfolio assessments: samples of children's actual work would be collected and scored on the basis of rubrics established by groups of teachers working with state education department representatives. Kentucky maintained, through the early 1990s, a mixed system of statewide tests combined with open-ended responses and some portfolio assessment. Some others, including New York, Connecticut, and Maryland, tried to move at least some distance away from testing of basic skills and established "balanced" assessments consisting of both multiple-choice items and problems requiring more complex answers, for which students were even allowed to show their work.

California completed its new testing program in 1993 after several hitches. The California Learning Assessment System was designed to be aligned with the state's new mathematics frameworks, and it comprised a set of tests that were administered to all students in the fourth, eighth, and tenth grades in 1993 and 1994. There were incentives to take the test seriously, for the results would be published. The state also offered professional development to enable teachers to learn about the new tests. These opportunities were rare before the first administration of CLAS in 1993: the state selected a few schools to pilot the new assessment and sent most districts information about the test only shortly before it was administered in the spring (interview with Ellen Lee, November 5, 1997). When faced with the scoring of thousands of student answers to some of the more complex questions, however, state officials contrived to turn scoring into a learning experience for teachers. They selected several hundred to work with math educators and assessment specialists during the summer months and score the open-ended items on the 1993 tests. The teachers spent a week grading those portions of the assessment, conferring about their grades and the students' answers, and discussing these matters with mathematics educators who ran the workshops. It was an extraordinary opportunity to learn about both math and students' understanding of math, and many teachers reported that it was the best professional learning experience they had ever had.

Some of these teachers returned to their districts and offered workshops for their colleagues. Other teachers in California reported that they had learned about performance assessment through the California Assessment Collaborative, the California Mathematics Project, or Lawrence Hall of Science. Teachers who responded to our survey reported that these in-service workshops consisted of looking at sample tests, developing rubrics, and scoring student work according to state-defined rubrics. Such learning about CLAS exposed teachers to the mathematics contained in the framework, to students' responses to challenging mathematics problems, and by inference, to the instruction that might prepare students to deal thoughtfully with such problems. Roughly one third of the teachers surveyed reported having had some professional development in association with the test, and two thirds of fourth grade teachers reported such learning. Even teachers who did not participate in formal professional development could have learned simply by watching their students complete the novel problems on the fourth grade mathematics CLAS.

The survey probed several issues concerning how CLAS may have affected teachers' work. Most generally, it investigated whether the tests affected practice: Did teachers who learned about or administered the mathematics CLAS report more framework practice and less conventional practice than others who did not? If so, we wanted to know why. Some have argued that instruction might change as a result of the opportunities to learn embedded in assessment, or that local publication of test results would provide an incentive for teachers to pay heed to the test or work harder, or both. Though these are not mutually exclusive, the alternative is important, for people have disagreed heatedly about whether tests influence practice through rewards and punishments or through learning. There were many opportunities for teachers to learn about the test, and though the incentive offered by CLAS was modest at best—scores only for schools, not for classrooms, were published, and the CDE threatened no action—teachers might have changed the curriculum and their instruction methods in anticipation that the scores would be published. A third issue concerns the relative weight of CLAS in the reforms: If it did affect teachers' practice, was it more or less important than other reform-related influences?

We constructed two variables to investigate these matters. One concerned whether teachers had learned about the mathematics CLAS,[11] and the other concerned whether they had administered CLAS. About one third of the teachers reported that they had learned about the mathematics CLAS, and another third reported that they had administered it.[12] Not all the teachers

Table 5.5. Teachers' Experiences with the CLAS

	Learned About CLAS		
	No	Yes	Total
Administered CLAS			
No	312	93	405
	(53%)	(16%)	(68%)
Yes	58	131	190
	(10%)	(22%)	(32%)
Total	371	224	595
	(62%)	(38%)	(100%)

who had learned about the mathematics CLAS said that they had also administered the test, and vice versa. Table 5.5 shows an association between these two variables. Teachers who administered CLAS were more likely to have had an opportunity to learn about it. The cases in which teachers had one experience and not the other, however, suggest that we could distinguish the effects of learning about the test from the effects of simply administering it.

The results of that analysis are presented in Table 5.6. Set 1 contains the results of adding both variables to our curriculum-time equations from the last section (Table 5.4). According to these results, administering CLAS improved the odds that a teacher would report having engaged in framework practices, as reflected in the statistically significant and positive association between having administered CLAS and reported framework practice. The relationship was quite modest, though; it did not come close to the importance of the association between attendance at curriculum workshop and teaching practice.[13] And administering CLAS was not associated with a decrease in teachers' reports of engaging in conventional practices like book work and computational tests. Furthermore, teachers who reported administering CLAS appeared no different on both scales measuring attitude (not shown) from those who did not. Any incentive associated with the administration of CLAS induced teachers to incorporate new practices into existing their conventional teaching practice. Rather than redecorating the whole

Table 5.6. Association Between Learning, Practice, and CLAS Measures

	Conventional practice	Framework practice	Conventional practice	Framework practice
Intercept	1.54***	1.92***	1.59***	1.70***
	(.19)	(.17)	(.20)	(.17)
Time in student curriculum workshop	−0.09***	0.13***	−0.08***	0.11***
	(.02)	(.02)	(.02)	(.02)
Past framework learning	0.10~	0.03	0.13~	0.05
	(.06)	(.06)	(.07)	(.06)
Attitude toward reform	−0.22***	0.23***	−0.17***	0.11***
	(.03)	(.03)	(.04)	(.03)
Familiarity with reform	−0.86***	0.38~	−0.63**	0.39*
	(.21)	(.20)	(.23)	(.19)
Learned about CLAS	0.05	0.01	0.11~	0.00
	(.06)	(.06)	(.07)	(.06)
Administered CLAS	−0.01	0.15*	0.06	−0.02
	(.07)	(.06)	(.07)	(.06)
Attended to CLAS			−0.15***	0.23***
			(.04)	(.03)
R^2 (adjusted)	0.18	0.22	0.20	0.30
N	583	583	528	528

~Indicates $p < .15$.
*Indicates $p < .05$.
**Indicates $p < .01$.
***Indicates $p < .001$.

house, teachers supplemented existing motifs with more stuff—a result that our colleagues found typical in earlier fieldwork (Guthrie 1990). In contrast, teachers who spent more time in curriculum workshops reported both less conventional and more framework practice.

That modest effect of test administration might disappoint supporters of assessment-based reform, because it suggests that the unique effects of testing were not great; but the CLAS lasted for only two years and published only school-level results, conditions that may not have been sufficient for strong incentives to develop.[14] In some communities, the political storms surrounding the CLAS may have encouraged local educators to ignore the aspects of the assessments relating to accountability, for many parents and

politicians opposed the test vocally. These results also seem to offer little so-
lace to advocates of the view that teachers' opportunities to learn will me-
diate the effects of assessment-based reform, for teachers' reported learning
about the CLAS fared even worse in these models. It showed no relation to
teachers' descriptions of their classroom practice in mathematics and a
slightly negative relation to teachers' agreement with framework ideas
($b = -.11$, $p = .02$; not shown). One might conclude that the "incentive" that
the CLAS offered to teachers who administered it caused only a mild change
in their math instruction and that the test promoted little independent
learning through its professional-development components. That would be
humble yet hopeful news for assessment-based reform: because teachers
could not "select" themselves into the test, the small effect associated with
test administration must be something like a "true" estimate of practitioners' response to this particular policy.

Given the weakness of the incentive and the voluntary nature of teachers'
opportunities to learn about the CLAS, however, the test's effects may have
been mediated by teachers' views of the test. To further probe that idea, we
cross-tabulated our measure of teachers' administration of the CLAS and
various measures of teachers' agreement with the test. Table 5.7 shows that a
significant number of teachers reported that the test agreed with the mathematics they wanted students to know, that they used performance assessments like the CLAS in the classroom, that the CLAS had prompted them to
change their teaching, and that learning new forms of assessment was useful for them in their teaching. The last item shows that more than six in
every ten teachers who reported administering the test said that they had
learned from it.

A comparison of responses in the two columns of the table also reveals
that a strong relation exists between administration of the CLAS, teachers'
view of the test, and adoption of classroom practices that the CLAS might
seem to encourage. Responses in the first column of the table also show, however, that not all teachers who reported administering the CLAS either agreed
with the test's orientation or tried to adjust their teaching to fit it. The response patterns strongly imply that teachers paid selective attention to the
new test. Many who administered the CLAS liked it and used it as a learning
opportunity, but others did not. The same can be said of those who did not
administer the test: even without the direct "incentive" supplied by the presence of the tests in their classroom, some found it instructive in changing

Table 5.7. Attitude Toward the CLAS by Test Administration

	Administered CLAS	Did not administer
The mathematics CLAS corresponds well with the mathematics understanding I want my students to demonstrate.*		
Agree	57%	50%
Neutral	32%	39%
Disagree	12%	11%
Total	101%	100%
I currently use performance assessments like the CLAS in my classroom.**		
Agree	48%	21%
Neutral	34%	33%
Disagree	18%	46%
Total	100%	100%
The mathematics CLAS has prompted me to change some of my teaching practices.***		
Agree	71%	39%
Neutral	15%	30%
Disagree	14%	31%
Total	100%	100%
Learning new forms of mathematics assessment like the CLAS has been valuable for my teaching.*		
Agree	64%	36%
Neutral	22%	32%
Disagree	15%	32%
Total	101%	100%

Note: Numbers do not always add up to 100, because of rounding.

*Seventy-four missing cases.

**Seventy-one missing cases.

***Sixty-nine missing cases.

their mathematics teaching, whereas others paid it little heed. The cross-tabulation of the variable "learned about CLAS" with these measures looks similar. Learning about the CLAS increased the probability that a teacher would look favorably on the assessment but did not ensure this result.

This returns us to the question whether learning or incentives increased the chance that teachers would feel positively toward, and attend instructionally to, the CLAS. Because the teachers in the categories "learned about" the CLAS and "administered" the CLAS overlapped a good deal, we used regression to sort out their effects on teachers' attention to the test. We began by making the four survey items in Table 5.7 into a scale called "attended to CLAS."[15] This scale measures the extent to which teachers felt that they had learned from the CLAS and the extent to which their reported instruction aligned with this test; it has a mean of 3.24, and a reliability of .85.

We carried out a regression for this scale on the predictor variables "learned about CLAS" and "administered CLAS," in an attempt to determine how much each had contributed to teachers' attitude about the test. We included as controls teachers' reports of their attendance at other professional-development opportunities. The results appear in Table 5.8. They show that both learning about and simply administering the CLAS had about the same positive effect on teachers' response to the test. By comparison, attending a student curriculum workshop added somewhat less, and attending a special-topics workshop was slightly negatively related to teachers' attitude toward the CLAS. Thus, official opportunities to learn about the CLAS and the simple act of administering it contributed equally to identifying oneself and one's practice with the new assessment. Yet neither could ensure that identification, as we saw in Table 5.7. Conversely, teachers may have identified with the test even if they had had no formal opportunities to learn or to administer the test.

To investigate whether this more personal measure of teachers' attitude toward the test ("attended to CLAS") corresponded to reported classroom practices, we reran the equations that probed the effects of testing on practice in Table 5.6, with "attended to CLAS" included. That rendered the two test-related variables we initially discussed ("administered CLAS," and "learned about CLAS") insignificant, or significant in the wrong direction (see Table 5.6, set 2). The new variable was significantly and strongly associated with teachers' reports of teaching practice based on the frameworks: teachers who scored relatively high on "attended to CLAS" reported engaging in more reform-based teaching practices, such as extended investigations and group work. They also reported relying on fewer conventional practices like computational practice and testing. This suggests a more thorough revision of practice and perhaps greater internal consistency in teachers' work. Similar results obtained for teachers' ideas about students and instruction (not shown).

These analyses throw more light on how statewide testing may influence

Table 5.8. Influences on Teachers' Self-Report of Attending to the CLAS

	Attended to CLAS
Intercept	2.79***
	(.07)
Administered CLAS	.49***
	(.09)
Learned about CLAS	.44***
	(.09)
Time in student curriculum workshop	.11**
	(.03)
Time in special-topics workshop	−.08~
	(.05)
Past framework learning	.09
	(.10)
R^2 (adjusted)	.16
N	533

~Indicates $p < .15$.
*Indicates $p < .05$.
**Indicates $p < .01$.
***Indicates $p < .001$.

instruction, at least in states whose policies and assessments resemble California's. Teachers were not compelled to teach the mathematics to be tested, so the incentive operated only upon teachers' sense of professional responsibility or their response to public pressure. In this more voluntarist scheme, the CLAS seemed to provide teachers with occasions to think about, observe, and revise their mathematics instruction.[16] In McDonnell's words, the test could persuade, but not coerce: some teachers seized the occasion, but others did not. The positive effects of assessment on practice appeared among those teachers who constituted themselves as a community of learners about and sympathizers with the test. Thus, in response to our earlier query about whether learning alone or incentives alone made a difference in teachers' practice, we found that a combination proved most effective. This link between learning and incentives also turned up in interviews with teachers. One reported: "The CLAS test. . . . It was a shock to me. They [students] really did fall apart. It was like, 'Oh! What do I do?' And I realized, I need to look at mathematics differently. You know, I really was doing it the way I had been taught so many years before. I mean, it was so dated. And I began last year, because of the CLAS test the year before, looking to see what other kinds of things were available" (Perry 1996, 87).

This suggests that the teacher's learning ("looking to see what other kinds of things were available") and her efforts to change her practice were associated with the incentive for change that was created when she noticed that her students "really did fall apart" when taking the new test. Her students' weak performance stimulated her to find ways to help them do better, even before she saw any scores.

A final question about testing is whether these effects of the CLAS overwhelmed the effects of workshop learning on teachers' practice. If they did, we might conclude that it was the test, not teachers' opportunities to learn about student curriculum, that drove any changes in instruction. In this scenario, teachers would have adopted student curriculum units as a response to the pressures of testing, and the significant relationships we saw in Table 5.4 would result from the CLAS rather than the units themselves. Table 5.6 shows that this was not so. When we ran models with only "administered CLAS" and "learned about CLAS" (Table 5.6, set 1), the coefficients on the curriculum workshop variables declined very slightly. When we entered "attended to CLAS" (Table 5.6, set 2), the "time in student curriculum workshop" coefficient declined somewhat more, a change suggesting modest overlap between teachers' learning about the CLAS and learning from curriculum. It was a small overlap, though: the coefficient on "student curriculum workshops" remained almost the same and statistically significant.[17]

This analysis suggests that the two approaches to improving instruction worked relatively independently, each contributing to teachers' revisions of classroom practices. It also suggests the joint power of policy instruments. When teachers attended student curriculum workshops, their classroom practices changed to reflect reformers' ideas, and when those same teachers also attended to the CLAS as a learning opportunity, their teaching methods changed even more. This result suggests the importance of using a variety of policy instruments in coordinated efforts to enable changes in practice, rather than placing all policy eggs in a single basket.

Curriculum. Student curricula consistent with the new math frameworks were a third method reformers used to promote change. It is reasonable to think those curriculum units might support teachers' implementation of the policy in any of several ways. Teachers who did not attend a student curriculum workshop may nevertheless have used a unit, and doing so might have increased their adherence to reform practices and decreased reliance on conventional practices. Teachers who did attend student curriculum workshops could have returned to their classrooms with relatively more elaborated plans for how to "do" policy, in contrast to abstract principles or one-day activities for students. Such concrete guidance could enable teachers to learn even after they had completed their student curriculum in-service work, as they daily observed the kinds of instruction that were possible with the new curriculum. There is a big difference, according to this view, between simply knowing that one should promote student discussion of mathematical topics and actually having more detailed knowledge of a curriculum, and of questions and possible student answers.

That makes particular sense because some of the units were designed in part to support teachers' learning about mathematics, student thinking, and mathematics instruction. Some developers of replacement units tried to build into their materials opportunities for teachers to learn, an aim remarkably different from that of most commercial math texts. Many commercial publishers claim that their texts are aligned with NCTM standards, because they include manipulatives or promote group work, but few ground these lessons in explanations of students' thinking, and, in 1994, none offered teachers guidance in helping students construct mathematical ideas. Some replacement-unit authors did try to help teachers learn such things. The *Seeing Fractions* unit designed by TERC, for instance, offered teachers guidance on such matters as unit pacing; the ways students might understand concepts like "equal parts" and "congruency," instructional activities and possible student responses, examples of student work, and other teachers' reactions to the materials. Both TERC and other developers consciously undertook to write curriculum that offered teachers opportunities to learn to use the materials well.[18]

If teachers did learn from replacement units, that learning should show up on our practice scales. Although these scales gauge only a narrow range of the material teachers might learn from the curriculum, the support these units provide for novel instructional practices should lead teachers who use more units to report more framework practice, and, perhaps, less conventional practice. Because the units explained instructional activity and student learning in relation to reformers' ideas about mathematics, teachers who used the units would also be more likely to report ideas about mathematics teaching and learning that accorded with the frameworks.

Table 5.9 shows precisely that result. "Replacement-unit use"—a measure

Table 5.9. Effects of Curriculum on Ideas and Practice

	Conventional ideas	Framework ideas	Conventional practice	Framework practice
Intercept	5.07***	2.95***	1.48***	1.86***
	(.18)	(.15)	(.19)	(.16)
Time in student curriculum workshop	−.04*	.03~	−.05*	.07***
	(.02)	(.02)	(.02)	(.02)
Past framework learning	−.07	−.02	.10~	.08
	(.07)	(.06)	(.07)	(.06)
Attended to CLAS	−.13***	.16***	−.10**	.20***
	(.03)	(.03)	(.03)	(.03)
Number of replacement units used	−.09**	.09***	−.12***	.18***
	(.03)	(.02)	(.03)	(.03)
Attitude toward reform			−.16***	.09**
			(.04)	(.03)
Familiarity with reform	−2.03***	.76***	−.55*	.30~
	(.22)	(.18)	(.22)	(.19)
R^2 (adjusted)	.26	.21	.22	.37
N	530	530	528	528

~Indicates $p < .15$.
*Indicates $p < .05$.
**Indicates $p < .01$.
***Indicates $p < .001$.

of the number of replacement units a teacher reports employing in her classroom (out of six possible)—is fully significant in the expected direction across all four equations. Teachers who used replacement units reported more of the practices reformers wanted to encourage and fewer of the practices reformers wanted to reduce or eliminate.

Use of replacement units also appears to decrease the effect associated with the student curriculum/time variable. That is not surprising, for the variable in part measured teacher attendance at replacement-unit workshops. It is likely that, in the absence of the replacement-unit count, the correlation between the two variables inflated the coefficient on the workshop marker. It also appears that, measured by comparing levels of significance, the size of the curriculum and workshop markers is about the same or that the curriculum marker is slightly more responsible for teachers' use of innovative math strategies. These observations, however, mask two complications. First, the teachers who used replacement units had elected to do so. Others may have attended a student curriculum workshop yet chosen not to use a replacement unit or chosen not to use as many units. The coefficient on "replacement-unit use" may therefore be artificially inflated, owing to selectivity.

Furthermore, our measure of attendance at student curriculum workshops covered only the year before the survey, yet "replacement-unit use" measured teachers' use of these *at any time* during the reforms. Hence, teachers who attended replacement-unit workshops in the first few years that they were offered are represented in the regression by the curriculum marker, not the workshop marker. Given this limitation of the survey design, we cannot accurately estimate independent effects of replacement-unit workshops and replacement units themselves.[19]

That limitation does not negate the evidence that teachers appeared to learn from replacement units alone, as well as from the workshops. It does suggest, however, that learning from one probably depends on the other. Even a high-quality curriculum that lacks a design for teacher learning is likely to fail if teachers do not know how to make good use of it on their own (Sarason 1982; Dow 1991; Cohen and Barnes 1993). Similarly, high-quality professional development is unlikely to help many teachers change practice substantially unless materials to support those practices are available. Observers of the California reforms corroborated this view by reporting that teachers who adopted replacement units without attending a full-length replacement-unit workshop implemented the curriculum more superficially (interview with Judy Mumme, September 17, 1997). Other teachers who became committed early to the view of mathematics in the frameworks reported frustration at the lack of quality materials available to support student learning.

Reform documents. Documents associated with the reforms were another potential means for teachers to learn. Reformers designed, printed, and disseminated nearly 180,000 copies of the 1992 frameworks, documents that advised teachers on mathematical content, student learning, and proposed instructional techniques.[20] Like NCTM documents from the same time, the documents included sample problems and student work. They also explicitly compared methods advocated by the reforms with conventional teaching.

Teachers were asked in the survey about their acquaintance with reform documents. They reported whether their districts or schools had given them a copy of the *Mathematics Framework for California Public Schools* and indicated whether they used it. They also reported whether they had read "much or all" of the two math frameworks. We found that:

- Two thirds of teachers had a copy of at least one of the frameworks.
- Half reported using one of these two documents.
- Nearly 20 percent reported reading much or all of one framework, and 30 percent had read much or all of both frameworks.

We entered the three different measures of teachers' attention to the documents separately into the ideas and practice models. Doing so also gives us some leverage on the selection question. Did merely receiving a copy of a framework document move teachers toward reformers' ideas, or, as we saw earlier with the CLAS, was it some combination of contact with the policy "instrument" and the teachers' own disposition? We probed this query in analyses that are reported in Table 5.10. We held constant the previously investigated variables in each equation affecting the opportunities for teachers to learn,[21] and we reproduce only the coefficients that appeared on the various indicators of document use described. The first column of the table shows that simply equipping teachers with framework documents did little to improve the odds that they saw mathematics instruction as reformers proposed. Holding all else constant, we find that teachers with these framework documents reported slightly more conventional practice than did those without. The direction of the effect runs contrary to what advocates of exposure would predict. Reporting use of a framework, in the second line of the table, has the same association with conventional practice, although teachers in this category do report more reliance on ideas and practices featured in the frameworks. These teachers were a subset of those who had been given a framework document; hence, we cannot be sure whether the effect represented true learning from the documents or some type of selection. The same holds true for teachers' reports of reading the frameworks (the third column in the table). Though this association runs in the expected direction, the effect may be spurious.

Our view of the influence of selection and policy here is similar to what we already reported regarding tests and curricula. Teachers do not transform their practice simply by virtue of coming in contact with a policy instrument. Policy documents alone are not forceful "teaching" agents and

Table 5.10. Associations Between Framework Documents and Teachers' Beliefs and Practices

	Supplied a framework	Used the framework	Read frameworks (1 or 2)
Conventional ideas	.07	.03	−.03
	(.06)	(.06)	(.03)
Framework ideas	.06	.11*	.00
	(.05)	(.05)	(.03)
Conventional practice	.17**	.13*	−.07*
	(.06)	(.06)	(.03)
Framework practice	−.01	.14**	.08
	(.05)	(.05)	(.03)**

Note: The column variables were not tested against one another; instead, each cell represents the effect of the column's variable in a separate regression model. See Table 5.9 for controls.

~Indicates p < .15.
*Indicates p < .05.
**Indicates p < .01.
***Indicates p < .001.

generally have quite a modest association with practice. Instead, if teachers choose to heed the policy documents, to learn and change, that transformation implies some combination of will, disposition to learn, and opportunity to do so.

Professionalism

Interest in teacher professionalism, and in the role that it can play in school improvement, has been a growing. As an example, much has been written about the role that teacher "networks" can play in increasing teachers' knowledge of policy, instructional methods, and subject matter (Lichtenstein, McLaughlin, and Knudson 1992; Lieberman and McLaughlin 1996). Such networks existed in California, and they devoted significant effort to supporting mathematics reform (Firestone and Pennell 1997). Teachers might have worked on policy-setting activities at the school or district level—for example, by chairing district mathematics committees or running workshops for other teachers. Teachers also might have learned from others at their school site, as professional communities developed or turned their attention to reform. Though these are not conventional policy instruments, other state-level reforms include such efforts, and some put enormous faith, not to mention monetary investment, in the service of their efficacy; therefore, it seems worthwhile to explore the possible effects of the reforms.

Leadership and networks. The survey asked teachers to report on the time they invested in several kinds of leadership activities, and these frequencies are displayed in Table 5.11.[22] There were three types of leadership opportunities. The California Math Project was a leadership development program with a strong learning component. Teacher participation in the CMP took several forms. Some teachers participated in two- to four-week summer institutes and weekend follow-ups, learning about a variety of topics related to the views of mathematics contained in the frameworks. Others were invited to participate in shorter workshops at one of the CMP's seventeen sites. Still others attended a workshop designed by a local teacher who had herself attended the CMP. The curricula for teachers in these workshops varied: teachers learned about new mathematics content and student learning, about the CLAS, about ongoing debates at the state level, about national reform movements like the New Standards Project and NCTM, about how technology and writing can be integrated into mathematics instruction, or about equity in math classes (Wilson, Lubienski, and Mattson 1996). All the workshops emphasized teachers' leadership skills and networking.

A second type of opportunity, shown in Table 5.11, was national or state leadership in the reform itself, or what we call professional activities. Teachers attended conferences offered by the NCTM or by the California Mathematics Council, its state affiliate. At either, teachers would have heard reformers and mathematics educators speak about mathematics reform, visited vendors of curriculum materials or manipulatives intended to support the standards, or attended workshops on particular materials or teaching techniques. Teachers who attended CMC activities might have heard about replacement units or the CLAS.

A third type of opportunity was local leadership, or "local policy." This included serving on district curriculum committees, teaching local math inservice workshops, or serving on Program Quality Review committees, which oversaw district mathematics curricula for state certification, among other things.

Table 5.11. Participation in Reform Leadership and Networks

Q: Which of the following mathematics-related activities have you participated in during the past year and approximately *how much total time* did you spend in each?

	None	1 day or less	2–6 days	One week or more
Participated in a California Mathematics Project	94.3	2.4	1.9	1.5
Attended a national mathematics teacher association meeting	94.2	5.0	.8	0
Attended a state or regional mathematics teacher association meeting, including California Mathematics Council affiliates	87.5	7.2	5.0	.2
Taught an in-service workshop or course in mathematics or mathematics teaching	86.2	10.4	2.7	.8
Served on a district mathematics curriculum committee	86.3	6.6	2.7	4.4

Note: Missing data treated as "none."

We averaged teachers' responses regarding each of these three types of opportunity to create new variables, which we then entered into the belief-and-practice models. The results appear in Table 5.12, and they are mixed. Time spent on the California Mathematics Project was negatively related to teachers' reports about conventional teaching practice, but it was not positively related either to reports about framework practices or to the ideas that reformers espoused. In other words, teachers who attended the CMP had their students less frequently practice computation or use conventional textbooks but did not appear to replace those activities with others favored by reformers. That may result from the fragmentation of the CMP workshops' curriculum (Wilson, Lubienski, and Mattson 1996), which might have made sustained learning about mathematics or instruction difficult.[23] The results for the other two variables fell flat across all models, except for the apparently negative association between local policy leadership and framework ideas. Though teachers who worked on policy at the state or local level participated more often in regular mathematics workshops than teachers who were not leaders (see Appendix D), the extra time spent on the leadership activities did not seem to yield additional gains in framework practice.

This finding may surprise some readers. They might expect that teachers

**Table 5.12. Association Between Leadership
Activities and Teachers' Ideas and Practice**

	Conventional ideas	Framework ideas	Conventional practice	Framework practice
Intercept	5.26***	3.15***	1.72***	1.83***
(standard error—se)	(.22)	(.18)	(.23)	(.19)
Time in student				
curriculum workshops	−0.03	0.04~	−0.04~	0.07***
(se)	(.07)	(.06)	(.02)	(.02)
Past framework learning	−0.05	−0.04	0.09	0.07
(se)	(0.07)	(0.06)	(0.07)	(0.06)
Attended to CLAS	−0.12***	0.16***	−0.10**	0.21***
(se)	(0.03)	(0.03)	(0.03)	(0.03)
Number of replacement				
units used	−.09**	.10***	−.12**	0.18***
(se)	(.03)	(.03)	(.03)	(0.03)
Professional activities	−0.08	−0.08	−0.05	0.02
(se)	(.10)	(0.08)	(0.10)	(0.08)
Local policy	−0.08	−0.11*	−0.06	0.08
(se)	(0.06)	(0.05)	(0.06)	(0.05)
California Mathematics				
Project	0.01	0.03	−0.10~	−0.05
(se)	(0.06)	(0.05)	(0.06)	(0.05)
Attitude toward reform			−0.16***	0.80*
(se)			(0.04)	(0.03)
Familiarity with reform	−2.07***	.75***	−0.60***	0.30~
(se)	(0.23)	(0.19)	(0.23)	(0.19)
R² (adjusted)	0.26	0.21	0.24	0.36
N	514	514	513	513

~Indicates p < .15.
*Indicates p < .05.
**Indicates p < .01.
***Indicates p < .001.

who volunteered to make an extra effort to participate in leadership and
network activities would be more highly committed to reform ideas before
undertaking their duties, and that teachers who enlisted in these reform activities were predisposed to practice as the math framework proposed, or at
least predisposed to learn. If that were so, self-selection into leadership and

networks could affect practice, but no such effects appeared. This is not the definitive test of learning from professional network activities or policy leadership, for there are enough weaknesses in the methodology of any survey that "no result" findings should be viewed with caution. Our evidence suggests, though, that many networks are less powerful than some suggest. We suspect that that was because the "curriculum" of such leadership activities was not centrally focused on mathematics, instruction, student learning, or student curriculum.[24] Instead, these workshops resembled those in our "special topics" category: they promoted single-lesson activities and committee meetings that introduced ideas but offered little or no guidance on how to put those reforms into practice.

Professional conditions in schools. Many scholars argue that teacher learning can and should take place at school sites, where learning can occur as a result of teachers' interaction with one another, students, and administrators (Darling-Hammond 1994; McLaughlin and Oberman 1996; Lord 1994; Newmann and Wehlage 1995; Perry 1996). These researchers reason that if teachers worked collaboratively on curriculum and had strong support from principals, they might be more open to new ideas about instruction and learn from each other. In Chapter 3 we considered the extent of administrators' and colleagues' support for the math framework, along with the extent of professional collegiality concerning mathematics and mathematics instruction, and the intensity of collaborative work within schools. Here, we link teachers' reports on these conditions with their reports on ideas about mathematics instruction and their classroom practices.

We constructed three new variables to explore that link. Administrators' support for the reforms was measured by the first two items in Table 3.9: the principal of this school is well informed about one or more [reform] documents, and there is a schoolwide effort to achieve the kind of mathematics education promoted by one or more [reform] documents. We averaged each teacher's responses to these two items and labeled the scale "administrative support." Its mean is 3.65, its standard deviation 1.18.[25] Teachers' perceptions of encouragement from colleagues and administrators for innovation in math teaching, and the extent to which teachers had school-based opportunities to learn from other teachers, were measured by another set of items on the survey, shown in Table 3.10. Averaged, these items make up the scale we call "math conditions"; the mean of this scale is 3.24, its standard deviation .91. Teachers' perceptions of more general norms of professional

Table 5.13. Association Between Professional Contexts and Teachers' Ideas and Practices

	Conventional ideas	Framework ideas	Conventional practice	Framework practice
Intercept	4.91***	2.83***	1.62***	1.62***
(standard error—se)	(0.26)	(0.21)	(0.27)	(0.22)
Time in student				
curriculum workshop	−0.04~	0.04*	−0.04*	0.07***
(se)	(0.02)	(0.02)	(0.02)	(0.02)
Past framework learning	−0.06	0.03	0.14~	0.08
(se)	(0.07)	(0.06)	(0.07)	(0.06)
Attended to CLAS	−0.13***	0.15***	−0.10***	0.16***
(se)	(0.03)	(0.03)	(0.03)	(0.03)
Number of replacement				
units used	−0.10***	0.10***	−0.12***	0.14***
(se)	(0.03)	(0.02)	(0.03)	(0.03)
Familiarity with reform	−1.91***	0.98***	−0.69**	0.36~
(se)	(0.24)	(0.19)	(0.24)	(0.20)
Attitude toward reform			−0.18***	0.11***
(se)			(0.04)	(.03)
Administrative support	−0.01	−0.02	0.02	0.04~
(se)	(0.03)	(0.02)	(0.03)	(0.02)
Mathematics conditions	−0.04	0.00	−0.04	−0.00
(se)	(0.04)	(0.03)	(0.04)	(0.03)
Norms of collaboration	0.11~	.00	0.04	0.02
(se)	(0.06)	(0.05)	(0.06)	(0.05)
R^2 (adjusted)	0.25	0.22	0.25	0.36
N	494	494	493	493

~Indicates $p < .15$.
*Indicates $p < .05$.
**Indicates $p < .01$.
***Indicates $p < .001$.

collaboration within their school were measured by a third set of items, shown in Table 3.11. When averaged, these items have a mean of 2.51 and a standard deviation of .58.[26] Higher scores on all three scales mean teachers perceive more support or collaboration within their schools.

Table 5.13 above reveals scant associations between professional conditions and teachers' ideas and practice.[27] Administrative support for the state reforms shows a small but positive association with teachers' reported framework practices. Teachers who perceived that their administration supported the reforms also reported slightly more of the practices reformers wished to see in classrooms. Because teachers who were more engaged in the reforms may have attended more carefully to principals' signals about them, we cannot tell if this is an effect of individual teachers' perceptions or of administrative support. In contrast, stronger and more broadly supported professional norms of collaboration were associated with conventional ideas, an outcome that shows that professional communities can be conservative as well as progressive. Collegiality around mathematics had no effect.

One explanation for the small and inconsistent effects of professional context is that survey research is not well suited to detect the effects such subtle contexts may have on ideas and practice. Both sides of the equation were measured only bluntly. An alternative explanation is that these contexts are simply not as important an influence on teachers' practice as are their learning opportunities and dispositions toward reform ideas. Still another view, which strikes us as most plausible, is that professional contexts are likely to bear on teachers' ideas and practices only when they create or actively support teachers' learning of matters closely related to instruction, and most professional collegiality and community in American schools is at present disconnected from such learning. If so, the interactions would have been both rare in fact and beyond the reach of the survey measures used here.

These analyses support our conjecture about the role of teacher learning in instructional policy. When teachers learned in and from the mathematics curriculum their students would use, and about students' work on the new assessments, teachers were more likely to report practices that were close to the aims of the state policy. Teachers who encountered a greater number of such policy instruments and who spent more time at any given opportunity to learn reported practices that were more closely linked to reform objectives. Policy success depended on learning—but not all opportunities to learn about policy were created equal. Some had weak or even negative associations with the mathematics ideas and practices reformers proposed. Those opportunities include teachers' reported professional community, or their encounters with mathematics networks, policy documents, and some professional in-service workshops.

Knowledge of this kind could have been helpful to those in California who sought to encourage new ideas and instructional practices. Resources could have been allocated differently, and change could have been accomplished more broadly. Our findings have more than short-term use, though, for the state reform can be thought of as a trial of several efforts to shape practice through policy, some of which worked better than others. We can learn something from the successes and failures.

The key point is that the *content* of teacher learning matters. The learning opportunities that appeared useful from our measures were grounded in the units students would study or students' work on the assessments students would take. As teachers often reported, actively working with student curriculum units or assessment was likely to deepen teachers' own understanding of mathematical topics like fractions, multiplication, measurement, and geometry. Teachers in these workshops would also discuss how students might respond to specific lessons and would see examples of student work. Such study was likely to strengthen their knowledge of different methods for teaching math. Teachers who learned more about mathematics from a new curriculum or assessment and about how to teach the subject would be more likely to make sustained, far-reaching changes in their instruction. Though such professional learning opportunities were effective, they are rare.

The content of reformers' unsuccessful efforts to encourage teacher change was more diverse, diffuse, and further removed from the actual practice of teachers' daily work. Special-topics workshops, for instance, offered general advice about classroom management or other matters, and some doubtless supplied teachers with a flavor of the framework views of teaching and learning. Still, student learning of mathematics, mathematical instruction, and mathematics itself were not the central focus. Reform documents did offer some particulars about mathematics learning and teaching but were removed from classroom work. Networks and mathematical leadership positions also lacked any "treatment" but focused instead on governance and issues removed from the direct work of teaching. It seems likely that the content of teachers' opportunities to learn in school-based professional communities—even the strong ones—was uneven, and perhaps unfocused as well.

Capable math teachers must know many things, but knowledge of mathematics and the ways it is taught and learned is central. The explanations already given add up to an unusual coherence between the curricula of students' work, assessments, and teachers' professional learning. It seems hopeful that nearly half the teachers reported attending a Marilyn Burns or replacement-unit workshop within the year before the survey. That is impressive breadth in the "coverage" of reform in the state, which gave many teachers at least some occasion to rethink their mathematics instruction. Breadth is not depth, though; many teachers' opportunities to learn were quite brief. Reinspection of Table 5.3 brings home that only about 5 percent of California elementary school teachers reported spending one week or more in either of the student curriculum workshops during 1993–94. This point is critical, because time spent on learning was such a significant influence on practice.

We also explored the role that voluntarism might play in teachers' adherence to the reforms. On one level this was a puzzle about selectivity: because our data were cross-sectional, there was a chance that teachers' will to change or their pre-existing views would influence the opportunities to learn they sought out or the results of those opportunities or both. The central issue was whether the associations between our key independent variables and our dependent measures of practice and ideas reflected learning that occurred in the opportunities or selection of atypically knowledgeable or motivated teachers into the workshops.

We found no evidence of strong selectivity by pre-existing practice or intense belief about preferred mathematics teaching. The two-stage least squares in Appendix D shows that teachers enrolled in student curriculum workshops independently of their views of the reform. The administration of the CLAS fell to fourth grade teachers, regardless of their beliefs about teaching or the test, and the effect of the simple "administered CLAS" measure can be seen as a "true" effect of that policy instrument. This evidence is supported both by other scholarship and by observers, who report that few teachers were using reform methods before the reforms.

Our evidence also suggests, however, that teachers' openness to learning and change played a role in the learning opportunities we examined. Studying student curricula itself, learning from the CLAS, and reading framework documents all posed opportunities to learn that teachers could choose to take up or ignore. That is what happened: a larger group of teachers learned about replacement units than reported using them in teaching; more teachers learned about the CLAS through workshops or administering the test than reported using it as a learning opportunity; more teachers received copies of the frameworks than reported using them or reading them. In these cases, we saw large effects not from the learning opportunity itself but from the combination of the opportunity and teachers' willingness to take up the ideas when the occasion arose.

Teachers' will or disposition to learn was thus important. This observation accords with other findings about the role of motivation, prior knowledge, beliefs, and capabilities on change in practice (Cohen 1990; Wilson 1990; Richardson 1996; Borko and Putnam 1995). Will was not an isolated influence but arose in combination with teachers' learning in workshops, their being persuaded by the ideas promoted in the workshops, and their having an incentive to think about the ideas contained in the reforms. The appreciable effect of the time teachers spent in replacement-unit workshops on their learning is crucial in our reasoning. The more time teachers spent in these workshops, the more they reported teaching practice consistent with the framework and the less conventional practice. It would have taken extraordinarily pervasive and clever self-selection by teachers to produce this effect. Given what we already know about the lack of such careful selection for professional development and the solid research on the effects of time on task in learning, it would be a real stretch to explain the effects of the replacement units by selection, not learning.

Our effort to understand the role of will in teachers' response to instructional policy has a broader significance, for it suggests that, at least in systems like California's, educational policies like those discussed here work more as opportunities to affiliate with change and learn than as directives. Such opportunities are constructed partly by reformers who supply them, and partly by the teachers who decide whether and how to make use of them. Teachers *can* be persuaded to change their views of mathematics instruction and make something of their opportunities to learn; there is ample evidence that this was important at least to the success of the CLAS as a learning opportunity. What happens inside opportunities to learn, though, is at least as important as what gets people into them.

Finally, government was only partly responsible for the limited success of the policy. State policymakers did not provide teachers with the opportunities to learn that enabled that success. Instead, they encouraged professional developers and curriculum writers to connect teachers with policy by devising and offering new curricula and opportunities to learn. In cases where the new state math policy succeeded, it was the result of both state efforts and the work of individuals and agencies in the private sector. A few state administrators played an important role in encouraging this work, but it

was the professionals who did it, and who did still more as teachers enthusiastically responded by using the materials and attending the workshops. In
many ways, these nonstate actors and the professionals whom they engaged
helped give official policy its content, by providing examples and materials
for teachers to use. In U.S. education, where government is relatively weak
and the private sector is relatively strong, state instructional reform requires
extensive participation by private agencies and individuals.

Chapter 6

LEARNING AND POLICY

The chief reason reformers sought to change mathematics teaching was to improve mathematics learning. We have shown that California's mathematics reform was a learning policy in the sense that some teachers learned new classroom practices. We now take the next step in probing the effects of instructional policy and ask whether California's mathematics reform became a learning policy in the sense that students' learning improved. Reformers aimed at this effect and designed their efforts with it in mind. They created and distributed new student curriculum units, encouraged professional development around these units, and used the state assessment program to prompt learning and change. Many reformers reasoned that teachers would respond to the initiatives by learning new mathematics and implementing different practices in their classrooms, and that students would learn as a result.

In what follows, we explore whether students in schools where teachers had substantial opportunities to learn, and where teachers' mathematics teaching was therefore more consistent with the state reforms, had higher math scores on the CLAS. We assume that if policy affected student performance, that effect would be mediated by what teachers knew and did in their own classrooms as a result of opportunities to learn. We probe these ideas using data from the 1994 administration of the CLAS.

Our analyses suggest that the California mathematics reforms of the 1980s and 1990s did improve student achievement—under certain conditions. Teachers figure critically in the story. When teachers in a school reported more use of framework practices and curricula or had learned about the CLAS, students in that school posted higher math scores on the 1994 CLAS. It appears that when teachers' professional development centered on the mathematics teachers would teach, and on what students would make of it, such professional learning in turn supported improved learning for students, at least indirectly. When teachers and schools reported having more opportunities to learn—either in time spent or additional practice-gounded ways to learn—student achievement was higher.

Before discussing statistical models and presenting results, we outline the origins of the state assessment and the difficulties that occurred during its implementation and during the publication of the results. This social history of the assessment provides a context for the technical and statistical work we present later in the chapter.

California Assessment Politics, Policy, and Design

The rise and spectacular fall of the CLAS holds lessons for politicians and psychometricians alike. Technical difficulties in the new assessment brought to the surface issues at the forefront of theory and statistics and occasioned more than one headache for test developers. Political difficulties stemming from increasing partisanship in California aggravated the technical problems and caused headaches of their own. The technical problems became political, the political problems technical, and policymakers eventually deserted the CLAS for more conventional and locally governed alternatives (McDonnell 1997b).

The student assessment program had operated for years with little fanfare, having begun in 1972 under the name California Assessment Program (CAP). State officials initially purchased tests from commercial publishers; yet this practice soon provoked complaints from teachers about the lack of congruence between what they taught and what the assessments tested. As staff and expertise grew within the California Department of Education, it took more control of assessment, first by writing "specifications" from which publishers constructed items and then, in the early 1980s, by supplying test items itself. Specifications and test items were developed by committees of CDE staffers and expert teachers who drew on the state's approved textbooks for guidance on the content and format of assessment. Because those textbooks were quite conventional, the assessment was too, consisting mostly of multiple-choice items testing student proficiency in basic mathematical operations, such as addition of whole numbers or subtraction with regrouping.

Because the legislation authorizing CAP required accountability of schools rather than of students, the assessment did introduce one innovation, matrix sampling, in its 1972 debut. Conventional individual-level assessments require the administration of the same items, or at least of items of equal difficulty, to every student, so that any individual's score is not affected by drawing "harder" or "easier" questions than their peer at the next desk. This requirement either limits the items on an assessment to a set that students can complete in the hour allotted for the test or requires relatively more complex empirical equating schemes to ensure comparability. By requiring school-level reporting only, however, CAP legislation freed test developers from this constraint and allowed them to increase the number of topics covered on the test. If schools rather than students were the unit of analysis and reporting, all students need not take the same test or encounter items of comparable difficulty. Test items could vary from student to student within the same grade in the school and thus cover more topics, as long as the total number of items represented the domains to be tested and as long as there were enough students answering each question to create a statistically reliable average. Matrix sampling decreased the number of items any given student had to complete, while at the same time increasing the number and type of test questions administered at any school—thereby furnishing a fuller and more reliable picture of the school's actual performance for an entire third or sixth grade curriculum. Results were reported by grade levels within schools and could be topically disaggregated to provide information on specific content areas like fractions. If a school were falling short in an area, the CAP results report would recommend specific page numbers from state-approved texts.

With Bill Honig's ascent to the state superintendency in 1982 and the passage of the Hughes/Hart Educational Reform Act the following year, state assessment policy began to change. The 1983 legislation authorized both new curriculum frameworks and new tests linked to the frameworks, and Honig did not delay in pressing new ideas about both. One idea was that if students should learn to think deeply about mathematics and engage with mathematical concepts, then tests should gauge the results. As we noted in Chapter 5, some scholars and policymakers argued that tests drive instruction and that changing the state assessment would advance reformers' goals. This implied a third big shift in state officials' reasoning: that they should use the frameworks, rather than existing textbooks, to guide decisions about assessment (interview with Tej Pandey, conducted by Penelope Peterson and Richard Prawat, California, 1989). Connecting the state assessment with the frameworks proved a substantial departure from conventional thinking about tests and testing and about the role tests play in the policy system.

Reformers faced several technical obstacles. They first had to decide what the new (1985 and 1992) state frameworks meant for student math performance at the grades to be tested, grades 4, 8, and 12. This was no easy matter: the frameworks, and in particular the 1985 version, contained little in the way of guidance regarding student performance in specific content areas for specific grades. Instead, the frameworks proposed that students should "understand" and be "mathematically powerful"—yet because these were desired properties in young children's minds rather than demonstrable outcomes, developing the test was a challenge. A committee headed by Tej Pandey worked through the 1980s to find test items open enough to require substantial student mathematical thinking and communication, yet with enough structure to allow for judgment of student responses. The effort turned out to be lengthy, difficult, and expensive.

The results were quite novel. Academics and reformers elsewhere in the country were trying to design performance assessments and move "beyond the bubble" of conventional multiple-choice testing, usually by executing small-scale studies of problem formats, scoring procedures, and such attendant statistical properties as reliability and generalizability (for a review of some, see Linn 1993). California testing experts experimented with these ideas statewide. The following, for example, is a two-part "performance task" on a sample fourth grade mathematics test designed by California test developers:

I. Your friend says she has 12 coins that add up to $1.00. She says that one of the coins is a quarter.
A. What coins might she have? Show as many possibilities as you can.

B. Could her 12 coins add up to $1.00 and not include one quarter? Explain your answer. (1993 Sampler of Mathematics Assessment)

Such open-ended problems were designed to hold student interest, to require them to construct responses and communicate about mathematical method, and to allow multiple solutions and solution methods. Raters could then score students' work on the basis of the depth of their understanding of a problem, rather than as simply right or wrong. These items were rounded out by so-called enhanced multiple-choice questions. Although these employed the conventional multiple-choice, choose-the-right-answer format, they were designed to go beyond assessing isolated skills to measure how students made connections between concepts and used more complex problem-solving strategies. Figure 6.1 is an example of enhanced multiple choice from the 1991 *Sampler of Mathematics Assessment.* In its second year, the assessment also contained a number of "constructed-response" problems designed to assess student's capability in more routine mathematics.

In addition to writing items, test developers also had to write guidelines for judging student work and for deciding which answers would count as satisfactory and which would not. The open-ended format of some test items made that endeavor more difficult, because state committees working on the math assessment had to anticipate the variety of ways young children might respond to novel problems and then create rubrics to score them. The open-ended format also meant that machine-scored tests would no longer suffice; instead, the state would need to locate and train cadres of teachers in both the mathematics of the framework and methods used to assess student work in that kind of mathematics. These methods were in their infancy at the time. Finally, the whole process—item development, rubric development, and scoring—had to yield measures that were valid, much as any test should, and could be consistently scored by well-trained but otherwise ordinary people. This arrangement entailed worrying about whether an item truly measured student understanding of mathematics or whether it measured other constructs (say, ability to read)—and whether different scorers would agree about a given student's performance on an item.

These technical difficulties associated with performance assessment would have given pause to even the best test developer of the early 1990s— and the CLAS had several of them—but the problems did not end there. The political system added further obstacles to the test designers' worries,

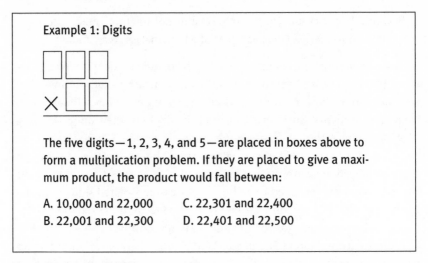

Example 1: Digits

The five digits—1, 2, 3, 4, and 5—are placed in boxes above to form a multiplication problem. If they are placed to give a maximum product, the product would fall between:

A. 10,000 and 22,000   C. 22,301 and 22,400
B. 22,001 and 22,300   D. 22,401 and 22,500

Figure 6.1. Sample CLAS Item

for when the new assessment system was authorized, the legislation required two separate kinds of accountability. First, by making CLAS scores public and by making schools' scores comparable to those of others with similar student composition, the state was to hold districts and schools publicly accountable—as the CAP had before it. In addition, the CLAS was required to provide schools and parents with individual student scores, thus allowing for some classroom-level accountability of teachers and for using the tests to monitor the progress of individual students and diagnose their problems. Governor Pete Wilson had promised such student scores during his original campaign for the governorship, and SB 662, the authorizing legislation for the CLAS, demanded it.

It was easier for politicians to promise both kinds of accountability than for testing experts to deliver it. Valid and reliable indicators of school achievement and year-to-year progress imply assessment of students in many components of the mathematical curriculum for a given grade. The CAP had solved this dilemma through matrix sampling, and the CLAS continued that tradition. According to some thinking, the CLAS required it, for grading students' performance on open-ended problems was hugely labor-intensive and costly, and testing individual students on the entire fourth grade curriculum would have been nearly impossible. Yet in the mid-1990s California's experts said they had found no way to use matrix sampling and report valid individual scores. In order to compare students with other students on this particular assessment, experts said, all should have tried the same items, or at least items of the same difficulty.

The small number of items taken by any single student on the mathematics CLAS meant that the accuracy of the assessment for that student would have been lower than was expected with conventional standardized tests. A student whose teachers had not provided instruction on coins and money, for instance, would perform significantly worse on the question about coins than would students whose teachers had covered that material. Unless the test contained more items to make up for this source of error in estimating that student's performance, the score would not represent actual math achievement. Further, test developers quickly saw that it would be difficult to cover the possible range of mathematical performance—from very high to very low achievement—with only six or eight items per student. Some students would get all six right, others would get none right, and for neither group could test developers gauge students' "true" achievement, for the students at either extreme would be simply off the charts.

Performance assessment advocates also faced the political challenge of securing public support. While they still were trying to iron out technical problems, state officials began an educational campaign to acquaint parents and teachers with the new assessment. Information sessions for parents and press releases to state newspapers helped in the former case. In the latter, the state employed a number of strategies, including recruiting teachers to help write, pilot, and score the assessment and arranging for educators experienced in open-ended mathematics assessment to offer workshops to colleagues through school districts, counties, and California Math Projects. The state also published two versions of *A Sampler of Mathematics Assessments,* which explained the assessment ideas the state was promoting and the performance standards by which student work would be judged. The samplers also supplied examples of open-ended and enhanced multiple-choice problems and of student work. We outlined in Chapter 5 the effects that some of these opportunities to learn had on teachers' practice and reported there that teachers who had an opportunity to learn *and* perceived it as such engaged in more reform practices than those who did not possess this combination. Yet only roughly one third of the teachers had an opportunity to learn about the CLAS, and only roughly one quarter judged that opportunity adequate. Our survey also asked teachers about their familiarity with the two sampler documents. In 1994, nearly half said they had never heard of the documents, and another fifth said they had heard of them but had not read them.

The politics of assessment were complicated, and technical work slowed, because of a feud between Honig and then-governor George Deukmejian, which at one point resulted in the governor's cutting the state education department's assessment development budget to zero. By 1991, when Pete Wilson was elected governor and SB 662 mandated that CAP be replaced with an assessment system that reduced reliance on multiple-choice items and increased the use of performance assessment, the California Department of Education, its contractors, and state educators had been at work for just under a decade. They had not perfected the product, though. Much remained unknown about performance assessment and how it would work on such an vast scale. Test developers and experts made major design decisions and modifications right through the 1993 and 1994 administrations of the CLAS, doing what they could under uncertain conditions, with tight budgets and an even tighter timeline. By the time the first new assessment was given, in spring 1993, some of the technical problems had been ironed out to a point many considered satisfactory. Other problems had not, including the lack of either individual student scores or the capacity to score student results.

Controversy erupted shortly after the inaugural CLAS administration in 1993. Conservative and religious groups began the fight, arguing that test items that asked students to write about their ideas and experiences violated families' privacy rights, and that other items threatened parents' moral teachings (McDonnell 1997a; Honig and Alexander 1996).[1] Others were upset because they felt that the tests assessed critical thinking and concepts at the expense of basic skills (McDonnell 1997a). This argument gained steam when the state refused to release the 1993 assessments to the public, on the grounds that it might be possible to reuse some of the expensive items if they were not made public. The release of 1993 scores in March 1994 did little to increase the popularity of the assessment, as some wealthy districts performed quite poorly, and sampling and scoring irregularities were soon uncovered by the *Los Angeles Times*. By May 1994, when the test was administered for a second time, Governor Wilson and his secretary of child development and education, Maureen DiMarco, had become outspoken critics of the test, calling the execution of the CLAS "disastrous" and questioning the validity of test items for measuring students' underlying understanding and skill proficiencies. Wilson complained in particular about the lack of student-level test scores.

The most devastating criticism, at least for educational professionals, came when a committee appointed to evaluate the assessment questioned its scientific soundness in a July 1994 report. Led by Lee Cronbach of Stanford University, a widely respected educational researcher and a gifted statistician, the committee noted myriad problems with the 1993 administration, from lost test booklets to unacceptably high levels of measurement error and imprecise scoring. Many of the problems stemmed not from incompetence or poor design, the committee was careful to note, but from the sheer difficulty of developing valid tests, sampling procedures, scoring rubrics, and an implementation infrastructure within the two-year time frame imposed by the 1991 legislation that had authorized the new assessment. Although the committee's report praised the creators of the test, it furnished ammunition to opponents.

As debate continued, CLAS supporters engaged in various defensive maneuvers intended to quell opposition to the assessment. State senator Gary Hart, a sponsor of the original CLAS legislation, designed an early 1994 reauthorization to deflect some of the criticisms leveled by conservative groups and school boards. His bill required test designers to add the constructed-response items to assess computational skills. And Bill Honig, whose conviction in a conflict of interest case forced his resignation from the state superintendency in early 1993, defended the assessment in the media, criticizing Wilson and DiMarco for abandoning a program the Republican administration had previously supported. Yet with Honig gone and only tepid support from other state education officials, the test had too few champions. The acting state superintendent of instruction, David Dawson, attempted to mollify religious conservatives by creating a parental-level opt-out program, while still requiring all school districts to administer the test, but these concessions were of little avail. Wilson vetoed the CLAS reauthorization bill in September 1994, citing some of the problems identified by Cronbach and the lack of individual student scores.

The test did have substantial professional support, at least from elementary teachers. Our survey, done several months after Wilson's veto, shows that outright disapproval of the CLAS was limited to about 10 percent of teachers, though a sizable percentage of them were on the fence. Only 7 percent agreed with a statement indicating that the CLAS conflicted with their preferred approach to mathematics teaching, and about 60 percent rejected this statement altogether. Half reported that the CLAS corresponded well to the mathematics skills they wanted their students to demonstrate, and half also reported that the CLAS identified topics the CAP missed. Table 6.1 shows reasonably solid support for the CLAS among school professionals in the state, even after a long controversy and the cancellation of the test. The popularity of the CLAS was probably related to teachers' general approval of reform, to efforts by the CDE to educate teachers about the test, and to the fact that many teachers had seen the CLAS itself as they administered it to their students. That is also fortuitous for us, because teachers' support for the CLAS makes it a more valid measure of student performance, and of the success of reformers' efforts. Had teachers not supported the test, there would be less reason to think its outcome would reflect local progress made toward state goals, because teachers would not have cared about what the test measured.

Technical Properties of the CLAS

We conjectured at the outset of the book that policy might affect student performance on the revised CLAS if teachers had substantial opportunities to learn, if they adopted the curricula or learned about the assessments designed to promote change, and if they taught math in ways that were more consistent with the state reforms. To explore this possibility, we merged student scores on the 1994 fourth grade mathematics CLAS into our data set. The scores were publicly available on the CDE website.[2]

The scores were the product of a novel process for assessing student performance, as we have mentioned. It started in spring 1994, when each nonexempted student[3] in the fourth grade took a mathematics test containing one open-ended task, eight multiple-choice items, and eight constructed-response items (*Technical Report,* 1-3).[4] The multiple-choice problems were machine-scored, and the constructed-response items were hand-scored as either right or wrong. Teams of teachers, test contractors, and others used scoring rubrics to assign student work a score of between one and four on the open-ended task. All student work was scored; there was no sampling. State officials and the main test contractor, CTB-McGraw Hill, tried to ensure agreement among readers by providing extensive training, allowing

Table. 6.1. Teachers' Support for the CLAS

	Strongly disagree				Strongly agree
The mathematics CLAS corresponds well with the mathematics understanding I want my students to demonstrate.*	6.1	5.2	36.6	31.8	20.3
The mathematics CLAS conflicts with my preferred approach to mathematics instruction.**	34.8	26.4	31.5	5.2	2.0
The mathematics CLAS can identify some mathematics understanding that the old (CAP) test missed.***	6.0	5.6	30.6	34.3	23.5

*Seventy-four missing cases.
**Seventy-five missing cases.
***Seventy-six missing cases.

only those who attained a certain standard to participate, and periodically giving readers "check sets" to ensure continued adherence to the standards. Between 83 and 89 percent of readers displayed perfect agreement on the four-point scale. Inter-reader reliabilities—a measure of agreement among raters—were calculated in double-blind readings of actual student tests, and the percentage of perfect-agreement correlations on these was in the low .80s (*Technical Report*, 1–8).

Once scoring of the open-ended task was finished, test officials assigned each student an overall performance level of between one and six, based on a "map" that related performance on the open-ended, multiple-choice, and constructed-response portions of the test. Correlations of these three item types ranged between .4 and .6, depending on the number of items being compared (*Technical Report*, 1-7). Although individual results were not released, school scores were reported as "percentage of students scoring [at] level 1" and "percentage of students scoring [at] level 2" at each level through six. To arrive at our dependent variable (CLAS), we established, for each school, an average of these percentages. Schools with higher scores on this measure had more proficient students, mathematically speaking. The mean for the CLAS in our sample of schools was 2.76, and the standard deviation at the school level .57.[5] Because assessment officials corrected problems that had turned up the year before, the 1994 assessment was improved, technically speaking—all student booklets were scored and measurement problems were reduced. Moreover, the test was administered in the spring of 1994, roughly six months before this survey, so our estimates of teachers' learning opportunities and practice corresponded chronologically with the assessment.[6]

Despite favorable timing, we faced several difficulties. Because the CDE reported only school-level scores, we had to compute school averages of all independent variables, including teachers' reports of practice and opportunities to learn. Use of aggregate data tends to increase any relationship found between variables, because aggregation reduces random error. Yet our survey sampled only four or fewer teachers per school, a very imprecise measure of school practices. Because classroom-level scores are not available, no known remedy to the former problem is available for this set of data, although we note that the individual-level models in Chapter 5 do not show much larger regression coefficients when run at the school level. We attempted to correct for the measurement error in a few models, and we present those results in Appendix F.

Reduced sample size compounded the problem of measurement error. Although the survey covered teachers in 249 schools, we lost nearly 100 from the CLAS analysis owing to various causes. Forty-five schools did have records but did not have CLAS data on the CDE database;[7] four schools lacked records altogether; and one more was lost because we could not assign it a matching I.D. The CDE reports that schools' CLAS scores were not published in cases where "error" in the score exceeded a threshold of acceptability,[8] when the school reported a sudden decrease in the reported number of gifted and talented students or a marked change in student demographics, when the number of students on which the score was based was low,[9] or when the number of students who opted out of taking the test was too high (see *Technical Report*, pp. 3-4 to 3-6).[10] Another thirty-seven schools were deleted from the analysis because only one out of four teachers responded to our survey. The final sample that we report on here contained 162 schools, each with between two and four teachers responding.

Our analysis is cross-sectional: we examine the relationships governing the different variables at a single point in time. Although this approach is typical of studies of school effects, panel data on student achievement would have been preferable, but they were not available. Even if they had been, we would not have had enough data points from the two-year administration of CLAS to model satisfactorily the relationships between policy, teaching practice, and student achievement. Nevertheless, we attempted to control for other factors that might contribute to student achievement, including students' socioeconomic background and general school conditions, by incorporating them into our model. We discuss these measures below.

Analysis

Our analysis is exploratory. These data are sufficient, and the issues important enough, to investigate the association between student achievement on this state assessment and the state policies meant to improve students' achievement. The data are not strong enough, however, for us to claim that any result is conclusive. If our conjecture about how instructional policy might operate is correct, teachers' reform practices should relate positively to student performance on the mathematics CLAS. So, too, should many measures of teachers' opportunities to learn about policy, for we saw in the last chapter that these opportunities to learn are substantially related to reforms in classroom practice. Furthermore, we might ask whether any of our policy instruments outweigh the others in their impact on student achievement—and whether they have any effects independent of the practice scales, as would be the case if the things they "taught" teachers were not wholly captured by the measure.

These questions are difficult to handle empirically. Reformers and researchers argue that the more actual overlap there is in policy instruments, the more likely teachers, students, and parents are to get the same messages and respond in ways that are consistent with policy. The more highly correlated any possible measures of those policy instruments are, however, the greater the problems of multicolinearity in the regressions used to sort out the independent effect of each. In multicolinearity, individual cases that have one characteristic, say replacement-unit use, also tend to have another, such as attendance at student curriculum workshops. If this happens in enough cases, the coincidence makes it difficult to sort out each variable's independent contribution to any dependent variable. Thus, the more successfully agencies "align" the instruments of a given policy, the more headaches analysts will experience in trying to discern either the distinctive contribution of each or the extent to which they operate in tandem.

Table 6.2 displays some evidence of such headaches. It reveals that the school-level correlations among the independent variables ranged from mild to moderately strong. At the strong end of the range, the average incidence at each school of replacement-unit use correlated at .44 with the average teacher participation in student curriculum workshops within the past year,[11] and at .47 with average reports of framework practice. This makes sense, given that student curriculum workshops should have provided teachers with replacement-unit materials and know-how and encouraged them to change their practices. At the weak end of the spectrum, average reports of teachers' learning about CLAS by school correlated at only the .13 to .16 level with schools' use of replacement units, teachers' reports of framework practice, and teachers' average participation in the student curriculum workshops. Special-topics workshops and conventional practices also produced low correlations with other variables. Finally, average student performance on the math CLAS by school correlated at the .14 to .29 level with markers for opportunities to learn that changed teachers' practices but did not at all correlate with special topics workshops. After inspecting this table, we drew up a strategy for analysis. We would first test our primary conjecture about student learning—that teaching practice in line with the reformers' ideas is associated with higher test scores. Since we have shown that changes in teaching practice result, at least in part, from the learning opportunities that reformers provided, a positive finding here would support efforts to change instruction. Still, because our scales for measuring practice are imperfect, in that they measure only one of the ways instruction might improve, we also tested the separate effects of each of the "policy" variables—teachers' learning about CLAS, use of replacement units, and learning via workshops—in successive models. We reasoned that these models would provide some overall impressions about the effect of different kinds of reform efforts on student performance, because each roughly summarizes a type of intervention that policymakers or others can organize.

Nevertheless, we thought that the coefficient estimates in these three "policy" models would be compromised by the high correlations among the variables, as shown in Table 6.2. In the absence of other closely related variables, each individual variable would garner not only its own effect but also the effects from its correlates. Hence, we devised a second strategy: that of putting all relevant variables in the base model at once, to see whether it is possible to sort out the independent effects of new student curriculum,

Table 6.2. Correlations Among Measures of Policy
"Instruments" and Mathematics Performance (School Level)

	Student curriculum	Special topics	Replace-ment units	Frame-work practice	Conven-tional practice	Learned about CLAS	CLAS
Student curriculum	1.0						
Special topics	.25	1.0					
Replacement units	.44	.03	1.0				
Framework practice	.37	.09	.47	1.0			
Conventional practices	−.33	−.02	−.32	−.41	1.0		
Learned about CLAS	.10	.02	.16	.13	.04	1.0	
School average CLAS score	.23	−.02	.27	.29	−.11	.14	1.0

teacher learning, and learning about the test and arrive at better estimates of the impact of each. If this enabled us to distinguish the relative importance of the different variables, it would offer evidence about which paths to reform might be most effective.

Finally, we want to know whether these policy activities are independently influential in improving student performance or whether they operate through teachers' practice as measured by our survey. So our third analysis strategy is to add the measure of practice to the fuller model.

We include demographic measures in all models, to control the influence of social and economic factors on student performance. One of these is "percentage FLE," a measure of a school's proportion of students eligible to receive free lunch. This measure is derived from the 1994 survey of school characteristics in the NCES Common Core Database; higher scores indicate schools with more impoverished students.[12] Another is "school conditions," a composite of three survey items measuring parental support for mathematics instruction, the rate of student turnover, and the maintenance of school facilities. Its mean is 2.77, its standard deviation .67 at the school level, and higher scores indicate more difficult working conditions. Though the two demographic measures correlate at .60, we include both, because both explain variation in students' test scores.

We also include the variable "past framework learning" in all models that weigh teachers' workshop attendance against student achievement. Although this variable is underspecified—we have no sense what those learning opportunities were—not including it would have biased the coefficients on the remaining variables, because teachers with some past opportunities to learn would be marked as zero and the "baseline" would be off. We did expect that this variable should relate positively, although not necessarily significantly, to student achievement.

We begin by modeling schools' scores as a function of their teachers' average reported practice and the demographic measures. Model 1 (column 1) in Table 6.3 shows a modest association: schools in which teachers reported classroom practice that was more geared to the math framework have higher average student scores on the 1994 fourth grade CLAS, once we have controlled for schools' demographic characteristics. This positive relationship between framework practice and student achievement offers evidence that teaching does link state policy with classroom practice, for students benefited from classes in which the teaching was more closely tied to state instructional goals. Though this interpretation is based on aggregate data, it is difficult to draw any other reasonable inference. If the conditions summarized in our model were satisfied, teachers' opportunities to learn paid off in their students' performance.

Model 1 also shows that no association was noticeable between our conventional-practice scale and students' scores. Schools in which teachers reported more conventional practices—book exercises and computational testing—did not have students who were more proficient on CLAS than schools whose teachers reported fewer of those practices.

We next investigate whether reformers' policies were associated with greater student achievement. We begin with the effect of teachers' learning on student achievement. On the basis of the analysis just given we expected to find a modest relation between teacher attendance at student curriculum workshops and CLAS scores, absent other factors, for we have seen that these workshops contribute significantly to changes in teachers' practices. After controlling for teachers' past framework learning, we did observe that relation, as is evident from Model 2 in Table 6.3. Teachers' opportunities to learn the subject matter they would teach did positively affect students' test scores.

Table 6.3. Association Between Teachers' Practice, Their Learning, and Student Math Scores

	1 CLAS	2 CLAS	3 CLAS	4 CLAS	5 CLAS	6 CLAS
Intercept	3.32***	3.74***	3.75***	3.76***	3.63***	3.33***
	0.24	0.13	0.12	0.12	0.21	0.23
Percentage FLE students	−1.36***	−1.41***	−1.39***	−1.43***	−1.38***	−1.35***
	0.13	0.13	0.12	0.12	0.12	0.12
School conditions	−0.125*	−0.11*	−0.11*	−0.11*	−0.11*	−0.12*
	0.05	0.05	0.05	0.05	0.05	0.05
Framework practice	0.16*					0.10~
	0.06					0.06
Conventional practice	−.01					
	0.05					
Time in student curriculum workshops		0.054*			0.037	0.028
		0.027			0.026	0.027
Time in special-topics workshops		0.025				
		0.042				
Number of replacement units used			0.10*		0.072~	0.048
			0.04		0.042	0.045
Learned about CLAS				0.22*	0.17*	0.16~
				0.09	0.09	0.09
Past framework learning		0.08			0.093	0.09
		0.10			0.095	0.10
R^2 (adjusted)	0.65	0.64	0.65	0.65	0.66	0.66
N	162	162	162	162	162	162

Note: All survey-based measures are school averages of teacher responses.

~Indicates significance at $p < .15$ level.

*Indicates significance at $p < .05$ level.

**Indicates significance at $p < .01$ level.

***Indicates significance at $p < .001$ level.

By contrast, Model 2 in Table 6.3 reveals no such positive association between teachers' attendance at special-topics workshops and student achievement. We observed in Chapter 5 that participation in special-topics workshops contributed little to explaining the differences between teachers' reports of framework or conventional mathematics practice. Consequently, one effect these workshops might have had on student achievement—that of increasing framework practices—could not occur. Special-topics workshops might have improved student achievement, however, along pathways not detected by this measure—for instance, by increasing teachers' knowledge of mathematical subject matter, helping teachers better understand student learning, or improving equity within classrooms. The nonexistent association between this variable and student achievement on the 1994 CLAS suggests that such influences on achievement did not operate outside the scales relating to practice that we devised. This is a very important result: whatever improvements these workshops might have brought to California's classrooms, they seemed unrelated to student performance.

Teachers' use of replacement units also positively predicts student achievement (Table 6.3, Model 3). Schools in which teachers used one replacement unit each had student test scores that averaged about a sixth of a standard deviation higher than did schools in which no teachers reported having used replacement units. This could reflect the additional teacher learning that accompanied the use of replacement units, the direct effect of quality curriculum on student learning, or "alignment" between students' curriculum and their test—or all three.[13]

Finally, there is a clear positive effect on achievement of teachers' learning about the CLAS (Model 4).[14] Schools in which all teachers learned about the test had average test scores roughly a third of a standard deviation higher than schools in which no teachers had learned about it. It is easier to report this result than to decide what it means. A skeptic might discount it as an artifact of schools' attempt to better their score on the mathematics CLAS by producing more test-savvy teachers and students. Even if that were so, teachers and administrators would have had to change the curriculum or introduce performance-based assessments in order to raise scores. That in turn would have required professional learning, which would have been reflected in teachers' reports of learning from the new assessment that we reported in the last chapter. We think that our conjecture is supported, even on the basis of a skeptical interpretation of the results.

In principle, then, both our practice and policy measures related positively to student achievement. That suggests that state efforts to improve instruction can affect not only teaching but also student learning. The relatively close links between some of these policy and practice variables call the point estimates in our models into question, however, for omitting any one variable will allow another to pick up its effects via their correlation. So we ask next about the "true" influence of each policy instrument on student achievement, after we have controlled for the others: Do the three policy instruments exert their influence jointly, each having some independent effect on performance, or does one predominate? This is an important theoretical and practical question, for if one were overwhelmingly influential, we would draw different inferences for action than if several were jointly influential. Thus we enter the markers for "learned about CLAS," attendance at a student curriculum workshop, and use of replacement units into the CLAS regression.

Model 5 offers a version of the joint-influence story. Schools in which teachers reported using an average of one replacement unit did come out higher in the distribution of CLAS scores than did schools in which no replacement units were used. The effect was modest, and statistically significant at the .15 level. Teacher learning in student curriculum workshops gave no statistically discernible boost to student learning, although the effect remained positive and just below statistical significance.[15] And schools in which teachers learned about CLAS itself continued to post scores about a third of a standard deviation higher than did schools in which teachers did not. Two of the three interventions organized by reformers were associated with higher student scores on CLAS.

One reason these policy variables might appear significant in this model is that they correlate with framework practice. If instructional policy is to improve student achievement, it must do so directly through changes in teacher practice, for students will not learn more simply because teachers *know* different things or have been exposed to new curricula or tests. Instructional interventions must change what teachers *do* in the classroom— including what they do with curricula and tests—even if very subtly, in order to affect student understanding. Teachers who used new curricula but understood nothing about how to use them would not be likely to help students learn significantly more. Following this reasoning, and assuming that we measured framework practices perfectly, we concluded that the addition of the measure of framework practice to Model 5 should produce an effect for that variable and zero out the three policy measures.

A partial version of that result appears in Model 6. The variables for replacement-unit use and student curriculum workshops do edge closer to zero, and the coefficient on our measure of framework practice is cut by about a third, an indication that it "shares" variance with the student curriculum workshops and replacement-unit use. Still, "framework practice" and "learned about CLAS" retain some modestly significant effect on CLAS scores. This evidence does not lead us to imagine that we have discovered a hitherto unnoticed magical effect of teacher knowledge or curriculum use. We are instead inclined to stick to the view that teachers' learning influences their practice, which in turn influences students' learning. One reason is that the three variables that split variance are the most colinear, an observation which suggests that the regression algorithm had difficulty sorting out their effects. We think it wiser to conceive the three as a package, not as independent units. An F-test of the three policy variables (student curriculum use, student curriculum workshops, CLAS learning) finds them jointly significant.[16]

A second reason is that our practice scale is imperfect. Recall the types of items that make up this measure: students do problems that have more than one correct solution; students make conjectures; students work in small groups. Although these tasks reflect the ways teachers' practices may change as a result of reform efforts, other changes in practice may also have occurred. The reforms might have helped deepen teachers' understanding of mathematics or student learning or shown teachers new ways to represent mathematical material. It is hard to imagine that reformers' interventions would not assist teachers in learning some of these topics, yet they are omitted from the framework-practice scale. If they do affect student achievement, as we expect, they would be picked up by the policy variables in Model 6. Model 6 teaches us as much about the limitations of survey research in instructional policy as it does about the pathways to improved student achievement.[17]

Through all six models, the coefficients on "percentage FLE" and "school conditions" remained significantly, and in the former case substantially, related to student achievement. A school enrolling 100 percent FLE students scored, on average, more than two standard deviations below a school with no such students.[18] Other factors associated with lower student scores were low parental support, high student turnover, and deteriorating school buildings. Controlling for students' social class strengthens our argument about policy interventions, for we can report that the relationships described earlier did not result from more advantaged students' getting better-educated teachers. It also helps put this analysis in perspective, for by comparison with some of the effects of student social class, the effect of policy instruments appeared modest. Yet the measures of student social status summarize a lifetime of inequalities and their effects in earlier grades, whereas the measures of curriculum and teacher learning address only a single year in students' school lives. Strong instructional interventions might have a cumulative effect over many years of schooling.

We investigate the robustness of these findings in several ways. We start by checking the stability of the regressions above. If, for example, the significant results in Table 6.3 depend on the particular specifications we chose, we might expect the effects to disappear when we make small changes such as using unweighted instead of weighted data, changing the specification slightly, or restricting the sample size to only schools where three or four teachers answered the survey. Yet the estimates seem reasonably stable, persisting through such checks. Dropping the measure of school conditions from the models changes the estimates on the other variables only slightly. Although not using the population weights caused the policy-and-practice variables in Models 5 and 6 to take slightly different-sized slices of the CLAS pie, the other models do not change greatly, and our interpretations would remain the same. Including only schools where three or four teachers answered the survey actually strengthens most point estimates of policy and practice on student achievement, although the smaller sample size also results in larger standard errors—and therefore the levels of significance do not rise. Checking the models for violations of the seven deadly regression sins, we find that most of the models have normally distributed residuals; all have tidy plots of predicted versus residual values; and deleting highly influential cases makes a difference to only two of the variables in Models 1 through 5.[19]

We checked on these analyses in another way, by probing the effects of other types of professional development on student mathematics achievement scores. We saw earlier that learning opportunities which concerned mathematics topics but not centrally focused on reformers' ideas about instruction and student curriculum did not have a salutary effect on student achievement. To offer further evidence for the claim that the content of teacher learning mattered, we tested the relation of two other learning opportunities to student achievement. One, called "nonmath professional development," measures the average time that responding teachers in a school reported spending on non-math-related in-service workshops within the year before the survey. The other, "other CLAS professional development," estimates the percentage of teachers in a school who had an opportunity to learn about the CLAS in a content area other than mathematics (reading or writing). Neither had any influence on student achievement, once we had controlled for student socioeconomic status and school conditions (see Table 6.4).

The results in this table reinforce our view that teacher learning that improves instruction and student learning is specific to particular subject matter and instructional approaches. Some readers might wonder whether both higher student test scores and greater teacher participation in professional development activities were caused by some unmeasured force like parent concern or overall school effectiveness. But these results support the claim that the effects observed in Table 6.3 stem from real teacher learning, and not from certain schools' general aptitude in taking advantage of tests and learning opportunities. Improved student learning does depend on teachers learning specific things about mathematics, math instruction, and student learning.

Our analyses support an instructional view of instructional policy. Teachers' opportunities to learn about reform do affect their teaching, when those opportunities are situated in curriculum and assessments designed to be consistent with the reforms, and which their students study or use. In such cases, a consistent relation exists between the purposes of policy, the professional curriculum favored by reformers, assessment and teachers' knowledge of assessment, and the student curriculum. When the assessment of students' performance is consistent with the student and teacher curriculum, teachers' opportunities to learn pay off in students' math performance. These conclusions are not ironclad, given that the data are cross-sectional, school-level, and based on a relatively limited sample. But they both confirm the analytic usefulness of an instructional model of instructional policy and suggest the significant role that the education of professionals can play in efforts to improve public education.

Table 6.4. Influence of Nonmath Professional Development on CLAS Math Scores

	CLAS	CLAS
Intercept	3.87***	3.77***
(Standard error—se)	(.18)	(.13)
Percantage FLE students	−1.44***	−1.43***
(se)	(.13)	(.12)
School conditions	−.12*	−.11*
(se)	(.05)	(.05)
Nonmath professional development	−.00	
(se)	(.03)	
Learned about CLAS mathematics		.22*
(se)		(.09)
Other CLAS professional development		−.01
(se)		(.09)
R² (adjusted)	.64	.65
N	162	162

Note: All survey-based measures are school averages of teacher responses.

~Indicates significance at p < .15 level.

*Indicates significance at p < .05 level.

**Indicates significance at p < .01 level.

***Indicates significance at p < .001 level.

It has been relatively unusual for researchers to investigate the relations between teachers' and students' learning, but when they have, it was even more unusual to find evidence that teachers' learning influenced students' learning. A few recent studies do report such work, and they are consistent with our results. Wiley and Yoon (1995) investigated the impact of teachers' learning opportunities on student performance on the 1993 CLAS and found higher student achievement in cases where teachers had had extended opportunities to learn about mathematics curriculum and instruction. Brown, Smith, and Stein (1996) analyzed teachers' learning, teaching practice, and student achievement data collected from four QUASAR project schools and found that students had higher scores when teachers had more opportunities to study a coherent curriculum that was designed to enhance both teacher and student learning. In a meta-analysis of the features of professional development that affect teaching practice and student achievement, Kennedy (1998) found that the content of teachers' learning influenced student achievement: teachers who had attended programs focused on student's mathematics learning or mathematics itself improved students' performance on mathematics assessments. Our results also are consistent with evidence from other studies examining the association between what is taught, what is tested, and what is learned (Leinhardt and Seewald 1981; Barr and Dreeben 1983; Berliner 1979; Linn 1983). Though the match between the CLAS and survey data is not ideal, the results are consonant with several other lines of related research. Although we cannot be sure of the effect sizes, we are confident that the nature and direction of the effects have been accurately established.

These results also bear on a possible criticism of our analysis. In Chapter 5 we noted that the relation between attendance at workshops on student curriculum on the one hand and framework practice on the other might result from teachers' simply learning to "talk the talk" of reform, rather than from their making substantial changes in the classroom. A critic might argue that that relation reflected teachers' rephrasing of their descriptions of classroom work to be more consistent with the reform lingo. Teachers, for example, who present new material through a conventional format—teacher asks, student responds, teacher explains—might continue to use this conventional method after attending a student curriculum workshop; yet they might report on our survey that they often had students "discuss" ways to solve mathematics problems. If teachers were merely learning a new way to talk, though, it is difficult to imagine how schools with teachers who report more framework-related instruction could post higher scores on CLAS. The association between framework practice and student scores not only seems to show the beneficial effects of reformed instruction; it also seems indirectly to confirm our earlier finding that teachers who had substantial opportunities to learn did substantially change their practice.

When educational improvement focuses on learning and teaching specific academic content, and when a curriculum for improving teaching overlaps with curriculum and assessment for students, teaching practice and student performance are likely to improve. Under such circumstances, educational policy can be an instrument for improving teaching and learning. Policies that do not meet these conditions—new assessments, for example, or curricula that do not offer teachers adequate opportunities to learn, or professional development that is not grounded in academic content—are less likely to have constructive effects. Unfortunately, most efforts to improve schools have focused on only one or another of the influences that we discussed. Challenging curricula have failed to have a broad impact on teaching and learning at least partly because teachers had few opportunities to learn and improve their practice (Sarason 1982; Dow 1991; Cohen and Barnes 1993; Cohen and Ball 1999). The difficulty with countless efforts to change teachers' practices through professional development has been that they bore no relation to central features of the curriculum that students would study and consequently have had no observable effect on students' learning. Many efforts to "drive" instruction by using "high-stakes" tests failed either to link the tests to the student curriculum or to offer teachers substantial opportunities to learn. These and other interventions assume that working on only one of the many elements that shape instruction will affect all the others. The evidence presented here, however, suggests that instructional improvement works best when it focuses on learning and teaching specific academic content, when there is a curriculum for improving teaching that overlaps with curriculum and assessment for students, and when teachers have substantial opportunities to learn about the content, how students are likely to make sense of it, and how it can be taught.

Chapter 7

MISSED OPPORTUNITIES

Teachers are not independent operators; they work in schools and districts, complex organizations situated within states, professions, markets for schooling, and the like. These organizations could encourage or inhibit the sorts of change the California mathematics policy sought to effect. That is especially important because the success story we have told thus far was atypical. The policy did lead to the creation of new opportunities for teachers to learn, rooted either in improved student curriculum or in examples of students' work, or both; but only a modest fraction of California elementary teachers—roughly 10 percent—had those opportunities. Most other teachers missed many connections between policy and practice and had no substantial chance to learn about new mathematics instruction. Though a minority of teachers did work together on serious problems of curriculum, teaching, and learning in short-term professional communities, most did not. They did not have access to the professional learning opportunities that would have enabled them to learn more about mathematics, about students' mathematical thinking, and about how teaching might be changed to improve learning. They did not have substantial opportunities to revise their teaching so that students could learn a more thoughtful version of elementary grade mathematics. Teaching often did change, but in ways that seem typical of U.S. education: a few new practices were added around a quite conventional pedagogical core. Teachers who had the extended professional learning opportunities of the sort we discussed in earlier chapters reported more innovative classroom practice, but most teachers in California adopted only a few fragments of elements of the state reforms, adding nothing that would disturb their solidly conventional practice.

If the success story we have told is important, no less important is the story of why success was confined to a small minority of teachers. In what follows we try to explain why so many teachers missed out on the opportunities that their more fortunate colleagues had. To do so, we offer an account of the California educational system and of the path of the policy through it. In order to appreciate what it took to create opportunities for a small minority of teachers to learn and change, one also must understand why those opportunities were lacking for so many others. One key point in our account is that California's system of public education is extraordinarily fragmented. The policy helped to create coherence among certain elements of curriculum, assessment, and professional learning, for certain teachers, but coherence is rare amid the blizzard of guidance for instruction that envelops U.S. public schools. As the new math policy filtered through the state school system, the reform became diffuse and incoherent. The missed opportunities were part of a broader pattern of often divergent response to this reform, as to many others.

That outcome leads us to a second crucial point of this chapter. The state reformers had to work within existing organizations and practices, for if the changes were not intelligible and compelling to those whose practice needed improvement, or if the opportunities to learn how to change were inadequate, little change would take place. Those who wished to effect a change, therefore, still had to operate in ways that made sense in the context of the fragmentation and decentralization in California and in the context of existing incentives, norms, and school culture. Otherwise, the reformers' ideas might be neglected, misunderstood, or underestimated. Unfortunately, though, those organizations, practices, incentives, norms, and school cultures were inhospitable to many kinds of change. California had a long history of innovative efforts to change mathematics teaching, but little to show for it. The organizations and professional culture in which innovators work often tend to diffuse change initiatives, marginalize them, or encourage adoption of only a few peripheral elements.

As this suggests, innovation confronts a dilemma: reformers have to work within the existing system, but that system often is a powerful threat to reform. If reformers are to succeed, they somehow have to work effectively enough within existing organizations and practices to bring about extensive change, but not so dramatically that they trigger rejection or marginalization. Innovation requires continual negotiation of that dilemma. The California math reforms were unrepresentative of state reforms in the sense that unusually rich resources for professional learning were mobilized, for a fraction of teachers in the state, for an entire decade, in support of a policy that departed sharply from conventional practice. The reforms were representative of others, however, in the sense that most teachers did not have access to those resources, because they were severely constrained by existing educational arrangements.

In what follows, we look within the state educational system for clues to explain why so many teachers in California missed the opportunities reform presented. We begin by exploring the nature and organization of the professional-development system. How did it affect the success of a reform that relied on professional development as its primary vehicle for helping teachers change? Next, we consider what the different components of the educational system made of state policy. Then we turn back to professional development to examine what impact teachers' autonomy had on the reforms as they played out. Finally, we look to teachers' reports of their ideas and practices, to probe what the interaction of reforms, systems, and individuals meant for California's schools.

Professional Development

Reformers in California envisioned an unusual kind of mathematics instruction and curricula. Because the reform model was much more deeply grounded in mathematics and aimed at more ambitious work, few teachers could have done on their own what reformers wanted. Reformers inside and outside the state education agency thus tried to teach teachers about the new mathematical ideas.

Teachers seemed well situated to learn, for they worked in the neighborhood of many organizations that might have helped—university teacher education departments, professional associations, private professional development agencies, and others. Yet while these organizations offered professional education in connection with the policy, few taught teachers in ways that deeply supported the changes that the policy entailed. Similarly, teachers worked in and for schools, districts, intermediate districts, and the state. If teachers were to learn the knowledge and skills that the policy required, they would need time, guidance, and encouragement as they learned and tried out new approaches to teaching. Money would be needed to support the enterprise. These things could come only from some combination of colleagues, principals, superintendents, union leaders, and governments. They were forthcoming in only a modest minority of cases. Even though the California Department of Education had proposed the policy change, and even though many who worked in the relevant agencies were sympathetic and helped, most teachers had neither the opportunities to learn nor the support for learning that would have been required.

The nonsystem. One reason for that result was the state school system, in which there was little coordination of instruction, teacher education, or other central aspects of public education. The fragmentation owed a good deal to decentralized authority: from the state to localities, and from local central offices to schools, and from school heads to teachers. It owed something more to the dissociation, at the state level, between governance and administration for K–12 schooling and teacher education. It owed a good deal to the delegation of public authority in curriculum, assessment, and professional education to private testing and publishing firms, with weak guidance from public authorities. Lacking coordination in these and other domains, local districts and school heads had lots of room to exercise choice about teachers' professional education, and they, in turn, left teachers many choices.

Guidance for teachers' professional learning was thus detached from guidance for students' learning; the student curriculum had little effect on the curriculum for teacher education in California. There were few incentives to focus teachers' learning on students' learning, and few efforts to do so. Professional education instead resembled a nonsystem, in which decisions about what professionals were taught and learned were coordinated neither with decisions about what students were to learn nor with incentives for teachers to learn approaches that would advance students' learning.

The market. Part of the explanation for that situation lay in the ways in which educators made decisions about teachers' professional learning. Providers and consumers of in-service professional education decide what to teach and learn in a market of sorts (Little and others 1987). Though districts and schools require teachers to complete a certain number of hours of professional development per year, teachers often choose the workshops. They usually do so from approved lists, but the lists include a panoply of district curriculum specialists, teachers, outside consultants and providers, university-based projects, and others. The length of the lists may be some function of the number of subject matter areas (math, science, language arts), special topics (diversity, time management, federal regulations, discipline, motivation), programs and approaches to material or classroom management (cooperative learning groups, assessment techniques, or integrating subjects across curriculum), and targeted student populations (Title 1 students, students who have limited English proficiency, or girls). Providers offer workshops that last for a few hours, or one or two days, with titles like "Cooperative Learning for LEP students," and teachers generally string several together to meet local requirements. Superficiality and fragmentation are the rule: the offerings rarely provide opportunities to learn in depth about anything central to instruction, and teachers at the same schools often study very different things.

Math reformers in California had to work within this system to accomplish anything, and some used it to good advantage. They began by offering a small number of workshops focused on a single substantial mathematical topic; the replacement unit on fractions that the state initially commissioned is a case in point. Teachers who enrolled learned about how a serious set of mathematical ideas could be understood, learned, and taught. The response was enthusiastic, and the state encouraged other developers to write additional replacement units and offer more workshops. Developers did, and the response continued to be very positive. State officials also helped to invent the California Mathematics Project (CMP), which offered extended teacher education at various universities throughout the state. These two innovations operated within the existing system of local lists and teacher choice, but they created opportunities to learn that were grounded in serious subject matter, that might extend for a week or more, and that concerned teaching and learning the subject matter. They were substantial innovations in the existing system, but they worked at least in part because there turned out to be enthusiastic markets for what they offered.

They reached only modest audiences. When a representative sample of teachers in the state responded to our survey in the fall and winter of 1994–95, most reported that their professional development in mathematics in the previous year had followed conventional patterns. A large majority had no opportunity to participate in the unusual workshops and professional communities in which teachers learned about new math curricula or students' work on the CLAS. Instead, they encountered reform ideas in district- or county-sponsored workshops and in-service programs, often with instructors who had little preparation, save having attended one of the more extended sessions offered by a replacement unit's developer. In these cases, mathematics was one of many subjects among many competing alternatives from which teachers could pick.

Most teachers' exposure to more typical professional development also was short and superficial. Although the value of more extended professional development had been clear from research by the mid-1980s, very few providers had the capacity to offer such opportunities to teachers, and they had space for only a few teachers in any given year. Marilyn Burns's workshops, for instance, accommodated 1.5 percent of the survey sample's elementary school teachers for one week or more in 1993–94, and the fraction of teachers attending the California Math Projects during that year was similar. In addition, though the replacement-unit workshops were designed by state officials to run for two and a half days, survey results indicate that more than half the enrolled teachers took a one-day version, most likely at their county or district. The same was true of other workshops that supported the math frameworks.

The evidence also shows that many teachers patched together professional development from two or more providers over the course of the year, thereby further fragmenting their experiences. Though nearly one in five teachers reported spending more than two days in mathematics professional development in California, only a small number spent more than a few days engaged in any one of the more intensive opportunities to learn. Most learned about the reforms by piecing together different kinds of workshops from the bewildering array that was available. Only a small fraction delved extensively into teaching and learning mathematics.

This limited capacity to supply extended opportunities for professional learning owed a good deal to the state and locally regulated market in which most professional development took place. For in such markets, the success of those who were teaching teachers depended on teachers' enrolling. This dependency generated strong incentives for offerings that brought teachers in, kept them in, and brought others in next month, next summer, and next year. Teachers, like other professionals, want practical help, and it is entirely rational for them to prefer professional development that helps them tomorrow, especially if they receive no guidance or incentives to the contrary. Making such choices in the short run means that most teachers' professional-development decisions will reflect their present problems and practice, and that the innovations that prosper will target that practice. The professional lore of professional development in the United States reflects that conclusion: everyone reports that teachers are looking for a workshop that will "help them Monday morning" and are averse to offerings that are not closely linked to ongoing practice. The professional lore even has a nickname for such workshops—"make and take"—that accurately represents the emphasis on activities, problems, or practices that can easily be brought to school. Our evidence shows that the lore misrepresents matters, because at least some of the state's teachers were enthusiastic about much more substantial fare, but it doesn't show how extensive that market might be.

Research on professional development in California during the reform showed that workshops oriented toward "Monday morning" were a substantial part of the effort to educate teachers about the new policies (Ball and Rundquist 1993; Wilson, Lubienski, and Mattson 1996). Even workshop leaders who favored the new frameworks felt it essential to offer specific activities, lessons, or manipulatives that would be immediately useful, along with ideas about the frameworks. That stance was familiar, for studies of instruction reveal that teachers often introduce a topic by stating some general rule or concept, providing a few concrete examples, and then leaving students with a few pages from the textbook or a ditto from which to work problems. In both classrooms and workshops, educators have assumed that learners make connections between conceptual underpinnings and specific examples or activities efficiently, correctly, and independently. Some educators believe that this paradigm of concept followed by example will further understanding and ensure proficiency.

Many California reformers would not have agreed with these assumptions; they argued that most students would not learn a topic in depth merely by looking at a few examples after listening to the general rules. Instead, reformers argued that learners need opportunities to explore the ideas, to see for themselves how generalizations relate to examples, and to investigate how examples incarnate a concept. Yet teachers were not offered such opportunities in most workshops concerning the reforms. Though the content of the frameworks was quite novel when compared with conventional practice, the new ideas were adapted by professional developers. Inherited ideas and practices were everywhere, and that was why reformers proposed change. Being everywhere, though, they permeated and sometimes overwhelmed the new ideas and practices.

The tension was ubiquitous. Suzanne Wilson and her colleagues (1996) found it in California Mathematics Projects that taught teachers about the framework. The CMP was innovative: teachers spent two to four weeks during the summer doing mathematical activities, learning mathematics from mathematicians, learning about students, discussing policy, and doing all of the above with each other. Still, the teachers who took part in these innovative projects worked within the existing system. Mathematics activities took up about half of teachers' time in their workshops, but there was little focus on mathematical ideas. Teachers were eager to engage with the practical and strategic aspects of the activities but did not examine the mathematics or discuss how individual problems related to more complex concepts. Wilson and her colleagues thought that workshop leaders shied away from trying to improve teachers' sometimes tenuous understanding of the mathematics: they note that "mathematics is respected and constantly pointed to. But seldom pushed on. Teacher leaders worry about embarrassing participants who offer wrong answers. Opportunities to discuss underlying mathematical ideas are missed. Repeatedly" (p. 28).

Even this atypically rich professional development did not probe the mathematics ideas that teachers were expected to help students learn—in workshops intended to help teachers learn how to do so. Wilson and her colleagues ascribed the meagerness of mathematical content to the "bargains" struck between workshop leaders and teachers who wanted to focus on the practical, logistical, and pedagogical aspects of the activities with which everyone was comfortable, to the leaders' wish not to embarrass teachers, and to the many items on the workshop agenda. In the negotiation between inherited practices and knowledge on the one hand and reform-based ideas on the other, many such compromises were struck. They weakened the reform as they opened access to the system and its professionals.

Weak evidence. There might have been more informed choice about professional development if there had been solid evidence on the effects and effectiveness of different approaches to it, if educators and policymakers had had ready access to such knowledge, and if there had been incentives to use it. Pitifully little evidence was available, though, and thus little solid basis for teachers or other school professionals to make informed choices about which experiences would improve student learning. The market for professional development was undisciplined by evidence on the effects and effectiveness of alternative approaches. There is no shortage of research about professional development, but little of it deals with the influence of particular programs on teachers' knowledge and practice, and on students' learning. Some government-funded and university-operated programs are evaluated, but most of them are NSF-funded teacher development programs, and the NSF required only that their operators evaluate them—a dismally weak standard. A far greater number of professional development programs—for instance, those operated by county or district staff or by private consultants—have no formal or independent evaluation. Teachers who attend may be asked to fill out a questionnaire about the value of the workshop, and project staff may even write a report. Follow-ups on teachers' classroom practice are rare, and follow-ups on their students' learning are virtually nonexistent.

The evaluation of larger, university-based programs also has serious problems. Most professional development programs have many goals, and most evaluations are done by the program operators or those they pay. Most evaluations are therefore specific to the design of each workshop, and far from independent. The result is a body of research that adds little to knowledge and does not inform action. One cannot say that teachers who attended Workshop A changed their practice more or less than otherwise similar teachers who attended Workshop B. When evaluations are done by the innovation designers each of whom uses different measures of different goals, the opportunities to gain rigorous and generalizable knowledge are greatly reduced. Because the evaluations usually focus on teacher practice as the sole dependent variable, evidence on student performance is rarely available.

The paucity of knowledge about the effects of professional development is particularly damaging because markets work more efficiently with better information. The infrequent evaluations of teacher in-service programs and workshops and the lack of a common criterion for judgment meant that producers and consumers had little rigorous knowledge about what was likely to be most effective for teachers and students. Teachers often heard about workshops from colleagues, but they were unlikely to learn from a reputable and independent source that one workshop had been successful in improving teachers' practice and student learning, whereas another had not. Teachers thus made professional-development choices based on some combination of what was available, what they wished to focus on, and what others recommended. One researcher described these choices as "random" (Lord 1994). In such ill-informed markets, producers are not influenced by consumers whose choices are based on solid knowledge about what works. Consumers have no incentives to choose workshops that might help to improve their students' performance, and producers have no incentives to offer education that might seriously influence teaching and learning. Parents and school systems have no way to use rigorous knowledge to set priorities or influence teachers' choices.

This situation means that professional development that produced no measurable improvement in teaching or student learning could persist, because no one knew it was inefficient. Teachers instead evaluated professional development on the basis of proximate criteria such as the material it provided for "Monday morning." Our research and that of others suggests that such decisions do not yield substantial opportunities to learn. The lack of information about workshops' effectiveness makes it harder for teachers and schools seeking academic improvement to find professional development that would help. Our research shows that only workshops that focused on the student curriculum of reforms enhanced teachers' implementation of key reform practices, but in 1993 teachers had no way to know that. Teachers interested in putting the mathematics frameworks into practice would have had little reliable information about what professional development would help them and their students. Policymakers who wished to improve schooling would have lacked guidance about how to invest in teacher learning.

One additional cause of this unhappy situation was the lack of agreement about what should be taught and learned. Research and evaluation on the effects of professional development would require common frameworks for measuring teaching, teacher learning, professional-development practices, and student learning. Such agreement would not be easy in the existing nonsystem of public education, but once states began moving toward frameworks and standards for teaching and learning, agreement might be more feasible, at least within states. If so, there may be hope for a better-

informed system. Given yearly expenditures on professional development—estimates range between 2 and 5 percent of total educational out-
lays[1]—the present nonsystem is a scandal.

The seeming randomness of teacher choice in the existing knowledge-
poor system is illustrated in Table 7.1. For the 350-odd teachers who attended a mathematics in-service program the year before the survey, we
forecast attendance at special-topics versus student curriculum workshops.
The table reflects the probability (estimated through logistic regression) that
a teacher would attend a student curriculum workshop, after we had controlled for school efforts to implement the framework (administrative support), availability of such workshops in the district, teachers' activism regarding mathematics policy (professional activities, California Math Project,
and local policy), and some contextual variables. Higher coefficients reflect
a greater probability that teachers would have taken a student curriculum
workshop. The strongest predictors of the workshop that the teachers did
attend were variables marking demographic distinctions between schools
and between teachers. Schools enrolling primarily impoverished student
populations were substantially less likely to have sent teachers to a student
curriculum workshop. White teachers were twice as likely as nonwhite
teachers to attend a student curriculum workshop. Second grade teachers,
for whom fewer replacement units were written, were less likely than average fifth grade teachers to go to a student curriculum workshop.

Teachers' opinions about the new standards and assessments, captured in
the variable "attitude toward reform," only weakly predict attendance at student curriculum workshops. Comparing two average white fifth grade
teachers in districts offering workshops, we found that the teacher who was
strictly neutral toward the standards had about a 48 percent probability of
going to a student curriculum workshop, whereas a very enthusiastic teacher
had a 61 percent probability of doing so. If there had been better information on the relative effectiveness of these workshops, it should have produced more of a difference in the percentages, as teachers who were more
enthusiastic would have been more likely to select the student curriculum
workshop.

Provision of framework-related workshops by the district improved the
odds that a teacher would attend a student curriculum workshop—a
teacher in a district offering a framework workshop was two and a half times
more likely to learn about student curriculum than a teacher in a district

Table 7.1. Influences on Teachers' Choice of Mathematics Professional Development

	Logistic regression parameter estimate (Standard error)	Odds ratio
Intercept	−2.00~ (1.03)	
Administrative support	.13 (.12)	1.13
District offered an opportunity to learn about the standards	.91** (.31)	2.48
Professional activities (NCTM, CMC, etc.)	.26 (.41)	1.29
Local policy	.46~ (.31)	1.59
California Mathematics Project	.44 (.34)	1.55
Attitude toward reform	.24~ (.15)	1.27
Teacher is white	.70* (.31)	2.01
Percentage of FLE students	−1.54** (.51)	.22
Teaches grade 2	−.95** (.37)	.39
Teaches grade 3	.22 (.34)	1.24
Teaches grade 4	.43 (.42)	1.53
N	358	

Note: This model predicts the likelihood that a teacher attended a student curriculum but not a special-topics workshop. Student curriculum workshop attendance = 271; special-topics attendance = 87. Estimated through logistic regression.
Log likelihood = −177.345; chi-square for covariates = 67.96.

~Indicates X^2 p < .15.
*Indicates X^2 p < .05.
**Indicates X^2 p < .01.
***Indicates X^2 p < .001.

without such an offering. Although this association appears striking, it is worth noting that influence of the district is roughly the same as that of teachers' race or the percentage of low-income students enrolled in a school. It is also worth noting that school-level support for the frameworks had no statistically discernible effect on the odds that a teacher would attend a student curriculum workshop. Teachers who reported that their schools were encouraging the framework were no more likely than others to attend the workshops that would aid framework implementation, and district provision of framework-related workshops improved those odds only modestly.

These results reflect the irrationality of decisions about professional development.[2] Teachers who wanted to improve instruction had developers' claims, colleagues' opinions, and their own interests, all of which can be valuable. But they could not support these with rigorous, independent evidence on the effects of various approaches.[3] Administrators and other leaders were in the same boat in that they lacked solid evidence to inform decisions. California state officials, education professionals, researchers, and reformers did nothing to remedy this knowledge drought.

Instructional Guidance

The incoherence described here was a major challenge to improving instruction. Teachers have grown accustomed to being bombarded by different and often contrary messages about teaching and learning and to receiving scant guidance from independent research. California teachers got conflicting messages from different and often contrary state and local tests, from curricula that often were unrelated to the tests, from state and federal programs (which often had different curriculum and assessment requirements), and from teacher education that was hardly related to any of these. This is no surprise, for American government was designed to frustrate central influence in domestic affairs; but it meant that local educators would be likely to see the math reform as just one more message—and attend to it accordingly.

State officials tried to solve that problem by making state guidance for instruction more coherent. They reasoned that strong and consistent messages about the methods and content of instruction would make clear what everyone needed to learn, teachers included. If everyone was on the same page, chances were better that they would learn. State policymakers tried to "align" state assessments of student performance and teaching through state-sponsored professional development, through state curriculum policy, and through state-mandated regulatory review.[4] Yet Sacramento is not California. State policymakers did not control many other local, regional, or nongovernmental influences on assessment, curriculum, and professional development.[5] Each district and county office had long operated as if it were nearly sovereign in these domains. In the decentralized and extensively privatized U.S. system, local and county districts, private publishers, professional organizations, and various interest groups have considerable influence, often much more than the state.

As a result, more coherent state guidance became less coherent as it played out in the complex array of agencies that we call the California school system. Most local and county districts, for example, offered professional development in mathematics, and many expanded these offerings as the reforms developed; expanding state action does not reduce local action (Cohen 1982; Spillane 1996; Porter, Floden and others 1986). Many localities also maintained or reintroduced basic skills testing, often the California Test of Basic Skills, and pressured teachers and administrators to bring about improvement on that measure (see Barnes 1997; Peterson 1990). Districts added a layer of instructional reform on top of existing practices, and many added a layer or two of conventional guidance on top of the less conventional reforms. In such situations, it is not uncommon for different local organizational subunits to broadcast conflicting messages and offer competing incentives to teachers (Cohen and Spillane 1993; Spillane 1998; Cohen, Spillane, Jennings, and Grant 1997). Some of these patterns are repeated in individual schools, whose staff were not mere recipients of policy but active agents who interpreted policy and created or limited opportunities and incentives for teachers to learn (Cohen and Spillane 1993; Cohen, Spillane, Jennings, and Grant 1997; Guthrie 1990).

Our discussion shows that to coordinate policy at the state level was not necessarily to coordinate it at lower levels. We considered teachers' reports of local policy instruments that they knew to exist, and we found both consistency and inconsistency. Four fifths of the teachers who reported that their district or school offered framework workshops also reported that printed frameworks were available. That pattern also held true for opportunities to learn about frameworks and replacement units: Table 7.2 shows that about four fifths of teachers reported that their district or school offered workshops related to the new framework and that replacement units were largely available for their use. That seems quite consistent, but there was inconsistency between other policy instruments. The existence of local framework workshops, for example, was only slightly related to opportunities to learn about the CLAS. Table 7.3 shows that three fifths of teachers who learned about the framework in a school or district workshop had no opportunity to learn about the CLAS. Since the CLAS was central to the reform, and a significant opportunity to learn, that could have been more troublesome than the lack of framework documents. If some policy instruments that had been made more consistent at the state level were employed fairly consistently in localities, others were much less consistent locally. To create coherence at the state level was not necessarily to create it elsewhere.

In fact, the closer we get to practice, the more pronounced the inconsistency. Table 7.4 reveals a moderately strong association between principals' knowledge of reform and schools' overall effort to change. Principals who were said to know more about reform worked in schools that were said to be doing more to put the reforms in place. We also considered teachers' reports of the relation between their own and their colleagues' views of the reforms, however, and Table 7.4 shows that it was weak: teachers who reported enthusiasm about the framework often reported that they worked in schools in which attitudes were quite different. Note the .00 correlation between teachers' reports of their own support for the framework and the efforts of others in their school.[6] Roughly a decade after the reforms began, there seemed to be no consistency within schools with regard to teachers' views about reform. The same pattern was repeated at the district level: schools that teachers described as enthusiastic about the framework were very often in districts that offered no opportunities to learn about such things (r = .51). Districts that were reported to offer opportunities to learn about the frameworks had teachers who did not take advantage of them, and some teachers who were enthusiastic about the framework reported that they went outside their districts to learn because they had no opportunities to do so within them.

The success of the California math reforms depended on many teachers' learning a great deal and adopting common ideas about mathematics, teaching, and learning. Reformers knew that and tried to make state instructional guidance more ambitious and coherent. Their efforts had some

Table 7.2. Local Framework Workshops and Availability of Replacement Units

	Replacement units not available	Replacement units available	Don't know	Total
District offered workshops	132	326	34	491*
	(22%)	(55%)	(6%)	(83%)
No district workshops	56	29	14	99
	(9%)	(5%)	(2%)	(17%)
Total	188	355	47	590
	(32%)	(60%)	(8%)	(100%)

*Totals not exact because of rounding.

Table 7.3. Local Framework Workshops and Opportunity to Learn About the CLAS

	CLAS opportunity to learn	No CLAS opportunity to learn	Total
District offered workshops	198	296	494
	(21%)	(50%)	(83%)
No district workshops	27	75	101
	(5%)	(13%)	(17%)
Total	224*	371	595
	(38%)	(62%)	(100%)

*Totals not exact because of rounding.

effect. In a few cases, teachers reported appreciable consistency between elements of their local opportunities to learn about the reforms. Given the organization of education in the state, these were remarkable accomplishments, but given the ambitions of the reforms, those remarkable accomplishments were only a beginning. If teachers saw moderate to strong consistency among a few elements of the state's instructional policy, they reported little or no consistency among others. As the state's revised guidance for instruction played out in California's nonsystem, it became fragmented. Inconsistency increased in the course of efforts to reduce it. One way to describe the system that encouraged such results is "loosely coupled," a term

Table 7.4. Teachers' Perceptions of Policy Coordination

	Principal	School effort	District effort	Teacher attitude toward reforms
The principal of this school is well-informed (about reform documents).	1.0	.61***	.36***	−.05
There is a schoolwide effort to achieve the kind of mathematics education promoted by (reform documents).		1.0	.51***	.00
Our district is providing extensive staff development based on (reform documents).			1.0	.01
How do you feel about the kind of mathematics education promoted by the new mathematics standards and assessments?				1.0

Note: Because of the high rate of "don't know" responses (see Table 3.9), these correlations have missing data ranging from between 9 and 33% of cases.

   ~Indicates $p < .15$.

    *Indicates $p < .05$.

  **Indicates $p < .01$.

***Indicates $p < .001$.

that organizational theorists use to describe weak connections and weak communication among organizations (Weick 1976). Teachers who work in such systems do not lack advice on instruction, for it comes at them from many different levels and sources, including state and local assessments, varied curricula, specialists in central offices and schools, their colleagues and supervisors, and many nongovernmental sources (Cohen and Spillane 1993). Much of the advice differs, some contradicts others, and most of it carries only modest authority. Reformers had made an impressive start on reducing those inconsistencies, but it was only a start.

Teachers' Autonomy and Opportunities to Learn

In the fragmented system that we have discussed, teachers have appreciable latitude to decide about instruction, their continuing education, and other matters. Fragmented authority and extensive conflict in guidance create room for teachers to exercise their judgment and pursue their preferences, for the conflicting advice tends to be self-neutralizing. Teachers can safely ignore or selectively attend to it, "closing the classroom door" and doing as they prefer. Moreover, systems that lack solid information on the effects of approaches to instruction probably further enhance teachers' autonomy, even though the lack of knowledge limits their effectiveness. Informal autonomy has become a very significant feature of teachers' professionalism in the United States. To be independent, to cultivate their own "style," and to disregard official guidance all figure prominently in teachers' professional norms. This attitude may compensate for teachers' lack of great formal authority and professional status, especially in a nation of individualists. In any event, teachers' autonomy has tended to set limitations on the implementation of policy. Until very recently, getting teachers to act in concert, to collaborate closely, and to coordinate instruction was thought to be impossible, perhaps even beyond the purview of official action. A common result of such attempts was to elicit still greater variation in teachers' response to policy, as they ignored a good deal and attended selectively to the rest (Porter and others 1986).

Professional development decisions. Decisions about teachers' continuing education are one case in point. If teachers' informal autonomy did give them considerable influence in choosing workshops or other learning opportunities, we would expect them to have weighed official influences only modestly in those decisions. Evidence from the survey bears out that expectation. In Table 7.5 we report that teachers' view of administrators' support for the new standards[7] had little influence on whether they had attended a framework-related workshop within the past year. District provision of such workshops was more influential, improving fourfold the odds that a teacher would have attended a workshop related to the framework within the past year.[8] Since districts provide and approve a large percentage of all professional development, it would be amazing if teachers' decisions did not show such an effect. It seems likely that this reflects whether workshops were provided or not, rather than the influence of higher-ups' preferences on teachers' decisions. This point is underscored when we see that teachers' experience with a professional activity like involvement in the California Mathematics Project was a better predictor of their attendance at a student curriculum or special-topics workshop within the past year than was district provision of workshops or an administrator's support for the framework. The same reasoning holds for the professional-development decisions teachers made, given that they had chosen to engage in a mathematics workshop in the past year. Recall that in Table 7.1 neither school nor district support for the frameworks, nor furnishing framework-related opportunities to learn, had substantial influence on the odds that teachers would take a student curriculum workshop over other workshops only generally associated with the reforms. Even teachers' reports of school leaders' enthusiasm about the framework had a modest influence on teachers' decisions about workshops. All this evidence supports the view that California teachers' decisions about their continuing education were only loosely affected by local priorities.

These analyses lead us to expect that the most significant influences on teachers' participation in professional development would be personal experience and preferences. The survey bears that out. Table 7.5 shows that one relatively strong predictor of teachers' participation in any kind of workshop was their involvement in a professional activity or the California Math Project. If state policy successfully made workshops available to resourceful teachers, those teachers' decisions to enroll occurred for reasons little related to school or district priorities. Access to and interest in mathematics, rather than local priorities, seemed to shape teachers' decisions about opportunities to learn.

To say that teachers' choices mattered as much as official preferences is not to say that teachers willfully enrolled in workshops meant to match their preexisting ideas about the framework, or even their ideas about how they might want to change in the future. As shown in Table 7.5, teachers' attitude toward reform did not necessarily jibe with their decision to attend a workshop. Additionally, the measure of teachers' attitude toward reform was just slightly above conventional significance levels in Table 7.1 and therefore carries only about two thirds the accuracy of measures of teachers' reported grade level or ethnicity. Though the changes teachers did make in their classroom appeared to rest on some combination of will and learning, there is little evidence these preferences shaped teachers' selection into workshops.

**Table 7.5. Influences on Teachers' Decisions to
Enroll in Mathematics Professional Development**

	Parameter estimate (standard error)	Odds ratio
Intercept	−4.76***	
	(1.24)	
Administrative support	.04	
	(.10)	1.03
District offered an opportunity to learn about the standards	1.47***	
	(.23)	4.34
Professional activities	2.53***	
	(.70)	12.55
Local policy	.57~	
	(.35)	1.76
California Mathematics Project	1.64	
	(.74)	5.17
Attitude toward reform	.11	
	(.12)	1.12
Teacher is white	−.63*	
	(.29)	.53
Percentage FLE students	−.09	
	(.41)	.92
Teaches grade 2	−.49~	
	(.30)	.61
Teaches grade 3	−.40	
	(.31)	.67
Teaches grade 4	−.82*	
	(.32)	.44
N	523	

Note: This table predicts teachers' attendance at a mathematics-related workshop in the year before the survey. By teacher reports, 358 teachers attended mathematics workshops in the year before the survey; 165 did not.
Log likelihood: −59.203.
~Indicates $p < .15$.
*Indicates $p < .05$.
**Indicates $p < .01$.
***Indicates $p < .001$.

Race and class differences. In a much less unequal world, students' social and economic class, and teachers' race, might not influence teachers' decisions about whether to invest in professional development, or what kind of learning to seek. In certain respects that expectation holds: Table 7.5 shows that teachers of children of low socioeconomic status (SES) were no less likely to report professional learning in mathematics than others within the same year, and teachers of color might have received slightly more professional development in mathematics. Still, there were differences. Teachers who were not white or who taught lower-income students were slightly more likely to enroll in special-topics workshops than in student curriculum workshops. Table 7.1 shows that, all else being equal, a white teacher was about twice as likely to attend a student curriculum workshop as a nonwhite teacher. This table also shows that teachers of low-SES students were less likely to attend a student curriculum workshop than their peers who taught high-SES students. Other analyses show that schools attended by students from economically advantaged families were slightly more likely to use replacement units than teachers in schools attended by students from less advantaged families.[9]

In short, teachers with more effective opportunities to learn worked in slightly better schools. One explanation could be the voluntarism that we discussed above: because workshops like EQUALS often focused on equity issues, and because those who cared about such issues tended to work in disadvantaged schools or to be minority teachers themselves or both, teachers' decisions may have stratified their learning. If so, reformers and educators have cause for concern. Workshops on equity may help teachers, for there are important things to learn about students' culture, language, and behavior. Yet teachers do not have endless time for professional development: a seminar on cooperative grouping could be one of a very few opportunities that many have to learn for a year. If that workshop did not deal with central subject matter, it would be less likely to improve students' learning. Disadvantaged students could be more disadvantaged by efforts to combat inequality if those efforts did not have an academic focus.

We have explained teachers' missed opportunities for substantial professional learning in terms of structural factors like fragmentation within the system, weak knowledge of effectiveness in markets for professional development, and the ensuing limitations on teachers' opportunities to learn. Additionally, teachers' own experience and preferences made a large contribution to missed opportunities, because the nonsystem left extensive room for choices based on experience and preferences. Those preferences took shape in an environment that included limited availability of replacement-unit workshops, fragmented and often contrary guidance for teaching, and weak knowledge about the effects of professional development. The norm of privacy allowed teachers to give little weight to local priorities, if they existed, and to interpret state priorities idiosyncratically or ignore them completely. The same norm seems to have encouraged nonstrategic decisions for the teachers of poor and minority students and enabled social and economic inequality to limit their access to opportunities to learn based on subject matter.

Individual and structural influences interact. The norm of autonomy is especially corrosive in the United States, where system fragmentation, weak knowledge of effectiveness, and limited opportunities to learn leave teachers with little consistent and constructive guidance. The same autonomy in much better-informed and coherent systems would almost surely yield more informed and productive decisions by teachers. If so, merely reducing autonomy—as opposed to greatly improving knowledge of effectiveness, opportunities to learn, and constructive guidance—would be unproductive.

Instruction Within Schools

Our analysis implies that state policy would pan out very unevenly. The combination of great variation in the way the policy reaches schools, other educational agencies, and providers of professional development on the one hand with the plethora of mixed messages, a professional norm of privacy, and a pervasive voluntarist stance toward interventions on the other all encourage variation in responses to the policy. Part of that variation stems from what providers of professional development notice and how they respond, as well as what catches teachers' attention in providers' offerings and how they decide among them.

This variation could have taken different forms. Schools could have taken advantage of the opportunities that fragmentation offered to exert influence on how teachers responded. Teachers and administrators in each school could have conferred about math instruction generally and the policy in

particular. They could have discussed their ideas, tried out classroom procedures, reported back, and settled on ways to teach math that suited them. If
they had done that, we would expect teachers' reports of their work to be relatively homogeneous within schools. Differences in instructional approaches
and responses to the policy would be linked to the places where teachers
were working, owing to the influence of school-level decision making.

Alternatively, schools might have done few or none of these things and
had little influence on how instruction turned out. Administrators could
have let each teacher fashion her own approach to instruction and state policy. Teachers and administrators would have conferred little or not at all
about the policy. They would not have discussed their responses to it, nor
would they have tried out classroom procedures, reported back, or settled
on a way of teaching math that suited them all. They would instead have
tried things out behind their classroom doors and would not have taken
each other's ideas and practices into account seriously. In this case, teachers'
reports of their professional learning or their work would vary a good deal
within schools. Differences among teachers in each school would tend to be
a microcosm of those in the entire teaching force, because the school would
not be a significant influence on instruction or instructional policy.

We dwell on this because teachers are crucial to the implementation of
instructional policy, as are school leaders, yet the nature of their influence
and its effects would differ radically in the two cases. We investigated which
of these models was closest to the truth, because the answer would reveal a
great deal about the extent of teachers' autonomy and the schools' role in
implementing instructional policy. We focused on teachers' reports of their
teaching, because we had relatively good evidence on that. Table 7.6 reports
the percentage of total variation in teachers' reports about instruction between schools, rather than between individuals within schools.[10] In the survey, we focused especially on reports of mathematics-related beliefs and
practices. The table's most remarkable feature is that only a modest percentage of the differences in those beliefs and practices—in the neighborhood of 15 percent—can be traced to the influence of school cultures or
conditions on teachers' work. Most of the variance in instructional beliefs
and practices we measured occurred from teacher to teacher within schools.
In other words, we picked up almost as much variation in instructional
practices, as teachers reported them, within schools as between them.
Teachers' instructional techniques were only slightly more likely to be sim-

Table 7.6. Variation Between Schools

	Variance between schools
Framework ideas	7%*
Conventional ideas	11%*
Framework practices	8.6%*
Conventional practices	21%**
Mathematics conditions	15%**
Norms of collaboration	19%**
Administrative support	31%**
School conditions	46%**

*T_{00} is significantly different from zero at $p < .05$.
**T_{00} is significantly different from zero at $p < .01$.

Table 7.7. Teachers' Reports of Mathematics Conditions in Their School

Q: Now consider conditions of mathematics teaching. How well does each of the following statements describe conditions in your school?

	Strongly disagree				Strongly agree
I feel supported by other teachers to try out new ideas in teaching mathematics.	3.8	8.6	26.8	26.8	34.0
The school administration promotes innovations in mathematics education.	6.2	11.6	24.0	29.7	28.5
Teachers in this school regularly share ideas about mathematics instruction.	8.2	28.4	29.2	22.6	11.7
I work regularly with other teachers on mathematics curriculum and instruction.	20.8	34.0	23.7	13.9	7.6

ilar to those of someone across the hall than they were to resemble those of someone they knew not at all, hundreds of miles away. Schools exerted only a modest influence over the instructional practices reported in this table; or, better, schools exerted their influence by not exerting it, by leaving teachers to decide.

Teachers' reports on collegiality fit this picture. Professions of collegial support were common: in Table 7.7, when asked if they felt "supported by other teachers to try out new ideas in teaching mathematics," teachers reported generous support. Yet only one in five reported, "I work regularly with other teachers on mathematics curriculum and instruction." Only about one third reported that "Teachers . . . regularly share ideas about mathematics instruction." The closer one gets to practice, the more influential privacy seems and the less collegiality is reported. California elementary schools seemed to have been extremely weak professional communities, at least when it came to math instruction.

A look back at Table 7.6 suggests that there also was little agreement within schools about collegiality and norms. When consolidated into one variable named "mathematics conditions," the items in Table 7.7 show that few teachers agreed about the environment within their own school. Only about 15 percent of the variance was between schools, the remainder resting between individuals within schools. A related variable, "norms of collaboration" (see Table 3.11), shows only a little more agreement between teachers. Only "administrative support" (see Table 3.9), a measure of teachers' perceptions about support from the principal and the school for the frameworks, does a bit better.

Professional individualism was not ironclad, however. Teachers' assessments of noninstructional matters ("school conditions" in Table 7.6) were much more similar within schools than were their reports on instruction. Teachers within a school, in other words, were much more likely to agree about such things as levels of parent support for instruction and student turnover than they were about instruction or norms of collaboration. Agreement among teachers within schools was entirely possible. This finding only highlights the lack of consistency among teachers in instructional matters. Teachers did not live entirely isolated, each under a bell jar. Their isolation was specific to math instruction. This shows how significant a role the norm of privacy played in instruction.

Our analysis implies that professionalism itself must be taken very seriously in efforts to explore how instructional policy pans out. For in the United States, professionalism means instructional individualism, and this affects how teachers apprehend and respond to external initiatives. From undergraduate education through professional service, teachers are encouraged to develop their own "style" and are told that such individuality is creative and constructive (Buchman 1993). Style covers work with students, content, classroom management, and a range of other matters. If a teacher's "style" does not include revised mathematics instruction, professional norms sanction the exclusion.

Instructional disagreements among teachers within schools are also important because they are likely to limit students' opportunities to learn by encouraging disagreements among teachers about how much or how well students could learn. They reduce the probability that instruction can be coordinated, for when teachers go their own ways, students' academic experience is more likely to be fragmented, either through the luck of the draw in teacher assignment within grades or as students pass from grade to grade. That lack of coordination, in turn, decreases the probability that students' academic experiences will be consistent, in the sense that Johnny's work with Mrs. Smith in second grade is of similar quality to Jimmy's work with Mr. Sanchez in the same grade. It also decreases the probability that students' academic experiences will be cumulative, in the sense that Jane's work with Mrs. Chang in grade four will build on her work with Mrs. Black in grade three. Both sorts of inconsistency can seriously disadvantage students. Professional individualism also inhibits teachers' learning. There is more to be learned from others, and to be gained from working with them, than most can learn from work alone. Coherent professional cultures are probably necessary to instructional coordination, and growing evidence indicates that professional community is a significant influence both on teachers' effectiveness as practitioners and on their students' performance (McLaughlin and Talbert 1993; Newmann and Wehlage 1995; Bryk, Lee, and Holland 1993; Perry 1996).[11]

When California reformers in the 1980s called for a significant departure from conventional mathematics instruction, it soon became clear that success would require a substantial improvement in teachers' knowledge of mathematics, of student learning, and of instruction. Policymakers and their professional allies designed instruments that would enable teachers to learn such things. They created new student curricula, stimulated workshops on those materials, and turned elements of CLAS into workshops for some teachers. They also tried to devise the instruments to be consistent with each other, as a way of reducing inconsistencies in instructional guidance. The resulting array of state policy instruments would be remarkable both for their sophistication and for their consistency.

These and other instruments of the policy had to operate within the existing system of school organization and governance, however, if they were to operate at all. That limitation frequently attenuated the instruments' quality and coherence. One of the key links in the chain connecting state policy to classroom practice was teachers' opportunities to learn; professional development, the activity that formally regulates those opportunities, is not centrally administered but occurs in the state and local markets where teachers, schools, administrators, and professional developers interact about the content of teachers' opportunities to learn. Weak evidence about the effectiveness of that content meant teachers and schools chose programs without regard to which experiences would improve student learning. Furthermore, teacher voluntarism and decentralized governance meant the reforms filtered unevenly through schools.

If we consider this matter in historical perspective, comparing state policymakers' efforts with previous state endeavors, we would say that the policy and its innovative instruments succeeded grandly. State policymakers did achieve a good deal of coherence among the policy instruments they could directly manipulate, they did frame an innovative and ambitious approach to mathematics teaching, and their efforts did influence some localities. If, however, we consider what might have been required to put the state policy into place across the board, policymakers and professionals had only begun. Ten years after the reforms began, changes in classroom practice occurred less in response to the priorities of school leaders, colleagues, the state, or districts than to complex interactions between teachers' choices and externally supplied opportunities to learn. Professional learning formed the crucial connective tissue between the elements of California's instructional policy, but teachers' decisions were a central determinant of their opportunities to learn, and those decisions, though not made on the basis of evidence, played a much larger role than official priorities. The norm of autonomy, so central to teachers' view of their role, significantly shaped their responses to the math reforms and made it difficult for state instructional policy to influence, in any consistent or influential way, teachers' decisions about what or how to teach. It seems to have been equally difficult for school and district leaders to exert such influence.

Broad implementation of state policy would have required more than California policymakers and their professional allies were able to do. It would, for example, have required making available to educators information about the relative quality of professional-development opportunities.

Instead of letting teachers' impressions of how workshops would "help on Monday morning" flow through informal networks, policymakers and professionals would have had to evaluate rigorously the effects workshops had on teaching and student learning. Findings from this research would have to have been validated and used in extensive professional education as part of efforts to improve the system. The education system in California had neither of these capabilities, however, and reform-centered curricula and professional development were absorbed into the extant system of weak information and underinformed choice. State education leaders were able to make professional learning a critical avenue for promoting the reforms in a significant minority of cases, but they had few of the tools needed to make far-reaching improvements in the content of that professional development or to encourage teachers and decision makers to make more rational choices about their participation.

We noted near the outset of this chapter that innovation presents a paradox: reformers must work within the existing system in order to get a hearing for their proposals and encourage their adoption, but that system can pose a potent threat to innovations that stray far from conventional practice. If reformers were to succeed, they would have to somehow work within the organizations and practices they proposed to change, by enabling extensive change but not triggering rejection or marginalization.

One reasonable inference is that the success of ambitious instructional policies depends on much more than hopeful visions of better teaching and learning. Success would require an array of richly developed initiatives: usable instruments for teachers, other professionals, and students; materials that incarnate the vision; suitable opportunities to learn in and from the materials; assessments that reflect them; better information about the effectiveness of different initiatives. The mixed messages in the environment and perverse incentives in the system would have to be ironed out, and school cultures would have to change if they were to support communities of teachers working to improve instruction.

Another inference that can be drawn from our account is that for instruction to improve, teachers must have the will to make it improve. Changing professional norms will be essential to reform. Some change programs now attempt to do so by requiring teachers to decide explicitly whether to elect instructional reform before the change program will be made available. Information systems and cultures within schools are created to encourage the will to improve. Some efforts are aimed at building professional communities within schools by urging teachers to focus on students' work and learning and on how teaching can improve them. Most California districts and schools dealt with the problem much more passively, by offering teachers lists of professional development from which to choose. They could have limited the entries on the list, but no agency even came close to setting standards for professional learning that would have restricted teachers' autonomy. Instead, they left the driving to the teachers. That made a certain sense in the professional and political contexts of U.S. schools, but it did not advance improvement in most classrooms.

Still another inference is that much more thoughtful and determined leadership would be required at the school level. Several researchers and professionals have argued that without such leadership, instruction becomes invisible within schools, and opportunities to improve quality and consistency are lost (Newmann and Wehlage 1995). Teachers have no chance to develop professionally, and students' learning often suffers. Leaving nearly all classroom issues to teachers' discretion has long been typical in U.S. schools. A few policymakers and reformers have tried to remedy this problem, but most administrators know little about teaching and learning, and teachers' norms are especially difficult to change when the profession makes change a matter of individual preference. If the evidence we have presented is at all typical, efforts to improve teaching and learning on a large scale still have a long way to go.

Chapter 8

POLICY AND LEARNING

Research has not been a source of great hope about policymakers' efforts to improve schools. Most studies report failures of implementation and insubstantial effects on classroom practice. This study departs from that pattern, for we found significant positive effects of California's effort to improve mathematics teaching and learning. Those effects did not occur across the board, though. The policy had a range of influences on classrooms, depending on the ways in which it was mediated by arrangements that professionals created. In order to understand the influences, we had to distinguish those arrangements.

Two things enabled us to do that. One was that we built a rough model of the conditions that, given the nature of the policy and the practices it sought to affect, would probably be required in order to influence practice. To build that model, we had to treat policy implementation as though it were a rational enterprise, and specify what it would take to change teaching and learning. One of us (Cohen) began studies with colleagues more than a decade ago that generated some of the hypotheses on which the current work has built. Those hypotheses furnished the basis for a rough model of policy implementation, which enabled the MSU research team to design a survey and collect data that later allowed the two of us to distinguish between the conditions that were likely to produce success and those which were not. Having that work and the survey data in hand enabled us to further specify the model and use the survey evidence to test the model's usefulness.

This set-up contrasts with many other evaluations of education policies and programs that have treated policy implementation more like a black box than like a range of differentiated processes. Rather than modeling implementation and distinguishing conditions that were likely to produce success from those which were not, previous analysts have asked whether the policy as a whole had its intended effect. Such studies shed little light on the conditions that afford success or lead to failure. Misunderstanding can arise when a package of very different processes is treated as though it were a single entity.

The second reason that we were able to differentiate between the conditions for success and those for failure was that some California policymakers and professionals deliberately tried to create conditions that, at least in some cases, would enable success. They had no formal model to follow, but they did have strategic ideas about how to improve instruction. Their efforts meant that there was more variety in how this instructional policy was implemented than often seems to have been the case. Not only were the policy instruments more coherent than usual, but some teachers had extended opportunities, grounded in practice, to learn about the proposed changes in teaching and learning. Many education policies and programs have been crudely framed and reflect little or no effort to build on research or professional knowledge about the conditions that are likely to lead to success. In this case, some policymakers and some professionals acted somewhat more rationally and produced a greater range of policy activity than often has been the case.

Those conditions created an opportunity for professionals and researchers to learn. We found that this instructional policy influenced practice under three conditions. One was that policy and its instruments provided opportunities for teachers to learn what policy implied for their practice. Teachers had all sorts of opportunities to learn, in a sprawling and unfocused system of professional development; but only those who learned from concrete, content-specific, and instructionally usable instruments of policy, and who spent at least a modest amount of time at it, reported the sorts of practice that we associated with significant departures from conventional math teaching. Teachers whose learning was not focused in those ways or who spent only small amounts of time learned only small scraps and made slight changes in classroom practice. Substantial professional learning is a key element in the implementation of instructional policy. It is not the only such agent, but both logic and evidence suggest that it is a necessary condition for any improvements in practice that depart appreciably from conventional classroom work. If policymakers or professional organizations propose seriously to improve teaching and learning but cannot create opportunities for teachers to learn how to improve, their proposals are unlikely to produce the desired improvements.

A second crucial condition, if instructional policy is to influence practice, is substantive coherence among the instruments of instructional policy. Reformers and professionals also created unusual coherence among the instruments of instructional guidance and among more direct influences on teachers' practice. Reformers fostered congruence between student curriculum and some teachers' opportunities to learn by grounding professional development in the replacement units. Coherence between the revised state assessments and some teachers' opportunities to learn was created because professional development was grounded in the teachers' study of the revised state math assessment. Coherence between teaching and learning was achieved by encouraging the teachers who graded the CLAS to study students' work on the assessment, and by encouraging teachers who studied the replacement units to consider how learners might approach the work in those units. Hence, a coherent association existed not only with regard to the purposes of policy, the state assessment, and state curriculum frameworks but also, closer to the classroom, among assessment, curriculum, and teachers' opportunities to learn; between state guidance and student curriculum; between assessment and teachers' knowledge of how students might approach the assessment; and between the student curriculum and teachers' knowledge of how students might approach that curriculum.

Many other states have tried to "align" assessments, curriculum frameworks, and, in a few cases, other instruments of education policy. Most of these efforts, however, have remained at the state level, and, as a result, important elements have been missing. Few states tried to develop or identify student curriculum that was consistent with state assessments and curriculum frameworks. Moreover, the day-to-day materials with which teachers and students work have not been an instrument of policy, were not included in efforts to ensure that those instruments worked coherently together, and were often at odds with state policy instruments (Neufeld 1996; Neufeld, Fickel, and Bennett 1998; Neufeld and Boothby 1999; Massell and Goertz 1999). That is a crippling problem, for coherence at the level of state guidance is only the first of many steps that could lead to coherence among the instruments and agents of instruction. Additionally, few states have invested much in using any instruments of instructional policy as a basis for professional learning (Neufeld 1996; Neufeld, Fickel, and Bennett 1998; Neufeld and Boothby 1999; Massell and Goertz 1999). The evidence from this study, when taken together with other research on standards-based reform, strongly suggests that coherence in instructional policy is unlikely to pay off handsomely for teaching and learning unless it is manifest both in the materials of instruction—especially assessment and curriculum—and in the curriculum for professionals' learning.

Rich opportunities to learn in and from policy of the sort we found in California are rare and difficult to organize, for they cut against the grain both of educational politics and of the industries that bear on schools. Because states and even districts have been unwilling to mandate curriculum, it has been difficult to ground professional development in the student curriculum. Teacher education programs prepare recruits in methods of teaching, but not in teaching a specific curriculum that their students will study. Textbook publishers may provide some introduction to their materials, but most such work has been shallow and short. The same is true of commercial assessments; teachers have few opportunities to learn from them. Professional development, which, by any reasonable standard should focus on improving teaching that will improve learning, does so rarely. These and other circumstances have inhibited the sorts of opportunities to learn that can pay off for teachers and students.

Creating more constructive conditions in California was not easy. In order to produce the effects that we observed, some professionals and professional organizations had to mobilize temporary communities to develop policy instruments and otherwise support change in practice. These efforts —a third requisite condition for policy to significantly influence practice— were unusual, often imaginative, and cut across conventional educational lines. They required considerable effort, and some risk-taking. These innovative features of the California reforms, though essential to them, were modest in scope. The student curriculum and CLAS workshops were significant departures from past practice and dramatic innovations, but they also were islands in a much larger and inhospitable sea. They reached only a minority of teachers, they dealt with only a few of the topics in the elementary math curriculum (in which, even at that, depth was lacking), they included modest follow-up at best in the classroom, and they dealt with only a small fraction of students' work.

Such conditions were briefly created in some sectors of the California math reforms, with relatively modest resources. Similar conditions could be created elsewhere. As we wrote near the outset, we suppose that these conditions would hold for any ambitious effort to improve teaching and learning, whether it aimed at the sort of ideas associated with the California math reforms or those associated with more traditional views of academic work. We hope that our research will encourage others to improve instructional policies and research on them. Such improvements would entail several different challenges.

One is the coordination of government and professional action. State government played a key role in the California math reforms, but private professional organizations were no less critical. The reform policy was inspired by professional ideas, supported politically by professional organizations, and advanced by professional activities, while policy enabled professional action for reform. When the reforms worked, it was because professionals and professional organizations had devised curriculum and professional development that fleshed out the state policy instructionally. Private professionals and professional organizations built an instructional infrastructure around the state's sketchy policy and skimpy resources. Improving instructional policy will require more substantial and artful coordination between private professionals, government, and professional organizations.

A second challenge is learning from efforts to improve instruction. Policymakers and reformers in California were not well informed about the effects of their endeavors; they made no attempt to learn systematically about how the reforms played out in schools and classrooms. As a result, they had no evidence to inform either their work or public debate, and when skeptics charged that the reforms were diluting instruction in basic math skills, state officials and professionals had no basis on which to investigate or respond. Our survey revealed no empirical support for the charges: even teachers who learned a great deal with the revised CLAS or replacement units still reported that their math teaching included frequent work with basic skills. Yet with systematic evidence almost completely lacking, even inaccurate ideas, repeated frequently, had weight and effect.

Creating better professional development and better knowledge about it is a third challenge. Professional development is an expensive undertaking, but little of it is calculated seriously to improve teaching or learning. As our survey data showed, little did. Only ineffectual efforts have been made to learn from experience in professional education. Most evaluations have been parochial in outlook and method, focusing at best on one project, narrowly defined, over a short time. Few studies relate professional learning to student achievement (Kennedy 1998). That so much professional development has gone on, with so little attention to seriously improving teaching and learning, is professionally indefensible.

States and professional organizations could sponsor and stimulate research to improve the design and execution of professional development: they have room for nothing but improvement. Standards-based reform has helped to build part of the base for such work in some states that have somewhat broader assessments and more highly developed state curriculum frameworks. There is a growing sense that better professional education will be a key to school improvement, yet the capacity to design or deliver better education to working professionals, or to conduct useful research on it, appears to be modest at best.

Progress on this front would require participation and support from professionals and researchers. Yet when we have made the suggestions above at a few meetings of education researchers and practitioners, colleagues have often objected, saying that such research would be tantamount to experimenting on teachers or children. We can imagine experiments that would shed a good deal of light on the sorts of teaching that improve learning and the sorts of professional development that would improve teaching. Carefully conducted experiments, along with other research, could usefully inform decisions about teaching and teachers' professional development, and doing such work well would be professionally more responsible than not doing it or doing it badly.

If our experience is representative, however, many researchers and professionals disagree. They do not seem troubled that education reformers often proceed as if their ideas about best practices had been handed down from some higher power and were inarguably correct. Many of the math reformers, in California and elsewhere, proceeded that way. Many of the colleagues who objected to our proposals for more evidence-based professional practice in education do not seem to think it odd to endorse and work for all sorts of educational reforms, most of which have little or no basis in evidence. Such reforms are experiments, even when they are grounded in much more research than was the case in California, and even though they rarely are called experiments. Failing to collect data does not make them any less experimental: they are experiments on teachers and other peoples' children. Few follow on systematic inquiry, and few include such inquiry as part of design, development, and implementation.

There is good reason to believe that better research could help improve teaching and learning, if it was designed to do that. Some already has helped, and more could yield still better results. Independent applied research should be a more regular feature of education policy and practice. Such work could contribute to efforts to improve instruction and to understanding improvement. Research of this sort could not determine decisions, but it can inform understanding, debate, and, in some cases, decisions. Another reason is ethical, or professional: in a democracy, the public deserves to know how efforts to change the schools affect teaching, learning, and children's well-being.

If educators do not do such work in a professionally responsible manner, sooner or later the reformers, their ideas, and perhaps their professionalism will be discredited. If research on teacher learning and professional development does not improve in these ways, pressure either to radically reframe or to do away with professional development will undoubtedly mount, precisely because it has been so ineffective and professionally unaccountable. Lacking better research in education, scholars from other disciplines will move in as they have already begun to do in early reading and a few other domains.

Near the beginning of this book we noted that education researchers often see a great gulf between educational policies and classroom practice. One researcher compared policies to storms on the oceans' surface, and practice to the calm beneath. We have offered a way both to understand that gulf and to reduce it. Whether the gap between instructional policy and classroom practice can be closed depends in good part on whether communications structures and knowledge to link the two can be built. The gulf between policy and practice has been created by politics, policy design, and professionalism, and they can remedy it.

Appendixes

Appendix A

One question about these findings is whether we can generalize them to the population of California teachers. Although the survey was designed so that, when weighted correctly, the sample would be representative of the state's population of second through fifth grade teachers, teacher nonresponse might impair this result. Those who responded might have felt more strongly about the reforms than those who did not or been more aware of what reform entailed. To assess that possibility, the authors of the survey compared data from the 559 teachers who responded to the questionnaire during the normal time frame, and the 185 teachers who responded either to the short-form survey or to the intensive follow-up explained in the opening of Chapter Three. Differences were noted along several dimensions:[1]

Demographics of teachers and students. Though teachers in the regular and short-form/intensive groups did not differ significantly in age, sex, or race, teachers who responded later (hereafter "late responders") did report more than a year's additional teaching experience (14.24 as opposed to 13.08 years, p = .09) than early responders. Late responders also reported having a higher percentage of LEP students in their classroom (32 percent as opposed to 27 percent, p = .06), and reported that more of their students were classified as Chapter 1 (45.6 percent as opposed to 39.8 percent, p = .06).

Staff development and professional activities. The regular and late responders did not differ in the rate of participation in any of the following mathematics workshops: attending a national meeting of mathematics teachers, attending state or regional meetings, teaching in-service workshops, serving on district committees, or participating in the California Mathematics Project. Teachers in the regular group were a bit more likely to report that they had not had in-service training within the past year (16.9 percent as opposed to 10.9 percent for late responders) but were also more likely to report completing thirty-five hours or more (8 percent as opposed to 2.7 percent).

Appendix B

Survey research cannot compare with classroom observation as a technique for investigating the subtleties of practice; however, properly sampled surveys allow estimates of practices within large populations of teachers—and also allow an estimation of the bias that occurs when some individuals are reluctant to participate in studies. Further, recent research into the validity of surveys like ours shows that on average, teachers' self-placement in relation to others agrees with outside observers' ranking of them. We shall discuss each issue—estimating nonresponse bias and the validity of survey measures like those used here.

Generalizability and bias. One question concerns the extent to which the results from our items on belief and practice could be generalized to the population of California teachers in 1995. Although the survey was designed to estimate the population values for various indicators, teacher nonresponse is a threat to the validity of these figures: those who responded to the survey might have had more favorable views of framework ideas or practices at the outset. To assess the possibility that this occurred, we compared data from the 559 teachers who responded to the questionnaire during the original response period, and the 185 teachers who either responded to the short-form explained in Appendix A or responded to intensive efforts to ensure completion of the long form. Differences between original and late responders were noted along several dimensions:[2]

Ideas about mathematics learning. Late responders reported stronger agreement than regular respondents with two statements concerning basic skills (out of three possible statements on basic skills), and averaged less agreement than original responders to the general statement about the reforms:

Table B.1. Differences Between Original and Late Responders' Ideas

	Mean of early responders	Mean of late responders	P-value
1. Students need to master basic computational facts and skills before they can engage effectively in mathematical problem solving.	3.04	3.42	.001
2. If elementary students use calculators, they won't learn the mathematics they need to know.	1.96	2.26	.002
3. How do you feel about the kind of mathematics education promoted by the new mathematics standards and assessments?	3.97	2.66	.001

The two groups' responses to four other items relating to ideas—including three that relating to "reform" ideas—were not significantly different.[3]

Teaching practices. We found no differences in use of any of the eight teaching practices included on both the long and short forms. These items included having students discuss problems, practice taking tests on computational skills, work in small groups on math problems, work individually on math problems from a text, work on individual or group projects over several days, write about how to solve a problem in an assignment, and do problems that have more than one correct solution.

Taken as a whole, the results of investigation into bias suggest that late responders and nonresponders to this survey are inclined to hold stronger beliefs in the necessity for student mastery of basic skills, perhaps disliking the reforms as a whole because of their deemphasis of these skills. These teachers were not, however, less likely to approve of reform-related ideas and practices than others.

Validity of self reports on practice. Some work has been done to investigate whether teachers' self-reports are reliable and valid measures of instructional practices. Burstein et al. (1995), for instance, compared high school math teachers' survey reports of instructional strategies with those reported in daily logs. The authors conclude that teacher surveys are likely to be a valid representation of the instructional techniques used but are valid because teachers in the study reported little variation in those techniques.

In his study of the relation between teachers' implementation of NCTM-aligned teaching methods and students' achievement in algebra, Daniel Mayer determined, using the following survey items, the percentage of time a given algebra teacher spent using NCTM methods: [students] listen to lectures; work from a textbook; take computational tests, practice computational skills; use calculators; work in small groups; use manipulatives; make conjectures; engage in teacher-led discussion; engage in student-led discussion; work on group investigations; write about problems; solve problems with more than one correct answer; work on individual projects; explain problems orally; use computers; discuss different ways to solve problems.

Although the teachers under study taught middle or high school, the items on the survey overlap substantially with the items affecting practice in our Table 4.4—hardly surprising, for Mayer culled items from a common pool used by many researchers on practice. Mayer determined the reliability of the instrument by administering the same survey to twenty teachers after a four-month lapse; the correlation between the first and second NCTM composite measures was .69.

Mayer investigated the validity of the survey items by observing nine teachers randomly selected from a sample stratified by their NCTM scale score (low, middle, high). After three observations of each teacher, he found observed and self-reported scores to be correlated at .85. Though most teachers tended to overreport their implementation of NCTM methods, their relative ranking was consistent with that made by an outsider.

A problem became evident during these observations, one that stems from teachers' lack of a common language to describe practice. Mayer illustrates the problem by comparing two teachers who both reported frequently requesting that students "orally explain how to solve a problem." One teacher asked students quite generic questions ("What answers did you get for number 5 $[-27x + -18 =]$?" Mayer 1997, 83) and seldom probed beneath the surface for evidence of student thinking or understanding. The other, according to Mayer, "insisted that students articulate each step of the problem and listened carefully to the explanation. Often he interjected, 'Please illustrate that more clearly?' or 'Why did you do that?'" (Mayer 1997, 83–84). So although both teachers considered themselves to be implementing the NCTM framework because they asked students to explain problems orally, the manner in which they did so was quite different.

Although Mayer's items relating to practice and his scale differ from ours, the extent of the overlap suggests that the reliability and validity of any measure constructed from the items in Table 4.4 might be comparable. This conjecture would imply that although they may have inflated practice reports, our own teachers' relative placement on a scale composed of our practice items will prove close enough to their "true" position that this measure can be used for multivariate analysis. Yet two caveats apply: these were for the most part high school teachers; and Mayer's study included only one district, where all teachers attended the same workshop on NCTM teaching practices offered jointly by the district and the College Board. Similarity in teachers' professional development might increase the consistency in teachers' reports over time and decrease the variability among teachers with regard to the definition of items like "students conjecture."

Appendix C

We conducted a check for the linearity of the independent variables "time in replacement-unit workshop" and "time in Marilyn Burns workshop" by breaking each categorical scale into four separate dummy variables, representing the response options "1 day or less," "2–6 days," "1–2 weeks" and "more than 2 weeks." We entered each separately against the dependent variables representing conventional and framework practice. The results show basic linearity, although the small number of teachers in the "more than 2 weeks" group didn't always behave as expected. By and large, lengthier stays in the Marilyn Burns setting led to greater increases in framework practice and decreases in conventional practice. This reinforces our points about the necessity of extended opportunities to learn in any kind of reform effort of this sort. The same general trend appears in replacement-unit workshops.

Table C.1. Practice Predicted by Time in Marilyn Burns (MB) Workshop

	Conventional practice	Framework practice
Intercept	1.49*	1.97*
	.19	0.18
MB 1 day	−.19~	0.27*
	0.10	0.09
MB 2–6 days	−0.21~	0.32*
	0.13	0.12
MB 1–2 weeks	−1.12*	0.69*
	.25	0.24
MB 2+ weeks	−0.78~	0.40
	0.47	0.46
Familiarity with reform	−0.79*	0.44*
	0.21	0.21
Attitude toward reform	−0.21*	0.25*
	0.03	0.03
R^2 (adjusted)	0.17	0.15

~$p < .15$
*$p < .05$

Table C.2. Teachers' Practice as Predicted by Time in Replacement Unit (RU) Workshop

	Conventional practice	Framework practice
Intercept	1.61*	1.90*
	.19	0.17
RU 1 day	−.15*	0.19*
	0.07	0.06
RU 2–6 days	-0.35*	0.62*
	0.08	0.08
RU 1–2 weeks	−.21	0.69*
	.21	0.20
RU 2+ weeks	−0.49*	0.65*
	0.18	0.17
Familiarity with reform	−0.86*	0.43*
	0.21	0.20
Attitude toward reform	−0.22*	0.23*
	0.03	0.03
R^2 (adjusted)	0.16	0.23

~$p < .15$
*$p < .05$

Appendix D

A two-stage least-squares analysis was performed on the student curriculum models to help mitigate "selection effects"—that is, the possibility that teachers who attended one of these workshops did so because they were already using the frameworks and the instructional techniques recommended. In order to do this, we identified variables that would affect the probability that teachers would attend a Marilyn Burns or replacement-unit workshop and estimated a logistic regression representing that relationship. We then took the predicted values from this first model and used them instead of the student curriculum workshop (SCW) marker in the student curriculum models.

To resolve endogeneity problems, we needed to identify factors affecting the probability that a teacher would select into the "treatment" condition but that do not affect the final outcome variable. In other words, we searched for factors that might encourage teachers to take the workshops but would not have a direct effect on their practice. Using both theory and empirical investigation, we have identified three such factors:

• Professional activities, a variable marking teacher attendance at national or regional mathematics meetings. Such participation should affect teacher practice if the content of meetings focuses on substantive matters of instruction and mathematics; where the focus is administrative or political matters, practice is less likely to be affected (Lichtenstein, McLaughlin, and Knudson 1992). The content of California's meetings was mixed during this period but tended toward more superficial treatments of mathematics and student curriculum. A regression analysis showed, after we had controlled for workshop and assessment-related learning, that this variable has little direct relation with conventional and reform practices.

• Local policy, a variable marking teacher participation in district mathematics committees or in teaching math in-service workshops. Again, knowledge of the content of those activities is key to predicting whether the variable should affect teacher practice or not. In the absence of this information, however, we proceed on the basis of results from a regression analysis that indicates that this marker is unrelated to teacher practices (Table 5.12).

• Administrative support, a three-item measure of teachers' reports of the extent to which their principal, school, and district were well informed about and favorable toward the frameworks. One item specifically asked about the amount of staff development supplied by the district. This measure has only a small effect on our scales describing teaching practice, net of professional development opportunities (Table 5.13).

We also chose to include two more variables in the first-stage selection equations—teachers' attitude toward reform, and teachers' familiarity with reform—in the expectation that these markers might indicate teacher desire to learn about both the reforms and children's curriculum as a vehicle for those reforms. To the extent these capture teacher "will," they will act as important controls.

Teachers' reports on all these measures were entered into the first-stage logistic equation predicting whether or not teachers attended a student curriculum workshop in 1993–1994:

Table D.1. First-Stage Logistic Regression Predicting Workshop Attendance

	Attended student curriculum workshop
Intercept	−5.26*
	.83
Attitude toward reform	.17~
	0.11
Familiarity with reform	1.84*
	.73
Professional activities	.97**
	.33
Local policy	.78***
	.23
Administrative support	.25**
	.08
N = 537	
Log likelihood	−333.56
X = 60.96, p = .0001	

~Indicates X^2 p < .15.
*Indicates X^2 p < .05.
**Indicates X^2 p < .01.
***Indicates X^2 p < .001.

All five proved moderately strong predictors of student curriculum workshop atten-dance. It is noteworthy that teachers' "attitude toward reform" is outperformed by other predictors in this equation.

Using the first-stage model above, teachers' predicted attendance at a student curri-culum workshop (zero or one) was generated for each observation in the sample, and this predicted value was entered into a pair of practice equations similar to those in Table 5.4. Table D.2 is not directly comparable to Table 5.4, because it uses a dummy variable, instead of a time variable, to represent student curriculum workshops. To simplify the comparison, we created Models 1 and 3, which show the effect of actual student curricu-lum workshop attendance on practice but use a dummy variable to do so. A comparison of Models 1 and 2 shows that the coefficient on student attendance at curriculum work-shops nearly doubles in the two-stage least-squares framework-practice regression. The increase in the coefficient is probably a result of the decreased precision with which our statistical package can estimate the two-stage equation, rather than of substantive dif-ferences in its real value. The coefficient on SCW in the conventional practice regression likewise dropped from −.30 to −.64 (se = .22), but it too was subject to higher standard er-

Table D.2. Second-Stage Regression of Predicted Workshop Attendance on Practice at Student Curriculum Workshop (SCW)

	Conventional practice— actual attendance	Conventional practice— predicted attendance	Framework practice— actual attendance	Framework practice— predicted attendance
Intercept	1.62***	1.84***	1.86***	1.89***
	.18	0.21	.17	0.19
Student curriculum				
workshop attendance	−.30***	−0.64**	.42***	.87***
	.06	0.22	(.05)	0.20
Attitude toward reform	−.21***	−0.22***	.22***	.21***
	.03	0.04	(.03)	0.03
Familiarity with reform	−0.85***	−.89**	.44***	0.25
	.21	0.25	(.20)	0.23
N	582	536	582	536
R-squared (adjusted)	.17	.17	.21	.17

~Indicates X^2 p < .15.

*Indicates X^2 p < .05.

**Indicates X^2 p < .01.

***Indicates X^2 p < .001.

rors. Despite the decrease in precision with which we could estimate both equations, we note that both measures of student curriculum workshop attendance remain significant, and related to the dependent variables in the expected direction.

The same procedure was carried out for the regressions using the variable "time in student curriculum workshop" instead of the dummy variable. Similar results obtained. For additional insurance, we also performed a two-stage least-squares using the item, "In teaching mathematics, my primary goal is to help students master basic computational skills," in place of "attitude toward reform," as the first-stage predictor of attendance at a student curriculum workshop. This item received some support from teachers and represented a sort of conventional thinking that later became a key part of the debate in the math wars. As a result, we thought, it might have better represented teachers' true disposition toward the reforms. Significance levels for SCW student curriculum workshop attendance, however, remained the same or increased in second-stage models.

Appendix E

Clogg, Petkova, and Haritou's test (1995) for difference in nested coefficients compares point estimates for models with and without one predictor or a set of predictors. Point estimates for the variable in question—here attendance at a student curriculum workshop—are compared with and without the "competing" explanatory variable(s) in the equation, to see if the difference in its effect is significant. If so, the regression is in fact *incorrect* unless the competitor variable is included. Here, we examined the point estimate on student curriculum workshop both with and without the CLAS variables—attended to CLAS, learned about CLAS, administered CLAS—both inside and outside the equation. For more details, see Clogg, Petkova, and Haritou (1995).

Table E.1. Clogg, Petkova, Haritou Test

	Restricted model (se of estimate)	Full model (se of estimate)	d (se of d)	t
Conventional practice				
student	−.088	−.080	.008	1.74
curriculum				
workshop	(.0191)	(.0196)	(.004)	
Framework practice				
student	.137	.114	.023	6.26
curriculum				
time	(.018)	(.0167)	(.0037)	

Appendix F

We improved the estimates in our CLAS models by employing a) knowledge of the variances and covariances of the observed data; b) assumptions regarding the nature of the variances and covariances of the measurement error; and c) multilevel modeling using HLM software. This work assumes that errors of measurement are independent of one another and of the true values.

The intuition behind the model is this: given that we have observed error-filled estimates of our dependent and independent variables and that we also have some knowledge of the error variance of each of these variables (obtained through HLM for all independent variables; for CLAS, the variance in student scores), we can obtain the "true" point estimates for the model. The math for the model that includes student curriculum workshop (SCW) follows: Level-1 observations are weighted by the variance of the measure. The models for our other independent variables are similar. Owing to multicolinearity, we could test only three- and four-variable models. We also could not work with the variable "Learned about CLAS," since it is a dichotomous variable at the teacher level. But we did this analysis with an expanded sample, since using HLM allowed us to readmit schools where only one teacher answered the survey back into the sample ($N = 199$).

$$CLAS = b_1 + e_1$$

$$SCW = b_2 + e_2$$

$$b_1 = \gamma_{10} + \gamma_{11} \,\% \, FLE + \gamma_{12} \, Past \, OTL + u_1$$

$$b_2 = \gamma_{20} + u_2$$

$$E \begin{bmatrix} b_1 \\ b_2 \end{bmatrix} = \begin{bmatrix} \gamma_{10} + \gamma_{11} \,\% \, FLE + \gamma_{12} \, Past \, OTL \\ \gamma_{20} \end{bmatrix}$$

$$\mathrm{var} \begin{bmatrix} b_1 \\ b_2 \end{bmatrix} = \begin{bmatrix} \tau_{11} & \tau_{12} \\ \tau_{21} & \tau_{22} \end{bmatrix}$$

$$E\,(b_1 \mid b_2) = \gamma_{10} + \gamma_{11} \,\% \, FLE + \gamma_{12} \, Past \, OTL + \frac{\tau_{12}}{\tau_{22}} (b_2 - \gamma_{20}) + \Sigma$$

$$\mathrm{var}\,(\Sigma) = \tau_{11} - \tau_{12} + \tau_{22}^{-1} \tau_{11}$$

Table F.1. HLM Models

	1 CLAS	2 CLAS	3 CLAS	4 CLAS	5 CLAS
Intercept	1.05	2.60	2.51	2.49	2.55
	0.64	0.18	0.26	0.25	0.31
Percentage FLE students	−1.30*	−1.35*	−1.35*	−1.36*	−1.34*
	0.09	0.09	0.09	0.09	0.09
School conditions	0.20*	0.24*	0.13	0.24*	0.06
	0.06	0.05	0.10	0.06	0.17
Framework practice	0.50*				
	0.21				
Conventional practice		−0.05			
		0.09			
Student curriculum workshop			0.43~		
			0.23		
Special-topics workshop				0.24	
				0.25	
Number of replacement units used					0.99
					0.73
Past framework learning			0.02	−0.08	
			0.07	0.07	

Note: In these models, higher scores on "school conditions" represent better estimates by teachers of their working climate.
~Indicates significance at $p < .10$.
*Indicates significance at $p < .05$.

The results of the models are as follows:

Most coefficients increase to between three and seven times their previous size, an outcome consistent with the observation that "true" coefficients are attenuated by 1/reliability of the variable when measurement error is present. The reliability of these measures—essentially a measure of agreement between teachers within schools—ranges between .15 (replacement-unit use) and .50 (conventional practice). Standard errors are likewise affected: since they are also functions of a the reliability of a measure at the school level, they also inflate when the measurement error fix is applied. Thus, we achieve more realistic point estimates with this method but cannot decrease the size of the confidence interval around these estimates.

Apart from the size of actual estimates themselves, there are several other things to note in Table F.1. Teachers' average reports of conventional practice continue to be statistically unrelated to student achievement on the CLAS, as does teachers' time spent in special-topics workshops. Though the coefficient on the latter does increase in size, it remains well below the level acceptable within conventional significance testing. Also, when we control for replacement-unit use and student curriculum workshop learning, the effect on "school conditions" disappears, suggesting that it serves as a proxy for these variables when they are measured more roughly. Finally, the coefficient on the replacement-unit variable does increase—but it is swamped by the increase in its standard error.

NOTES

Chapter 1: Policy, Teaching, and Learning

1. Our work draws on earlier studies in California (Guthrie 1990), other work we have done on practice and policy (Cohen 1989; Cohen and Spillane 1993), and several lines of research in which researchers have tried to observe teachers' response to policy (Schwille and others 1983), in which the researchers have tried to devise indicators of quality in teaching and curriculum (Murnane and Raizen 1988; Shavelson, McDonnell, Oakes, and Carey 1987; Porter 1991), or in which they have probed the nature and effects of professional education (Kennedy 1998).

Chapter 2: The New New Math in California

1. For an exception, see McDonnell (1994).

2. Because the assessment design included matrix sampling, scores were available only at the school level, not for individual students.

Chapter 3: Learning About Reform

1. The number of schools also rises above 250, because in some locations, fifth graders attend middle schools, and these were included in our sample.

2. See Weiss, Matti, and Smith (1994), Kennedy and Ball (no date).

3. For more information on the technical aspects of this survey, see Lash, Perry, and Talbert (1996).

4. Except as otherwise noted, we report missing data for statistics only when the percentage of cases missing exceeds 5 percent of our data—about thirty teachers.

5. The CCD is a dataset produced and maintained by the National Center for Education Statistics in the U.S. Department of Education.

6. Kirst, Hayward, and Koppich (1995, p. 96) shows that in 1994, 42.4 percent of California's student population was white, 37 percent Hispanic, 8.3 percent Asian, 8.5 percent black.

7. Chapter 1, now known as Title 1, provides funds to schools on the basis of their enrollment of students from low-income families.

8. This estimate exactly matches the one provided for all of California by the National Resource Data Center and the National Center for Education Statistics, U.S. Department of Education (1993).

9. Because of our sampling frame and weighting scheme, we can estimate how teachers in the California elementary school population would answer the questions in this survey. Presenting such population estimates, however, also requires some mention of confidence intervals or other indicators of uncertainty. Because of the burdensome nature of presenting such results, we report results only for the teachers who took the survey and let readers make their own judgments about where a true population estimate might lie.

10. A related item on the survey asked teachers whether their district or school made a personal copy of the California mathematics framework(s) available; 68 percent said yes, and nearly 75 percent of those reported using them.

11. We also asked teachers whether they had had any opportunities to learn about the new standards. Sixty-five percent reported that they had at some time attended school or district workshops related to the new mathematics standards, and 45 percent said they had been given time to attend off-site workshops or conferences related to those standards. Nearly seven out of ten teachers had attended one of these two activities, and many both.

12. Identification of content was one reason that we excluded workshops at the county and district level.

13. Interview with Ellen Lee, November 5, 1997. The CMC also published a parent information newsletter, and promoted other local and regional activities.

14. One problem inherent in any attempt to study teacher networks is selection. Combined evidence from Wilson, Lubienski, and Mattson (1996) and from this survey, for instance, shows that teachers who joined the California Mathematics Project were, by their own estimation, more pro-reform at the outset than the average teacher in California. At many CMP sites, teachers applied and were selected on the basis of their promise as leaders. Since teachers cannot be randomly assigned to networks, it will prove difficult to determine to what extent networks "add value" to teachers' work, given that many may have made similar changes in their practice anyway.

15. This report is based on review of a sample of teachers' responses to the open-ended portion of the question.

Chapter 4: Teachers' Ideas and Practices

1. This finding runs counter to the response bias of the survey; teachers were asked to circle reform ideas and to leave blank items not considered part of reform.

2. In the reform context, this statement refers to the idea that teachers should try to understand how their students make sense of mathematical ideas, and then take students' understandings and misunderstandings as a starting point for teaching.

3. These two categories are collapsed in the table, as are two complementary categories "Strongly disagree" and "Disagree." Teachers were responding on a five-point scale, from "Strongly Agree" to "Strongly Disagree." The middle category designated a neutral attitude—what we refer to as being on the fence.

4. Conventional instruction aside, most teachers become distressed when their students seem to be confused: if teachers succeed only in befuddling their students, what kind of success can they be having?

5. On the first sort of teacher, see Barnes (1994) and Cohen (1994); on the second sort, see Wilson (1990) and subsequent notes, Jennings Weimers (1990), and Jennings (1996).

6. *Beyond Activities* actually consists of three different replacement units.

7. A caveat is in order, however, about the less-adopted pieces of the reform. It is difficult to tell from reformers' documents how often teachers are *expected* to engage their students in these time-consuming activities.

8. The correlation between the framework-practice scale and the framework-belief scale is .39; the correlation between the conventional-practice scale and the conventional-beliefs scale is .32. Although this may strike the reader as low, there is little reason to expect they will be higher. In addition to measurement error, these scales gauge different ways teachers might have responded to reformers' ideas. See Chapter 5.

Chapter 5: Teachers' Opportunities to Learn and Classroom Practice

1. We will not explore the relation between demographic characteristics of students or schools and reform. For a consideration of this issue, please see Hill, Cohen, and Moffitt (in press).

2. This correlation differs from the one between the ideas about reform and conventional ideas reported in Chapter 4 because we used only a subset of the Chapter 4 items here.

3. This correlation differs from the one between the items concerning reform and conventional practices reported in Chapter 4 because we use only a subset of the Chapter 4 items here. Some items from Table 4.4 did not appear in either factor, and were not used in the analysis. These were:

- Using manipulative materials or models to solve problems
- Using calculators to solve problems
- Using computers in mathematics
- Doing mathematics in conjunction with other subjects or class projects

These classroom practices are technically included in the reform movement, for the 1992 framework recommends them. Yet we suspect, partly on the basis of these factor analysis results and partly on earlier fieldwork carried out by MSU researchers, that not only the reforms but also other forces in schools, like the availability of money and training for technology, served to promote these activities.

4. "Ordinary least squares" asks a statistical package to determine the effect of a one-unit change in a given independent variable on a dependent variable, holding other independent variables constant. Thus, when we try to predict a dependent variable like "conventional ideas" using an independent variable like "days spent in math workshop,"

we shall see the effect of the latter on the former as a number, say –.12. In this instance, we would say that for every day a teacher spent in a workshop, her score fell by .12 on the conventional ideas scale. For more information on OLS, see Hanushek and Jackson (1977).

5. Our scale actually had six levels: 1 to 5 (negative to positive) and a level 6 for "no opinion." A statistical comparison showed that individuals who answered "6" were quite similar to those who answered "3" (to indicate mixed feelings) on the scale. Because those who answered "6" would otherwise be classified in missing data, we transformed the response "no opinions" into "mixed" responses. The regression results presented here do not change in the absence of this fix.

6. Thanks to Susan L. Moffitt for pointing this out.

7. This is a slightly revised version of Table 3.7.

8. The survey asked teachers to circle an amount of time ranging from "one day or less" to "more than two weeks," rather than write down the number of days they spent at each activity. To calculate time spent, we assumed the following.

"One day or less" = 1 day
"2–6 days" = 4 days
"1–2 weeks" = 7.5 days
More than 2 weeks = 14 days

9. See Appendix D, and for more detailed information on the workshop selection process, Chapter 7.

10. We took several other statistical precautions in this analysis. We checked each workshop individually against our four dependent measures, to ensure that our categorization did not obscure unexpected benefits of any particular kind for belief or practice. We checked the models we used for stability and sensitivity to changes in specification and weighting and for a host of regression sins like outliers and heteroskedasticity. Few of these tests and fixes changed our substantive conclusions.

11. The question asked whether teachers had "participated in any activities that provided [them] with information about the CLAS (e.g., task development, scoring, pilot testing, staff development)."

12. In our sample of 595 second through fifth grade teachers, almost a third reported actually administering the fourth grade math CLAS. Though this may seem illogical, remember that the test had been administered in both 1993 and 1994. It appears that at least some teachers had taught fourth grade in 1992–93, but had moved to a different grade by the time the test was administered in 1994. Their inclusion thus raised the total number of teachers who had administered the test.

13. The coefficients on administered CLAS and time spent in student curriculum workshops are not directly comparable because they appear on different scales. By "size," we are referring to significance levels, a conventionally accepted measure for comparing differently scaled measures.

14. Thanks to Jennifer O'Day for this point.

15. This scale runs from 1 (CLAS did *not* correspond, etc.) to 5 (CLAS corresponded well, etc.). Its mean is 3.24, its standard deviation 1.02, and its reliability .85.

16. See also Kirst, Hayward, and Koppich (1995), 88, for a focus group in which teachers tell much same story.

17. According to the test suggested by Clogg, Petkova, and Haritou (1995), the change in one of the two coefficients in question is nonsignificant. See Appendix E for details.

18. See Ball and Cohen (1996) and Collopy (1999) for arguments concerning learning from curriculum. Also see the TERC *Seeing Fractions* unit.

19. This is also the reason we did not attempt a two-stage least-squares analysis here, as we did earlier for student curriculum workshops.

20. Statistic furnished by Roberta Hendry, analyst in Publications Division of California Department of Education.

21. In only one case do the coefficients and significance levels change. "Used frameworks" decreases the coefficient on "time in student curriculum workshop" from .0298 to .0244 in the "framework ideas" equation, and the significance level falls to p <.15.

22. This table appeared earlier as 3.8.

23. Alternatively, teachers who participated in this network activity might have a more focused definition of some of the items on our practice scale. Such teachers would be less likely to report that their students conjectured daily if all that was going on in the classroom was teacher-directed guessing—whereas teachers who had not attended these workshops might not distinguish between the two. If this hunch is correct, these teachers' framework-practice scores would appear lower than those of teachers who held looser definitions. We do not think this unlikely, although there is no way to be sure.

24. These results fit with Lichtenstein's observation that increases in teacher participation in decision making and advocacy yield improved professional knowledge and capacity only when such opportunities are designed with these goals in mind (Lichtenstein, McLaughlin, and Knudson 1992, 55).

25. We treated "don't know" responses as missing data.

26. We treated "don't know" responses as missing data.

27. Using a hierarchical linear model would have been more appropriate, because we employed school-level indicators to predict teachers' practice. The low reliability of the intercept indicating average school practices precluded this approach, however.

Chapter 6: Learning and Policy

1. Some conservatives, for instance, claimed a reading item featuring a snowball fight was too violent (Honig and Alexander 1996).

2. *http://www.cde.ca.gov*

3. Exempted students included those of limited English proficiency who had been enrolled in U.S. schools for under thirty months, students whose parents had requested opt-outs, and some students with disabilities or with special education needs.

4. Elsewhere in the *Technical Report,* the test is described as consisting of two open-ended problems, three constructed-response problems, and four enhanced multiple-choice questions (*Technical Report,* p. A-76).

5. The same statistics for all elementary schools in the state are:

N	Mean	Std Dev	Minimum	Maximum
4228	2.8135951	0.6242373	0	5.0200000

The student-level standard deviation for our sample (constructed from schools' reports of student distributions) is 1.728. Thanks to Steve Raudenbush for help with this statistic.

6. To the extent that teachers' learning at workshops occurred in the summer of 1994 (after the administration of the test), we could underestimate the effect of such workshops on student learning.

7. Thus the no-report rate for schools in our sample is 18 percent. For elementary schools across the state, the no-report rate was 12 percent. One explanation might be our sampling scheme: we oversampled smaller, rural schools, which were perhaps more likely to have not met CDE's score publication criteria.

8. The standard error on the "percent scoring 4 or above" measure had to be at or above 10 percent to be eliminated on these grounds (*Technical Report*, pp. 3-4 to 3-5).

9. The state-level student opt-out rate for the fourth-grade mathematics assessment was 3.7 percent (*Technical Report*, p. 3-4). The opt-out rate had to be above 25 percent in an individual school before it was flagged for removal from the public release scores.

10. *Technical Report, California Learning Assessment System.*

11. It is likely that this correlation would rise if we had careerlong estimates of teachers' attendance at student curriculum workshops.

12. *http://nces.ed.gov/ccd/ccddata.html*

13. We are inclined to favor the first two explanations, because replacement units were aligned with the framework and approved by the state, yet not specifically designed to overlap directly with the abilities tested by CLAS.

14. We tried both "Learned about CLAS" and "Attended to CLAS" in this model, for both could be measures of teachers' attempts to prepare students for the test. "Attended to CLAS" was not significant; it also showed evidence of colinearity with "framework practice."

15. There is reason to expect that the coefficient in this model—and elsewhere—concerning time spent on student curriculum is actually underestimated. Remember that the survey asked teachers to report workshop learning of this type within the last year—and thereby left teachers who attended student curriculum workshops in past years and now use replacement units represented by only the replacement-unit marker. This factor will bias the effect of replacement-unit use upward, and that of time on student curriculum downward.

16. The F-statistic is 2.57, with df (degrees of freedom) in numerator = 4 and 163 in the denominator.

17. Because we had at most a sample of four teachers from which to construct each school's profile, all estimates in Table 6.3 are adjusted downward for measurement error. We attempted to correct these models for this error using Hierarchical Linear Modeling and a latent-variable approach. By examining information generated by that program about the variance and covariance of both errors and variables, we were able to arrive at better point estimates for models with one independent regressor. The size of the "effect" on the student curriculum time marker, for instance, rises to .43 when we hold constant both school conditions and the percentage of students who are FLE. Although we have arrived at this more reasonable point estimate, however, we cannot be more certain of its accuracy, for standard errors do not also improve with this method. Furthermore, our at-

tempts to test more comprehensive models that included competing policy-and-practice variables were frustrated by the low reliability and multicolinearity of the survey measures. For these reasons, we consign both the technical details and the presentation of the models to Appendix F. We are indebted to Steve Raudenbush for masterminding this fix for measurement error but reserve the prerogative to claim all mistakes as our own.

18. We chose not to use this data to examine the independent or combined effects of student race and class on achievement. Without individual student achievement scores, it would be difficult to differentiate the effects of actual student ethnicity from the characteristics of schools enrolling students of a certain ethnicity. This observation also conditions what we can conclude from the "percent FLE" variable. Exploratory regressions do suggest, however, that incorporating markers for student ethnicity into these regressions does not change our substantive findings about policy and its effects.

19. "Replacement-unit use" became insignificant in Model 5. "Special-topics" workshops became marginally significant in Model 2 ($b = .088$, $se = .044$) when about 10 percent of schools were deleted from the sample. Schools deleted included five where the school average for time spent in these workshops is over 1.5 days (out of seventeen schools total with values over 1.5); further analysis shows that deleting these five observations alone yields the positive result. It is difficult to explain why deleting schools that averaged more time in the workshops should result in a positive outcome for this variable. The result was not robust across models without weighting, either, when schools with only two teachers responding were deleted from the sample or when *all* schools that averaged more than 1.5 on special topics were deleted from the sample.

Chapter 7: Missed Opportunities

1. Tom Corcoran estimates that it may be up to 7 percent. See Consortium for Policy Research in Education, 1997.

2. They also support our earlier claim (Chapter 5) that teachers did in fact "learn" from the curriculum workshops, for they show that teacher selection into workshops is modest at best.

3. These other influences often are crucial, but given the importance of teachers' decisions for students, the lack of independent evidence tends to dissipate rather than strengthen professional judgment.

4. The last review was carried out by way of the Program Quality Review, a state-mandated, local peer review of educational quality.

5. Reformers had little or no influence over such other relevant state education policy domains as criteria for entry into higher education or the content of preservice teacher education; both were governed by other state agencies.

6. These items actually asked how different educational actors related to documents listed in an immediately previous item. The documents listed were both NCTM standards documents (1989; 1991); the California frameworks (1985; 1992); the California samplers of mathematics assessment (1991; 1993); and the *Mathematics Model Curriculum Guide* (1987).

7. A combination of principals' familiarity with reform documents and schoolwide efforts at reform.

8. This estimate must be qualified: districts might have offered framework-related workshops for several years, and teachers might simply have been working on reading or social studies the year we administered the survey. It is difficult to get a solid estimate of the influence of district priorities on teacher decisions, but our evidence is consistent with others' estimates of fairly modest district influence despite their formal control. See Little (1993) and Lord (1994).

9. We discuss these differences at length in Hill, Cohen, and Moffitt (in press).

10. We arrived at these estimates by using HLM to estimate a simple ANOVA on our two-tier data and partitioning the variance into that between schools on the one hand and that between teachers on the other. Only schools in which three or more teachers responded to the survey were used, and population weights were not. See Bryk and Raudenbush *Hierarchical Linear Models* (Newbury Park, Calif.: Sage, 1992).

11. Lack of agreement within schools also can encourage conflict, especially when change is attempted. For a case in point, see Carol Barnes's 1997 study of instructional approaches in reading at one California school, which she tracked over several years.

Appendixes

1. Details of these design and nonresponse features are taken from the technical report for the study, Lash, Perry, and Talbert (1996).

2. For a more extended discussion, see Lash, Perry, and Talbert (1996).

3. Only six items measuring beliefs were on the short form—and thus available for comparison.

REFERENCES

Ball, D. L. 1990. "The Mathematical Understandings That Prospective Teachers Bring to Teacher Education." *Elementary School Journal* 90 (4): 451–466.

———. 1992. "Magical Hopes: Manipulatives and the Reform of Math Education." *American Educator: The Professional Journal of the American Federation of Teachers* 16 (2): 14–18.

———, and D. K. Cohen. 1996. "Reform by the Book: What Is—or Might Be—the Role of Curriculum Materials in Teacher Learning and Instructional Reform?" *Educational Researcher* 25 (9): 6–8.

———, and S. S. Rundquist. 1993. "Collaboration as a Context for Joining Teacher Learning with Learning About Teaching." In *Teaching for Understanding: Challenges for Policy and Practice*, edited by D. K. Cohen, M. McLaughlin, and J. Talbert, 13–42. San Francisco: Jossey-Bass.

Baratta-Lorton, M. 1976. *Math Their Way.* Boston: Addison-Wesley.

Barnes, C. A. 1994. "The Case of Anita Lorenz." Paper presented at the annual meeting of the American Educational Research Association, April 4–8, 1994, New Orleans, La.

———. 1997. "Understanding Curriculum Reform in One School: A Competition of Ideas and Commitments." Ph.D. diss., College of Education, Michigan State University.

Barr, R., and R. Dreeben. 1983. *How Schools Work.* Chicago: University of Chicago Press.

Berliner, D. 1979. "Tempus Educare." In *Research on Teaching: Concepts, Findings, and Implications*, edited by P. Peterson and H. Walberg, 120–135. Berkeley, Calif.: McCutchan.

Borko, H., and R. T. Putnam. 1995. "Expanding a Teacher's Knowledge Base." *Professional Development in Education*, 35–65. New York: Teachers College Press.

Brophy, J. 1991. Introduction to Volume 2. In *Advances in Research on Teaching*, vol. 2: *Teachers' Knowledge of Subject Matter as It Relates to Their Teaching Practice*, edited by Jere Brophy, iv–xv. Greenwich, Conn.: JAI Press.

Brown, C. A., M. S. Smith, and M. K. Stein. 1996. "Linking Teacher Support to Enhanced Classroom Instruction." Paper presented at the annual meeting of the American Educational Research Association, New York, New York.

Bryk, A. S., V. E. Lee, and P. B. Holland. 1993. *Catholic Schools and the Common Good.* Cambridge: Harvard University Press.

Bryk, A. S., and S. W. Raudenbush. 1992. *Hierarchical Linear Models.* Newbury Park, Calif.: Sage.

Bryk, A. S., P. B. Sebring, D. Kerbow, S. Pellino, and J. Q. Easton. 1998. *Charting Chicago School Reform.* Boulder, Colo.: Westview Press.

Buchmann, M. 1993. "Role over Person: Morality and Authenticity in Teaching." In *Detachment and Concern: Conversations in the Philosophy of Teaching and Teacher Education*, edited by M. Buchmann and R. E. Floden, 145–157. New York: Teachers College Press.

Burstein, L., L. M. McDonnell, J. Van Winkle, T. H. Ormseth, J. Mirocha, and G. Guiton. 1995. *Validating National Curriculum Indicators.* Santa Monica, Calif.: RAND.

California Department of Education. 1985. *Mathematics Framework for California Public Schools.* Sacramento, Calif.

California Department of Education. 1992. *Mathematics Framework for California Public Schools.* Sacramento, Calif.

California Department of Education. 1993. *A Sampler of Mathematics Assessment.* Sacramento, Calif.

California Learning Assessment System. 1994. Appendices Accompanying the CLAS *Technical Report.* Monterey, Calif.: CTB/McGraw-Hill.

Carpenter, R. P., E. Fennema, P. L. Peterson, C.-P. Chiang, and M. Loef. 1989. "Using Knowledge of Children's Mathematics Thinking in Classroom Teaching: An Experimental Study." *American Educational Research Journal* 26 (4): 499–531.

Clogg, C. C., E. Petkova, and A. Haritou. 1995. "Statistical Methods for Comparing Regression Coefficients Between Models." *American Journal of Sociology* 100 (5): 1261–1293.

Cohen, D. K. 1982. "Policy and Organization: The Impact of State and Federal Educational Policy on School Governance." *Harvard Educational Review* 52 (4): 474–499.

———. 1989. "Teaching Practice: Plus Ça Change . . . " Contributing to *Educational Change: Perspectives on Research and Practice*, edited by P. W. Jackson, 27–84. Berkeley, Calif.: McCutchan.

———. 1990. "Revolution in One Classroom: The Case of Mrs. Oublier." *Educational Evaluation and Policy Analysis* 12 (3): 311–330.

———. 1994. "Listening to the Music of Reform." Manuscript, School of Education, University of Michigan, Ann Arbor.

———, and D. L. Ball. 1999. *Instruction, Capacity, and Improvement.* Philadelphia: Consortium for Policy Research in Education.

Cohen, D. K., and C. A. Barnes. 1993. "Pedagogy and Policy." In *Teaching for Understanding: Challenges for Policy and Practice*, edited by D. K. Cohen, M. W. McLaughlin, and J. E. Talbert, 207–239. San Francisco: Jossey-Bass.

———, and J. P. Spillane. 1993. "Policy and Practice: The Relations Between Governance and Instruction." *Designing Coherent Education Policy: Improving the System,* edited by S. H. Fuhrman, 35–88. San Francisco: Jossey-Bass.

———, N. Jennings, and S. G. Grant. 1997. "Reading Policy: The Enactment of Reading Reform in Michigan Schools." Manuscript, School of Education, University of Michigan, Ann Arbor.

Collopy, R. M. B. 1999. "The Educative Potential of Curriculum Materials and Their Contribution to the Learning of Elementary Mathematics Teachers." Ph.D. diss., School of Education, University of Michigan Ann Arbor.

Consortium for Policy Research in Education. 1997. *Policies and Programs for Professional Development of Teachers: A Fifty-State Profile.* Philadelphia: University of Pennsylvania.

Corcoran, T. B. 1995. *Helping Teachers Teach Well: Transforming Professional Development.* New Brunswick, N.J.: Consortium for Policy Research in Education.

Corwin, R. B., S. J. Russell, and C. C. Tierney. 1990. *Seeing Fractions: A Unit for Upper Elementary Grades.* Sacramento, Calif.: California Department of Education.

Cronbach, L. J., N. M. Bradburn, and D. G. Horvitz. 1994. *Sampling and Statistical Procedures Used in the California Learning Assessment System.* Palo Alto, Calif.: CLAS Select Committee.

Cuban, L. (1993) *How Teachers Taught: Constancy and Change in American Classrooms, 1880–1980.* 2nd ed. New York: Teachers College Press.

Darling-Hammond, L., ed. 1994. *Professional Development Schools.* New York: Teachers College Press.

Dow, P. B. 1991. *Schoolhouse Politics: Lessons from the Sputnik Era.* Cambridge: Harvard University Press.

Firestone, W. A., and J. R. Pennell. 1997. "Designing State-Sponsored Teacher Networks: A Comparison of Two Cases." *American Educational Research Journal* 34 (2), 237–266.

Fuhrman, S., W. H. Clune, and R. F. Elmore. 1988. "Research on Education Reform: Lessons on the Implementation of Policy." *Teachers' College Record* 90 (2): 238–257.

Fuhrman, S., and R. F. Elmore. 1990. "Understanding Local Control in the Wake of State Education Reform." *Educational Evaluation and Policy Analysis* 12: 82–96.

Grant, S. G. 1998. *Reforming Reading, Writing, and Mathematics: Teachers' Responses and the Prospects for Systemic Reform.* Mahwah, N.J.: Erlbaum.

Guthrie, J. W., ed. 1990. *Educational Evaluation and Policy Analysis* 12 (3).

———. and M. W. Kirst. 1985. *Conditions of Education in California.* Berkeley, Calif.: PACE.

Hanushek, E., and J. E. Jackson. 1977. *Statistical Methods for Social Scientists,* San Diego, Calif.: Academic Press.

Heaton, R. M., and M. Lampert. 1993. "Learning to Hear Voices: Inventing a New Pedagogy of Teacher Education." In *Teaching for Understanding: Challenges for Policy and Practice,* edited by D. Cohen, M. McLaughlin, and J. Talbert, 43–83. San Francisco: Jossey-Bass.

Hill, H. C., D. K. Cohen, and S. L. Moffitt. In press. "Instruction, Poverty and Performance." In *Hard Work for Good Schools: Making Federal Programs Work in High-Poverty Schools,* edited by G. Orfield and E. DeBray. Century Foundation.

Honig, W., and F. Alexander, in collaboration with D. P. Wolf. 1996. "Rewriting the Tests: Lessons from the California Learning Assessment System." In *Performance-Based Student Assessment: Challenges and Possibilities. Ninety-Fifth Yearbook of the National Society for the Study of Education,* edited by J. B. Baron and D. P. Wolf, 143–165. Chicago: University of Chicago Press.

Jennings, N. E. 1996. *Interpreting Policy in Real Classrooms: Case Studies of State Reform and Teacher Practice.* New York: Teachers College Press.

Jennings Weimers, N. 1990. "Transformation and Accommodation: A Case Study of Joe Scott." *Educational Evaluation and Policy Analysis* 12 (3): 281–293.

Kennedy, M. M. 1998. "Form and Substance in Inservice Teacher Education." Paper presented at the annual meeting of the American Educational Research Association, April 1998, San Diego.

———, and D. L. Ball. "Teacher Education and Learning to Teach Project." College of Education, Michigan State University, Lansing, Mich.

Kirst, M. W., G. C. Hayward, and J. E. Koppich. 1995. *Conditions of Education in California, 1994–95.* Berkeley, Calif.: PACE.

Kirst, M. W., and C. Mazzeo. 1996. "The Rise, Fall, and Rise of State Assessment in California, 1993–96." *Phi Delta Kappan* 78 (4): 319–323.

Lash, A., R. Perry, and J. Talbert. 1996. *Survey of Elementary Mathematics Education in California: Technical Report and User's Guide to SAS Files.* Stanford, Calif.

Leinhardt, G., and A. M. Seewald. 1981. "Overlap: What's Tested, What's Taught." *Journal of Educational Measurement* 18 (2): 85–95.

Lichtenstein, G., M. W. McLaughlin, and J. Knudson. 1992. "Teacher Empowerment and Professional Knowledge." In *The Changing Contexts of Teaching: National Society for the Study of Education Yearbook,* edited by A. Lieberman, 37–58. Chicago: University of Chicago Press.

Lieberman, A., and M. W. McLaughlin. 1996. "Networks for Educational Change: Powerful and Problematic." In *Teacher Learning: New Policies, New Practices,* edited by M. McLaughlin and I. Oberman, New York: Teachers College Press.

Lin, A. C. 2000. *Reform in the Making: The Implementation of Social Policy in Prison.* Princeton, N.J.: Princeton University Press.

Linn, R. L. 1983. "Testing and Instruction: Links and Distinctions." *Journal of Educational Measurement* 20 (2): 179–189.

———. 1993. "Educational Assessment: Expanded Expectations and Challenges." *Educational Evaluation and Policy Analysis* 15 (1): 1–16.

Little, J. W. 1989. "District Policy Choices and Teachers' Professional Development Opportunities." *Educational Evaluation and Policy Analysis* 11 (2): 165–179.

———. 1993. "Teachers' Professional Development in a Climate of Educational Reform." *Educational Evaluation and Policy Analysis* 15 (2): 129–151.

Little, J. W., W. H. Gerritz, D. S. Stern, J. W. Guthrie, M. W. Kirst, and D. D. Marsh. 1987. *Staff Development in California: Public and Personal Investments, Programs, Patterns, and Policy Choices.* Berkeley, Calif.: Far West Laboratory and PACE, paper #PC87–12–15-CPEC.

Lord, B. 1994. "Teachers' Professional Development: Critical Colleagueship and the Role of Professional Communities." In *The Future of Education: Perspectives on*

National Standards in Education, edited by N. Cobb, 175–204. New York: College Entrance Examination Board.

Massell, D., and M. Goertz. 1999. "Local Strategies for Building Capacity: The District Role in Supporting Instructional Reform." Paper presented at the annual meeting for the American Educational Research Association, April 1999, Montreal, Canada.

Matti, M. C., E. H. Soar, S. B. Hudson, I. R. Weiss. 1995. *The 1993 National Survey of Science and Mathematics Education: Compendium of Tables.* Chapel Hill, N.C.: Horizon Research.

Mayer, D. 1997. "New Teaching Standards and Old Tests: Dangerous Mismatch?" Ph.D. diss., Graduate School of Education, Harvard University.

———. 1999. "Measuring Instructional Practice: Can Policymakers Trust Survey Data?" *Educational Evaluation and Policy Analysis* 21 (1): 29–46.

McCarthy, S. J., and P. L. Peterson. 1993. "Creating Classroom Practice Within the Context of a Restructured Professional Development School." In *Teaching for Understanding: Challenges for Policy and Practice,* edited by D. K. Cohen, M. McLaughlin, and J. Talbert, 130–166. San Francisco: Jossey-Bass.

McDonnell, L. M. 1994. "Assessment Policy as Persuasion and Regulation." *American Journal of Education* 102 (4): 394–420.

———. 1997a. "Local Testing Controversies: The Case of CLAS." CRESST manuscript. Santa Barbara, Calif: University of California, Santa Barbara.

———. 1997b. "The Politics of State Testing: Implementing New Student Assessments." CRESST manuscript. Santa Barbara: University of California, Santa Barbara.

McLaughlin, Milbrey. 1991a. "Learning from Experience: Lessons from Policy Implementation." In *Education Policy Implementation,* edited by A. R. Odden, 185–195. Albany, N.Y.: SUNY Press.

———. 1991b. "The RAND Change Agent Study: Ten Years Later." In *Education Policy Implementation,* edited by A. R. Odden, 143–155. Albany, N.Y.: SUNY Press.

———, and I. Oberman, eds. 1996. *Teacher Learning: New Policies, New Practices.* New York: Teachers College Press.

———, and J. E. Talbert. 1993. "Understanding Teaching in Context." *In Teaching for Understanding: Challenges for Policy and Practice,* edited by D. K. Cohen, M. W. McLaughlin, and J. E. Talbert. San Francisco: Jossey-Bass.

Murnane, R. J., and S. A. Raizen. 1988. *Improving Indicators of the Quality of Science and Mathematics Education in Grades K–12.* Washington, D.C.: National Academy Press.

Murphy, J. 1989. "Educational Reform in the 1980s: Explaining Some Surprising Success." *Educational Evaluation and Policy Analysis* 11 (3): 209–222.

Neufeld, B. 1996. *Standards-Based Reform: Baseline Data Report, Jefferson County Public Schools.* Cambridge, Mass.: Education Matters.

———, and J. Boothby. 1999. *Standards-Based Reform: Baseline Data Report, Jefferson County Public Schools.* Cambridge, Mass.: Education Matters.

Neufeld, B., L. Fickel, and A. Bennett. 1998. *Standards-Based Reform: Baseline Data Report, Jefferson County Public Schools.* Cambridge, Mass.: Education Matters.

Newmann, F. M., and G. G. Wehlage. 1995. *Successful School Restructuring.* Madison, Wis.: Center on Reorganization and Restructuring of Schools.

O'Day, J., and M. Smith, M. 1993. "Systemic Reform and Educational Opportunity." In

Designing Coherent Policy, edited by S. Fuhrman, 250–312. San Francisco: Jossey-Bass.

Perry, R. 1996. "The Role of Teachers' Professional Communities in the Implementation of California Mathematics Reform." Ph.D. diss., School of Education, Stanford University, Stanford, Calif.

Peterson, P. 1990. "Doing More in the Same Amount of Time: Cathy Swift." *Educational Evaluation and Policy Analysis* 12 (3): 261–280.

———, E. Fennema, and T. P. Carpenter. 1991. "Teachers' Knowledge of Students' Mathematics Problem-Solving Knowledge." In *Advances in Research on Teaching, vol. 2: Teachers' Knowledge of Subject Matter as it Relates to Their Teaching Practice,* edited by J. Brophy, 49–86. Greenwich, Conn.: JAI Press.

Porter, A. C. 1991. "Creating a System of School Process Indicators." *Educational Evaluation and Policy Analysis* 13 (1): 13–29.

———, R. E. Floden, D. J. Freeman, W. H. Schmidt, and J. R. Schwille. September 1986. *Content Determinants (with Research Instrumentation Appendices).* Institute for Research on Teaching. Research series #179. East Lansing: Michigan State University.

Resnick, D. P., and L. B. Resnick. 1985. "Standards, Curriculum, and Performance: A Historical and Comparative Perspective." *Educational Researcher* 14 (4): 5–21.

Richardson, V. 1996. "The Role of Attitudes and Beliefs in Learning to Teach." In *Handbook of Research on Teacher Education,* 2nd ed., edited by J. Sikula, T. J. Buttery, and E. Guyton. New York: Simon & Schuster.

Sarason, S. 1982. *The Culture of the School and the Problem of Change.* 2nd ed. Boston: Allyn and Bacon.

Schifter, D., and C. T. Fosnot. 1993. *Reconstructing Mathematics Education: Stories of Teachers' Meeting the Challenge of Reform.* New York: Teachers College Press.

Schwille, J. A. Porter, R. Floden, D. Freeman, C. Knapp, T. Kuhs, and W. Schmidt. 1983. "Teachers as Policy Brokers in the Content of Elementary School Mathematics." In *Handbook of Teaching and Policy,* edited by L. Shulman and G. Sykes, 370–391. New York: Longman.

Shavelson, R. J., L. M. McDonnell, T. Oakes, and N. B. Carey. 1987. *Indicator Systems for Monitoring Mathematics and Science Education.* Santa Monica, Calif.: RAND.

Spillane, J. P. 1996. "School Districts Matter: Local Educational Authorities and State Instructional Policy." *Education Policy* 10 (1): 63–87.

———. 1998. "State Policy and the Non-Monolithic Nature of the Local School District: Organizational and Professional Considerations." *American Educational Research Journal* 35 (1): 33–63.

———. 2000. "Cognition and Policy Implementation: District Policymakers and the Reform of Mathematics Education." *Cognition and Instruction* 18 (2): 141–179.

———, and C. L. Thompson. 1997. "Reconstructing Conceptions of Local Capacity: The Local Education Agency's Capacity for Ambitious Instructional Reform." *Educational Evaluation and Policy Analysis* 19 (2): 185–203.

Stallings, J., and E. M. Krasavage. 1986. "Program Implementation and Student Achievement in a Four-Year Madeline Hunter Follow-Through Project." *Elementary School Journal* 87 (2): 118–138.

Steinberg, J. Dec. 3, 1999. "Academic Standards Eased as a Fear of Failure Spreads." *New York Times,* A1.

Stone, Deborah. 1988. *Policy Paradox and Political Reason.* Glenview, Ill: Scott, Foresman.

Talbert, J. E., and M. W. McLaughlin. 1993. "Understanding Teaching in Context." In *Teaching for Understanding: Challenges for Policy and Practice,* edited by D. K. Cohen, M. McLaughlin, and J. Talbert, 43–83. San Francisco: Jossey-Bass.

Technical Report: California Learning Assessment System. 1994. Monterey, Calif. CTB/McGraw-Hill.

Thompson, A. 1992. "Teacher Beliefs and Conceptions: A Synthesis of the Research." In *Handbook of Research on Mathematics Teaching and Learning,* edited by D. A. Grouws, 127–147. New York: Simon & Schuster.

Tyack, D., and L. Cuban. 1995. *Tinkering Toward Utopia: A Century of Public School Reform.* Cambridge: Harvard University Press.

Webb, N. L. 1993. *Mathematics Education Reform in California.* Madison: Wisconsin Center for Education Research.

Weick, K. E. 1976. "Educational Organizations as Loosely Coupled Systems." *Administrative Science Quarterly* 21 (March): 1–19.

Weiss, I. 1993. *A Profile of Science and Mathematics Education in the United States: 1993.* Chapel Hill, N.C.: Horizon Research.

Weiss, I., M. C. Matti, and P. S. Smith. 1994. *Report of the 1993 National Survey of Science and Mathematics Education.* Chapel Hill, N.C.: Horizon Research.

Welch, W. W. 1979. "Twenty Years of Science Curriculum Development: A Look Back." In *Review of Research in Education* (7), edited by D. C. Berliner, 282–306. Washington, D.C.: American Educational Research Association.

Wiley, D., and B. Yoon. 1995. "Teacher Reports of Opportunity to Learn: Analyses of the 1993 California Learning Assessment System." *Education Evaluation and Policy Analysis* 17 (3): 355–370.

Wilson, S. M. 1990. "A Conflict of Interests: The Case of Mark Black." *Educational Evaluation and Policy Analysis* 12 (3): 293–310.

———, and J. Berne. 1999. "Teacher Learning and the Acquisition of Professional Knowledge: An Examination of Research on Contemporary Professional Development." In *Review of Research in Education,* vol. 24, edited by A. Iran-Nejad and P. D. Pearson. Washington, D.C.: American Educational Research Association.

Wilson, S. M., S. T. Lubienski, and S. M. Mattson. 1996. *What's the Role of Mathematics? A Case Study of the Challenges Facing Reform-Oriented Professional Development.* Paper presented at the annual conference of the American Educational Research Association Annual Conference, April 1996, New York.

Wilson, S. M., C. Miller, and C. Yerkes. 1993. "Deeply Rooted Change: A Tale of Teaching Adventurously." In *Teaching for Understanding,* edited by D. K. Cohen, M. McLaughlin, and J. Talbert, 84–129. San Francisco: Jossey-Bass.

INDEX